Kwaio Religion

Kwaio Religion

The Living and the Dead
in a Solomon Island Society

Roger M. Keesing

Columbia University Press
New York
1982

Library of Congress Cataloging in Publication Data
Keesing, Roger M., 1935–
    Kwaio religion.

    Bibliography: p.
    Includes index.
    1. Kwaio (Melanesian people)—Religion.
2. Solomon Islands–Religion.   I. Title.
BL2630.K85K43   299'.92   82-4122
ISBN 0-231-05340-1 (cloth)   AACR2
ISBN 0-231-05341-X (paper)

Columbia University Press
New York   Guildford, Surrey

Contents

Contents

Kwaio Orthography

KWAIO VOWELS ARE pronounced roughly as in Italian. Doubling of a vowel indicates doubling in length. Consonants have approximately their English quality, with these exceptions:

The glottal stop, ?, is a common consonant. It represents a closure of the glottis which, between vowels, is manifest as a break (as occurs in the Polynesian pronunciation of Hawaii—Hawai?i). When the glottal stop occurs at the beginning of a word it is difficult for English speakers to hear, except as a preceding vowel makes it audible. (In most dialects of American English, a glottal stop is inserted in some contexts prior to a word that starts with a vowel, to keep the vowels from running together—as in "I'm going to Omaha," where a glottal stop is inserted before "Omaha." In Kwaio, though not in English, these initial glottal stops distinguish words from one another (thus *abu* is "taboo," and *?abu* is "blood").

Another complication is that voiced stops in Kwaio are "prenasalized." That is, when preceded by a vowel, *b* is pronounced *mb*, *d* is pronounced *nd*, *g* is pronounced *ŋg*. Thus *abu* is pronounced "ambu," *wado* is pronounced "wando," and *laga* is pronounced "laŋga." (The *ŋ* here represents the final consonant of "sing.")

In Kwaio, *r* and *l* are allophones of a single phoneme (*l* occurring preceding *a*, *e*, and *o*, and *r* occurring preceding *i* and *u*); but I have written them separately to ease the task of the reader and comparativist.

Preface

STUDY OF KWAIO culture has been a much longer and more sustained project than I could have anticipated when I began my Ph.D. research in 1962. That work, funded by the National Institute of Mental Health, enabled me to get a solid understanding of Kwaio social structure, but my data on religion was relatively thin. In 1969–70, a grant from the National Science Foundation enabled me to undertake a further year of fieldwork focused on religion and symbolism as well as continuities of social structure and economy. After my move to the Australian National University in 1974, I was able to do another seven weeks of Kwaio fieldwork in that year, looking closely at religion and the women's realm; and then to do nine months of fieldwork in 1977, and a week at the time of independence in 1978. Finally, after the first draft of *Kwaio Religion* was written early in 1979, I was able to spend two more months in the field, and resolve some remaining questions and ambiguities. I owe thanks to all—the National Institute for Mental Health, the National Science Foundation, the University of California–Santa Cruz, the Social Science Research Council, and the Australian National University— who have supported my research.

The book has had a rather longer birth-process than I had first anticipated. The first draft was written, under contract to Mayfield Press for the Explorations in World Ethnography series, between January and March 1979. After two months of further fieldwork in mid-1979 I produced an extensively revised draft, still sharply constrained by Mayfield's length limitations.

The manuscript was read and reviewed, in this period, by Cambridge University Press and Columbia University Press. Although in the end I chose to have Columbia produce the book, I am grateful to Walter Lippincott, and particularly to Robert McKinley, who read the manuscript for Cambridge University Press, for assistance. Dr. McKinley went far beyond what Cambridge, or I, could have expected from a reviewer. His comments, almost fifty pages of careful and reflective reanalysis of the Kwaio data, were not only useful in my revision, but represent a substantial interpretive work in its own right. Where Dr. McKinley's ideas have been incorporated quite directly into the revision, I have cited or quoted his comments. At this stage of revision, I also drew on the suggestions of Professor Mervyn Meggitt, who read the manuscript for Columbia, and Professor Donald Tuzin, who commented on it at length. Others whose comments in seminars and suggestions on the manuscript have substantially affected the revision include Ron Brunton, F. K. Lehman, Rodney Needham, and Marie Reay. Shelley Schreiner, coparticipant in Kwaio fieldwork since 1974, has contributed so centrally to ethnography and interpretation that her ideas and mine are intertwined in the chapters to follow.

My deepest debts are to the Kwaio friends who have shared their lives and homes and friendship and have tried patiently to make what to them was obvious about their world clear to an often obtuse but sympathetic outsider. If I have described Kwaio religion as if ancestors did not exist, it is because as an anthropologist I know no other way. The *adalo* may exist, may impose the rules Kwaio follow. An ultimate sceptic about matters theological, I can only say that I find Kwaio theology at least as convincing as Christian theology. Among the many Kwaio who have tried to teach me about the *adalo* and their rules, my greatest debts are to ʔAika, Booriʔau, ʔElota, Faʔafataa, Fenaaori, Folofoʔu, Louŋa and Talauŋaʔi.

Through the years I have been dependent in many ways on administrators, missionaries, and others in the Solomons for support and hospitality. I wish to express special thanks to Len and Betty Larwood of the Atoifi Adventist Hospital. Len Larwood's accidental death, in August 1979, is a tragic loss to the Kwaio, for whose health and well-being he had worked tirelessly for thirteen years. For Christian and non-Christian alike, his passing leaves a gap that cannot be filled.

Royalties from the book, as from my other publications on the Kwaio, go to the Fataia Development Fund, administered by Kwaio trustees. I hope that these resources will help the Kwaio people to preserve what they most value, to free themselves from exploitative systems of plantation labor, and to maintain a sufficient degree of political cohesiveness to resist the pressures that would unnecessarily impose alien ways on them.

Kwaio Religion

Introduction

JET AIRLINERS now land at Henderson Field, prize of the Guadalcanal campaign of World War II. They carry diplomats, development experts, businessmen, and tourists to the UN's 150th member nation, and its prosperous, bustling capital, Honiara.

Yet a scant seventy-five miles away, in the central mountains of Malaita Island, young men carry bows and arrows; girls and women, nude except for customary ornaments, dig taro in forest gardens; valuables made of strung shell beads are exchanged at mortuary feasts; and priests sacrifice pigs to the ancestral spirits on whom prosperity and life itself depend.

Life goes on in these mountains much as it has for the fifty years since pacification; outwardly, only steel tools and the cessation of blood feuding make this world strikingly different than it was a century ago. Yet the Kwaio-speakers of central Malaita and their ancestors now inhabit a beleaguered enclave, the largest remaining pocket of defiant religious and cultural autonomy in a militantly Christian and rapidly westernizing young country. The Kwaio traditionalists are beleaguered not only by a government committed to Western-style development in a Christian mold, and evangelists whose weapons of conversion now include antibiotics and airplanes, but by their own militantly Christian kin along the coast, seeking to gain control over mountain lands and reluctant souls.

Following the dictates of one's ancestors in a Christian

country in the latter twentieth century is in one sense perpetuation of old ways; but as a people's commitment to autonomy it is very different from the religious commitment of
their parents fifty years ago, when the Pax Britannica was imposed by brute force (Keesing and Corris 1980); and more
different still from that of their grandparents a hundred years
ago, when Kwaio men were taken on sailing ships to the cane
fields of Queensland and Fiji. For a century Kwaio have known
the power of Europeans, have heard the Christian message.
Their conservatism has been born of struggle, not isolation.
As other Solomon Islanders progressively capitulated to Western cultural pressures, what had been a collective stance became a singular one; what had been a powerful majority
melted into a powerless minority. The grandparents, even the
parents, of contemporary Kwaio lived in a world the ancestors
controlled, surrounded by manifestations of ancestral power;
today Kwaio traditionalists live in a narrow, shrinking world
beyond which Europeans' ways of life, their God, and their
power and wealth hold sway.

The commitment of the Kwaio to ancestral ways poses a
twofold anthropological challenge. On the one hand, this is
one of few areas in island Melanesia where a traditional religious system is still fully flourishing. We have only a handful
of substantial ethnographic accounts of island Melanesian religions; and those from groups speaking Eastern Oceanic Aus-
tronesian languages, in which concepts of *mana* and *tapu* are
central, are of particular comparative interest. As we will see,
Kwaio conceptions of ancestral power and sacredness are a
revealing variant of this much discussed complex. On the
other hand, the sheer persistence of Kwaio religion through
some 110 years of contact with Europeans, and into the post-
colonial present, poses a challenge to interpretation. Why,
and how, has Kwaio religion endured?

In the chapters to follow I will seek to describe Kwaio
religion in a way that captures the phenomenological reality
of a world where one's group includes the living and the dead,
where conversations with the spirits, and the signs of their

presence and acts, are part of everyday life. Then, stepping back, I will probe for deeper meanings, will ask how and why such a universe has been created across the generations. And in the process, I will question some currently fashionable anthropological approaches to symbolism, myth, ritual, and cosmology. The quest in symbolist/structuralist anthropology for hidden formal patterns, for structures of meaning, makes ethnographic analysis a kind of cultural cryptography. This quest too easily leads the analyst to create a formally elegant system, spuriously coherent, that distorts the subjective realities of individual experience, the sociology of religious knowledge in small-scale communities, and the political uses of religious dogmas as ideologies. I will try to situate Kwaio religion not on some abstract plane of formal structure, but in the minds and acts of individuals and in the social life of communities.

Here a theoretical clarification is in order. I have recently argued (Keesing 1981) that the anthropological conception of culture entails a fundamental perspectival ambiguity. Some anthropologists (e.g., Goodenough 1957, 1961) have taken culture to be a generalization from, or characterization of, the cognitive worlds of individuals: what individuals know that enables them to participate in the ordered social life of a community. Other anthropologists (e.g., Geertz 1973; Schneider 1968, 1976) have seen culture as situated in the community, as a public and shared symbolic system, a system of meanings that cannot be situated in, or reduced to, the minds of individuals.

I take the view (1981) that this perspectival ambiguity cannot be resolved by insisting that either view is "correct" (e.g., by advancing arguments to demonstrate that the culture disappears when the last brain in which it is stored ceases to function, or that "the culture" exists, like a Beethoven quartet, regardless of who knows and enacts or performs it). Rather— as with the fundamental ambiguities in theoretical physics— each perspective is "correct" but does not negate the salience of the other. We need, I argue, to take *both* vantage points. There are many aspects of the cultural process, of meaning and communication within communities, that can best be grasped if we see the culture as public, not private, if we take a Geertzian view of shared meanings. But I will suggest that there are other aspects of the cultural process that are obscured by this perspective; there are some questions we are led not to ask, from this symbolist direction, which I believe to be crucial in understanding what I have recently called the "political economy of knowledge" (1981). Symbolic systems change, and not simply the way coral reefs change, by a kind of accretion of ideas deposited upon the cumulated meanings that are a culture. Ideas have histories, I will suggest, that must be situated both in individual minds and knowledge, and in political contexts. Men and women, young and old, experts and nonexperts, participate in different ways in the symbolic process; they have different views of, access to, and commitments toward "the culture" as a community's symbolic resources. To ask such questions does not preclude our understanding these symbolic resources as shared and public as well. Both perspectives, I will argue, are needed if we are to understand how a people such as the Kwaio understand, organize, and enact their lives together.

The categories of Kwaio religious thought, and their expression in the arrangement of settlements and the patterning of everyday social relations and ritual, have a coherent, global, and elegant structure. In these respects, the Kwaio cosmos is ordered in ways that invite analysis in the theoretical tradition of Durkheim, Mauss, Hertz, and, more recently, Lévi-Strauss, Needham, and Douglas. For the Kwaio, who have little interest in ultimate origins or systematic theology, such a symbolic scheme must be pieced together from the myriad rules that govern everyday life, and the detailed procedures of ritual. The analyst must discover such coherent structures, implicit in the conduct of social life; but it is dangerous to leave things at that. Our task includes, but goes beyond, cultural cryptography. If such symbolic schemes have meaning in Kwaio life, it is not only at a level of "cultural symbols."

We must resituate these structures in everyday life and experience.

Much anthropological writing about "primitive" religion has been based on a year or two of fieldwork, on incomplete mastery of a local language, and on heavy reliance on one or several especially gifted or knowledgeable informants. After almost five years of fieldwork on seven trips over a seventeen-year period, and intensive work with dozens of Kwaio individuals—men and women, young and old—my data will no longer sustain an idealized, neatened-up view of Kwaio religion derived from one or two philosopher informants. Some Kwaio individuals command very broad knowledge, both open and esoteric, have a commitment to systematic understanding (if not ultimate explanation), and have access to deep symbolic structures. The majority know less than they could, apparently understand only superficial layers of symbolism, and assume a pragmatic approach to the spirits they seek to live with in harmony, not understand. Given this distribution of knowledge, interest, and commitment in the community, some common assumptions about culture and symbolism, about rituals and meanings, wear uncomfortably. "Kwaio religion," indeed "Kwaio culture," emerges as a composite; or, to change the image, as a pool from which individuals draw in different ways and degrees, and to which they contribute in different ways and degrees. The historical development of "Kwaio culture," and the preservation and progressive modification of coherent symbolic structures across generations, become problematic—questions about social and political processes within communities, as well as intellectual operations of *la pensée sauvage*.

In these and other respects, the Kwaio of the Malaita mountains illuminate the general from the particular. Human nature emerges not from universals, generalizations, or stereotypes, but from the distinctive, local ways in which peoples have understood their place in the scheme of things, have conceptualized life and death, have created order and meaning in a universe we can ultimately control only in our minds. The strikingly Tylorean[1] world of the Kwaio, where shades wander in dream, where the living and the dead together spin out the ancient designs of life, can teach us much about humankind.

1. Reference is to the great British anthropologist Sir E.B. Tylor (Tylor 1871).

Chapter One

The Kwaio of Malaita

1.1 Malaita: Peoples and Languages

WE CAN BEGIN by moving back in time to the first half of the nineteenth century, when direct European influence in the southeast Solomons was negligible. Sketching the precontact languages and cultures of Malaita will provide a needed background for narrowing the focus in to the Kwaio, and for sketching the transformations of the past century.

Malaita is a mountainous island, about a hundred miles in length, running northwest to southeast, as part of a double chain of islands that comprises the Solomons group (figures 1.1 and 1.2). Separated from Malaita proper by a narrow channel is the island of Maramasike, or Small Malaita. On Malaita, variations on a common cultural heritage are substantially shaped by geographic factors. Most of the island is mountainous, rising to 4,000 feet in the central massif, and drained by rain-fed rivers. Along much of the east[1] coast, there is no flat coastal land; the mountains rise steeply from undercut coastal cliffs punctuated by harbors. The west coast has a flat shelf, in some areas several miles in width, below the mountain flanks. Long stretches of this coast are relatively sheltered by mangrove islands or reefs. On the east side, only the northernmost strip is sheltered from the heavy southeast seas that

---

1. By convention, for Malaita, the coast that faces northeast is referred to as "east," and the coast that faces southwest is referred to as "west."

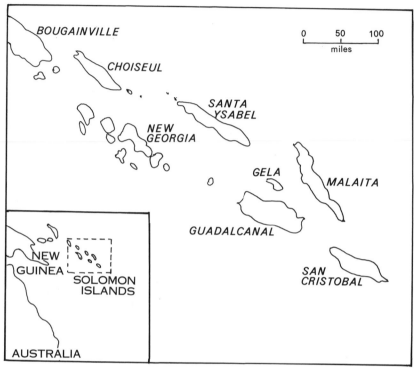

Figure 1.1 The Solomon Islands

pound the coast; there, fringing reefs have created a sheltered lagoon.

The peoples of Malaita share a single broad cultural pattern—the same religious system, a broadly common system of social organization and, in the interior, the same subsistence economy. We will see shortly that the major variants of this common pattern are found in areas with a maritime orientation and adaptation: the shallow lagoons of northeast and west central coasts, and the island of Maramasike.

Local descent groups, throughout the main island, have blocs of territory centered around ancient shrines where ancestors were propitiated. Settlements in pre-European times were tiny, scattered, and shifting—two or three houses clustered on a ridge, relocated every few years. Stability in

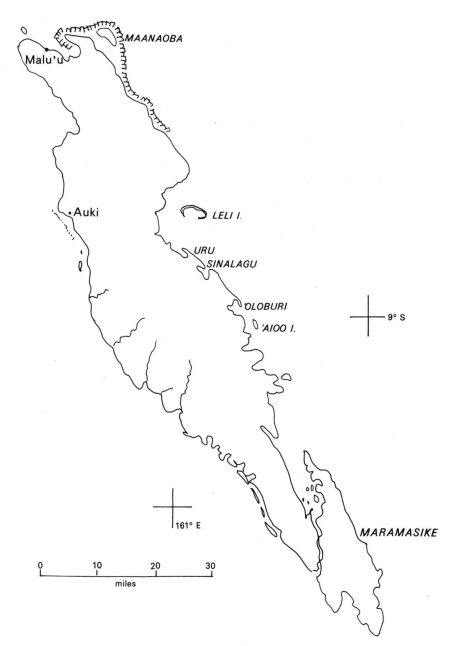

Figure 1.2 The Island of Malaita

this shifting scene was provided by the shrines that were the foci of religious congregations.

Throughout Malaita, both agnatic descent—down through lines of men from the founding ancestors—and cognatic descent—through links of out-marrying women—are important. Descent in the male line from the founding ancestors of the group conveys inalienable primary rights to land, and primary ritual interests. But the descendants of out-marrying women have secondary interests in land, and in ritual. These entail rights of residence and land use; and they can be—and often are—converted to de facto primary rights through long-term residence. Each individual has ties to, and interests in, a number of descent group territories.

Political organization and ritual relations between local descent groups varied considerably. In the northern zone (comprising a set of closely related languages and dialects) local descent groups were grouped together into regional clusters, united in ritual hierarchies, conceptualized in terms of descent from ancient ancestors. Politically, local descent groups seem to have been largely autonomous, despite the conceptualization in terms of regional clusters reminiscent of the much larger-scale phratries of highland New Guinea. In the central zone that includes Kwaio—geographically the most mountainous and fragmented sector of the island— small-scale local descent groups are fully autonomous (although linked together by ritual interconnections, as we will see for Kwaio in chapter 6). The southeastern end of Malaita narrows, and the high mountains give way to lower hills, then the sheltered Maramasike Passage. The west coast, mangrove-fringed, forms a network of sheltered waterways. In this setting, ?Are?are speakers developed a distinctive adaptation: a more hierarchical political organization, and a more maritime and outward orientation, than the "bush" peoples of most of the island (de Coppet and Zemp 1978). On Small Malaita, the outward orientation to the open sea and political hierarchy were more pronounced; hereditary chiefs, elaborate male initiations, a cult centering around bonito, and ritualized overseas voyaging highlighted a cultural tradition distinctive in Melanesia (Ivens 1927).

Further distinctive variations on the mainland Malaita pattern emerged where, in the sheltered lagoons, specialized maritime traditions and concentration of population on islets and platforms built up from the coral of the lagoon floor changed the spatial and subsistence orientation. Lau speakers of the northeast coast (Ivens 1930; Maranda 1976) specialized in bartering fish for taro. Concentration of population and resources led to a distinctive variation on the neighboring mainland pattern from which it was derived, with a more rigid agnatic descent system and more sharp polarization of the sexes. The Langalanga speakers of the west central coast concentrated both on fishing and on fabricating strung shell discs, exported around the southern and central Solomons (Cooper 1971).

Throughout Malaita, local descent group congregations propitiated their ancestors at shrines presided over by ritual officiants. In northern Malaita, these "priests" are referred to as *fataabu* ("speak-sacred"). A second leader, at least in the ideal model Malaita peoples have of their own social order, is a Melanesian-style big man, an entrepreneurial feastgiver (Keesing 1978a; Hogbin 1939; Ross 1973). The third in the triumvirate of traditional leadership was the *ramo* or warrior: an assassin, a bounty hunter, a war leader. Blood feuding was pervasive.

Although no solid linguistic subgrouping has been established, the linguistic relationships appear fully consistent with the cultural patterns. Northern Malaita comprises a single cluster of dialects and closely related languages. The languages of the lagoons are close to those of the adjacent mainland mountains. The central zone, of Kwaio and related dialects, stands somewhat apart, but apparently groups more closely with the northern languages than with adjacent ?Are-?are (although the Kwaio-?Are?are border zone shows evidence of much linguistic and cultural borrowing in both directions). The dialects of Small Malaita and the nearby island

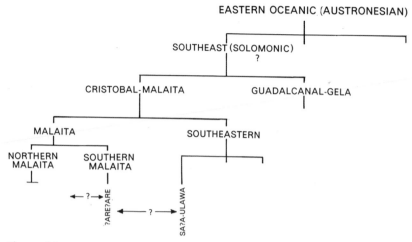

Figure 1.3a   Eastern Oceanic Languages of the Solomons

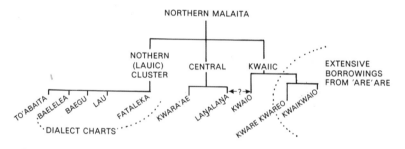

Figure 1.3b   The Northern Malaita Languages
NOTE: The asterisks indicate reconstructed or hypothetical parent languages. Major gaps in knowledge where I have made guesses are indicated by question marks.

of Ulawa stand apart quite sharply, a separation consistent with the cultural evidence. Probable subgroupings of Malaita languages, and their distribution, are outlined in figures 1.3 and 1.4.

We can now focus more closely on the mountainous central zone of Malaita, as it was 150 years ago, when sailing ships first began to appear on the distant horizon.

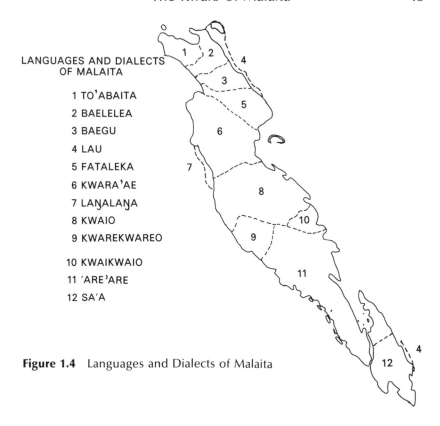

LANGUAGES AND DIALECTS
OF MALAITA

1 TO'ABAITA

2 BAELELEA

3 BAEGU

4 LAU

5 FATALEKA

6 KWARA'AE

7 LAŊALAŊA

8 KWAIO

9 KWAREKWAREO

10 KWAIKWAIO

11 'ARE'ARE

12 SA'A

Figure 1.4 Languages and Dialects of Malaita

1.2   Kwaio Society: A Window Into the Past

Between five and ten thousand speakers of Kwaio (one can only guess at their number, which is now about seven thousand) lived scattered through the rugged interior mountains and on the coastal ridges and slopes. These brown-skinned, frizzly-haired Melanesians (Howells 1973) carved their gardens from densely forested mountain slopes using crude chipped adzes and fire for felling and clearing. Taro was the main staple. A single crop was planted, weeded, harvested, then the shoots replanted in a new swidden, in a continuous cycle without seasons. This continuity was reinforced by year-round rains, punctuated only by a diametric shift in wind directions. Yams, planted annually, marked the passing of the years and a season of sorts. But yams, plantains, leafy greens, and other wild and cultivated food plants were an embellishment of starchy taro corms, the daily staff of life. Birds, insects, fish, cuscus opossums, and other morsels of protein-rich food were only periodic supplements to a mainly vegetarian diet.

On the coastal slopes and ridges and the broken plateau country inland from the east coast, the tiny settlements were dotted fairly close together, although the infertile mudstone, limestone, and clay militated against high population density. The central massif of Tolobusu and the precipitous river valleys of the interior are an unstable basalt; there, population was very sparse.

The Kwaio speakers inland from the east coast, with whom this study will be primarily concerned, were very much a bush people. In Uru Harbor and in several coastal colonies, there were some saltwater[2] people who bartered fish with mountain dwellers. But the economic complementarity of the Lau and Langalanga coasts was much less developed in Kwaio. Peoples of the coastal slopes and ridges netted tiny fish, using lift nets (Keesing 1976: cover and 105) and bamboo rafts, gathered shellfish for food and shells for manufacture of valuables, and prepared salt and lime. Trade with the peoples of the further bush was carried on as much by these downhill people as by the saltwater people, who spoke a different dialect.

The interior border zones, between Kwaio and Kwara?ae to the northwest, and between Kwaio and ?Are?are to the southeast, were on the whole sparsely populated, though they were filters through which cultural and linguistic borrowings passed. The Kwaio heartland inland from Sinalagu (figure 1.5) is a land of steep, broken ridges, peaks, and ravines where

2. The designations "bush" and "saltwater" are conventional on Malaita, characteristically labelled in local languages with the terms *tolo*, "bush" (Kwaio *fataia*), and *asi*, "sea." Kwaio add a third category, *ta?a i sifola*, "downhill people," who inhabit the coastal slopes and harbor margins, and augment taro and yam production with fishing.

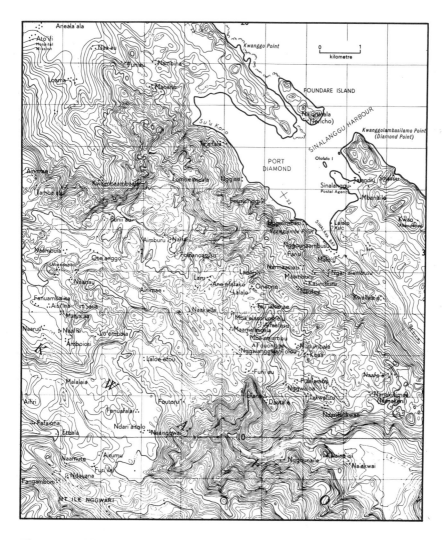

Figure 1.5 The Kwaio Heartland (Courtesy of the Solomon Islands Lands Department.)

ten consecutive steps on level ground are seldom possible, a land of sticky red clay and limestone outcroppings and sinkholes, of dense jungle laced with rain-fed streams. An orientation inward, to small neighborhood clusters of settlements within which security lay, was a circumstance as much of geography as of culture.

The cultural grid laid on this natural environment crystallized the past in the present. According to Kwaio traditions of their past, the land was first cleared some twelve to twenty generations ago. The pioneer settlers cleared primary forest for gardens, and in doing so they and their descendants progressively established title over named tracts of secondary forest. The founding settlers, coming from an established territory, established a shrine to their ancestors, linked to the parent shrine. These shrines are not physically elaborate, consisting simply of a grove or thicket in which sacrificial ovenstones are kept. But old shrines stand out from the surrounding secondary growth as groves of towering forest.

In time, a patchwork of named tracts and associated settlement sites, with a focal shrine and often several branch shrines, expanded to the margins of another group's territory. Such a cluster of land tracts, title to which was held by descendants of the founding ancestors, comprises a *fanua*, 'shrine territory'[3]—usually referred to by the name of its original or focal shrine (thus *taʔa i Gaʔenaafou*, "Gaʔenaafou people," whose land and ritual interests center around Gaʔenaafou shrine). Partial separation of the lands within a territory, and partly divided land title could result from sociological segmentation and patterns of residence and land use.

Each *fanua* is, or once was, the estate of a small descent group, comprising those descendants of the founding ancestors who have a primary commitment to that territory and shrine. In theory, and very often in practice, these are agnatic descendants of the founders: people "born of men" have primary rights of residence and land use, which are not contingent on their residence. However, other nonagnatic descendants, and especially the children and grandchildren of women who were agnatic members of the group, have sec-

---

3. Following anthropological convention, I use single quotation marks to indicate glosses of Kwaio categories. Double quotation marks around a rendering of a Kwaio term indicate that I am giving the literal meaning of the term.

ondary rights and interests which can be strengthened by residence in the *fanua* and active participation in the affairs of the descent group (Keesing 1970). In practice, childhood residence exerts a very strong influence on adult residence and social affiliation; if children grow up with their mother's kin in her *fanua* (because of parents' uxorilocal residence or maternal custody after the father's death or divorce) they are likely to form their primary attachment to her group. Descent groups may then include nonagnates, people "born of women"; and because multiple attachments are possible the boundaries of descent groups may be fuzzy and partly overlapping. An individual may have a clear primary attachment to a particular descent group and secondary attachments to three or four others; or, in some cases, a dual or multiple and diffuse attachment may be sustained through changes of residence and flexible social participation (Keesing 1968, 1970, 1972).

As of late 1927, when the Kwaio mountains were first pacified, the mean number of adult men per descent group was 8.68, the range 3 to 20—small even by the standards of seaboard Melanesia (Hogbin and Wedgwood 1953).[4] Being small, Kwaio descent groups are vulnerable to demographic fluctuations: the male core of a group can virtually disappear within the span of a generation if men do not marry (permanent bachelorhood is common) or if they beget few sons who survive to adulthood. Groups that proliferate characteristically segment, with one segment often assuming control over another territory (sometimes an adjoining one) whose agnates have died out or dispersed. Such lateral expansion, usually predicated on a cognatic tie, makes the distribution of land rights much more fluid across the span of generations

4. One of the few positive byproducts of the disastrous events of 1927–28 (Keesing and Corris 1980), in this case a boon to the ethnographer rather than the Kwaio themselves, is that I was able to reconstruct with a very high degree of accuracy a household-by-household census as of October 4, 1927. This, combined with residential histories and a continuous record of demographic events, marriages, and moves over the past eighteen years, gives me a record of more than fifty years of social continuity, a record possibly unique in the ethnography of traditional Melanesian societies.

than the ideal model would suggest, flexible to the vicissitudes of demography and politics.

Kwaio settlements were tiny, even by Melanesian standards. A settlement may consist of one or several separate clearings, immediately or closely adjoining. Usually only very close kin, most commonly ones who have grown up together (Keesing 1980b), share the same clearing: as we will see, they expose one another to the danger of ancestral punishment. As of 1927, Kwaio settlements ranged in size from 2 to 28, with a mean of 9.95. The number of component households ranged from 1 to 8, with a mean of 2.19. Usually settlements were moved every few years, although a few old settlement sites had been occupied continuously for several generations. The fluidity of residence meant a circulation through the named land tracts of a *fanua*; each tract has an old settlement site, characteristically reoccupied several times in a lifetime. A man's adult residence in his natal *fanua* often was punctuated by periods of residence with his wife's kin, his maternal kin, or other cognatic relatives, most often because of a quarrel or feud.

Marriage, with rare exceptions, was serially monogamous. Most first marriages joined a man, often in his thirties or beyond, with a girl aged sixteen to twenty-five, to whom he had no close kin relationship. The most common and favored pattern was for the man to bring home a girl with whom he had had a chaste dating relationship (often a girl his parents had picked out or at least approved of, since he was dependent on them and their close kin to finance the marriage). Child betrothal, and 'seizure' of a girl on behalf of an older (or reluctant) man, were less common variants. Relatives too close to have an approved dating relationship could have a secret sexual affair only at great risk. If they were third or fourth or fifth cousins, they had a strong chance of getting to sanctuary with kin who would protect them (if the affair came to light through discovery or pregnancy) until tempers cooled and a marriage payment could be arranged; if they were first or second cousins, or coresidents, they would more often be killed. If a virtuous girl was propositioned (even by an eligible suitor), she was supposed to go into her father's men's house to report it: she would then have to be killed by her own kin. Adulterous or incestuous relationships were usually dealt with by the summary killing of both parties, although an adulterous wife was sometimes spared (on the cultural premise that a man is the active instigator of sexual intercourse).

Such sexual violations, precipitating killings, usually led to blood feuds. The aggrieved kin group or groups might exact vengeance themselves to redress the balance. Alternatively, they could put up a bounty of pigs and blood money, which could be claimed by the man or men who killed an approved victim (the cause and ramifications of such blood feuds are discussed in more detail in Keesing 1978a). A group against which vengeance was sought might retreat into palisaded defenses, relatively protected against arrows, spears, and clubs; or they could scatter individually into sanctuary with cognatic or affinal kin. Killings were also precipitated by curses, insults, thefts, and confrontations. There was always a danger of violence where male pride and honor, and the glorification of violence and homicide, encouraged escalation.

The type-roles of secular leadership reflected this pattern. The *lamo* (*ramo* in other Malaita languages) was an intimidating warrior, a bounty hunter and executioner (often of the weak and defenseless). In contrast, entrepreneurial leaders such as ʔElota (Keesing 1978a) and his father not only mobilized wealth in Melanesian big-man fashion, but kept peace within the group and, as best possible, between groups.

The main focus of the prestige economy was mortuary feasting. The death of an important man or woman plunges the bereaved group and other close kin into liminal sacredness, most marked when the group's 'priest' dies.[5] This sacredness is progressively removed in a sequence of rites, cul-

---

5. I will gloss as 'priest' the Kwaio term *wane naa ba ʔe* (lit., "shrine-man"; the north Malaita term *fataabu* is rarely used in Kwaio). This man, although not a full-time religious specialist, acts as the principal officiant in sacrifices to descent group ancestors.

minating in an *omea*, 'mortuary feast', in which the living reenter into normal social relations. The *omea* is a means of acquiring and maintaining prestige, although the presentation of valuables ostensibly rewards several male kin of the decedent for their services in burying the dead. Death of a child or unimportant adult calls for a smaller scale feast. Sponsoring of mortuary feasts is partly geared to cycles of pig breeding, taro production, and the accumulation of investments. If an important man has lost no appropriate relatives by the time his resources are ready to be invested in a mortuary feast, he may stage an *omea* ostensibly in honor of some other decedent (often someone who died years earlier) or to reward some act of kinship.

The medium of exchange, in the prestations of feasting and marriage, in compensation growing out of litigation, and in the mundane buying and selling of taro, fish, pigs, areca nuts, magical spells, etc., is *bata*. *Bata* consists of tiny beads, fabricated by the Kwaio from cone shells, and strung on fiber into conventional lengths and denominations.

This was a world where the humans on the periphery spoke closely related languages, shared a common cultural heritage: a relatively closed world in which the generations went by, in which the ancestors and the living patterned their relations in an ancient design. The sailing ships that had begun to pass in the distance every few years did not intrude.

But all this was to end forever when, about 1868, two Kwaio men were taken from their canoe. Their loss was mourned, the feasts given . . .

1.3   The Kwaio Enter the World Beyond

These first Kwaio travelers returned, laden with steel tools and trinkets, describing far lands, wonders beyond imagining. And soon afterwards, other young Kwaio went on these strange ships, perhaps kidnapped at first, but later embarking for adventure and its material rewards (Corris 1973). The Europeans and Pacific Islanders on these ships brought to the Solomons the experience of traffic in human cargo elsewhere in the Southwest Pacific, and the pidgin lingua franca ("Bichelamar") of the labor trade. They were supplying a demand for workers who could toil in the tropic sun of Queensland and Fiji from dawn to evening, and cost a pittance: humans, barely accorded humanity, fit to clear, plant, and harvest the expanding cane fields (Saunders 1975).

The mortality rate among the early plantation recruits was high, the living conditions appalling (Saunders 1975). But the potential rewards, not only of adventure but of hardware, were high enough to guarantee a stream of recruits from Uru, Sinalagu, ?Oloburi, and the Kwaio passages of the west coast. The recruits were in many cases sent off by their senior kin, who held power of life and death (and marriage rather than bachelorhood) over them. The seniors controlled the boxes of goods brought back by the recruits, and collected the recruiting bounties that were paid once the labor trade became established.

The goods the Kwaio found attractive included cloth, pipes, twist tobacco, and gewgaws such as mirrors. But the important new items that made the lure of the labor trade irresistible, despite its dangers, were steel tools and firearms. Steel knives, tomahawks, axes, and plane blades had by the 1890s revolutionized Kwaio technology. Important men claimed the first steel tools; but after twenty years of the labor trade, virtually every family apparently had an axe and bush knives. Although the open importation of firearms into what was viewed as the most dangerous island in the Pacific was prohibited early, the demand for guns on one side and for cheap labor on the other made it inevitable that Malaita warriors would be steadily armed (mainly with long-obsolete muskets, muzzle-loading or converted to breech-loading). Steel tools probably had a more profound impact on the Kwaio subsistence economy than in some documented New Guinea cases. To fell giant trees and cut firewood, Kwaio had only small adzes with roughly flaked chert blades, which look like crude toys in comparison to the big polished stone tools of the New Guinea highlands.

With the introduction of firearms and much less time spent on garden work, blood feuding was apparently escalated and transformed. The power of the prominent *lamo* seems to have increased, and changed somewhat. By controlling the supply of labor and the flow of introduced goods, the leaders of descent groups commanded a more central position than they had before. The *lamo*, controlling stocks of ammunition and firearms, seem to have turned more squarely to bounty-hunting for profit; the bounties assured them obligated retainers and control over the prestige economy.

The death of Kwaio men overseas called for vengeance; and the recruiting ships laden with trade goods for "beach payments" offered tempting targets. Not surprisingly, Kwaio strongmen with access to the coast tried their hand at combining vengeance with profit. In 1880, the strongman Maeasuaa from Uru Island attacked, looted, and burned the recruiting ship *Borealis*, and two years later he did the same to the *Janet Stewart*. Punitive action was misdirected and ineffectual. In 1886 ?Arumae, a *lamo* from Tetefou in Sinalagu Harbor, organized an attack on the *Young Dick*, which was repulsed with considerable loss of life.

The Kwaio working in Queensland and Fiji experienced the wonders of port towns, trade stores, and nineteenth-century frontier culture. Some were exposed to the Christian message, but all but a handful remained committed to traditional patterns of religion, fighting, and the ways of the men's houses. The founders of the Queensland Kanaka Mission faced a crisis in keeping their small Christian flock together when Solomon Islanders and New Hebrideans were deported from Queensland in the early years of this century. They decided to follow their Malaita converts back to the islands, redesignating their group the South Sea Evangelical Mission (SSEM). From 1906 to 1920, tiny SSEM enclaves were established in the lowlands around Sinalagu, Uru, and ?Oloburi on the east Kwaio coast, under threat from the powerful bush descent groups.

The first SSEM missionary who worked in Kwaio territory was assassinated in 1911 by two Kwaio men (who were ostensibly purifying a curse, but actually were striking at what they saw as a threat to ancestral ways). A punitive expedition killed five villagers, but the power of the descent groups of the interior and their formidable *lamo* remained unchallenged (Keesing 1978a; Keesing and Corris 1980).

The first strong threat to autonomy came in 1922, when a brave, forceful, and able Australian District Officer, W.R. Bell, sought to extend the Pax Britannica to the then "wild" east Malaita coast from his base at Auki. He appointed village constables at Uru, Sinalagu, and ?Oloburi, and through them he organized a system for collecting an annual head-tax. Bell, who had opposed imposition of the tax, saw as his main task the disarming of the powerful *lamo*, their enforced retirement from bounty hunting. But when the tax came, Bell saw it as a means to force the bush strongmen, through payment of what they viewed as a tribute, to capitulate to the Pax Britannica. On the fifth annual tax collection, Bell, his British cadet, and a police patrol were set upon by Kwaio warriors. The two white men and thirteen Solomon Islanders were killed in the October 1927, massacre. Although the later investigations sought specific provocations and motives, the underlying issues were sovereignty and power: the autonomy of a proud people, the power of the Kwaio *lamo*, who were prepared to face disastrous reprisals rather than meekly accept submission (Keesing and Corris 1980).

A massive punitive expedition led, directly or indirectly, to the death of more than a hundred people from the interior. Malaita members of the punitive expedition, mainly police and volunteers from north Malaita, seeking vengeance for kin slain in the massacre, and determined to break forever the ancestrally-conferred power of the Kwaio, systematically desecrated sacred things and places (Keesing and Corris 1980). Ancestral skulls were thrown in menstrual huts, the bark mats from the menstrual huts were thrown into shrines; ritual objects and relics were scattered, desecrated, or destroyed.

During the massive invasion of the interior, and the arrest and nine-month imprisonment of almost two hundred men, the women, children, and peoples from groups not implicated in the massacre took refuge in the Christian villages. These, and the west coast Catholic settlements around the mission at Buma, were filled to overflowing. The non-Christian men who took refuge in the Christian villages were exposed to menstrual and childbirth pollution. Hundreds on east and west coasts (the number can only be guessed at) adopted Christianity rather than face the ancestors and try to repair the massive breach of relations caused by desecration and their own exposure to pollution.

It took commitment and courage for the men from the interior, when finally repatriated, to move back into the mountains with their families. They faced the task of rebuilding ritual ties with the ancestors, and social relations sundered by the death of many men, women, and children, including most senior leaders. Many members of descent groups from the coastal slopes became Christian at this stage.

Throughout this period, young men continued to work on plantations as indentured laborers, on copra plantations that had been established in the Solomons in the first two decades of this century. Plantation labor had become an almost universal way station on a young man's path to adulthood: an adventure and coming of age for young men, a source of tools and trade goods for those at home. But pacification and the routinization of internal labor migration had, by the 1930s, begun to give young men an increasing independence from their elders.

In the 1930s, Kwaio traditionalists smouldered with resentment against their loss of independence, and against what they viewed as an erosion of morality under pressure of alien laws. The hostility surfaced in the form of a cult movement in 1939. A priest named Noto?i told his kin he had received a message from the ancient and powerful ancestress, La?aka:

American soldiers would come, would destroy the British capital at Tulagi, and expel the colonial masters. To ensure fulfillment of the prophecy, Noto?i and his followers built a palisaded village, and raised a pig consecrated to La?aka. Messages from the ancestress, spoken in tongues, were translated by Noto?i. The arrest of Noto?i and his followers, and failure of the Americans to arrive as prophesied, led to disillusionment although the movement continued underground for several years (Keesing 1978b, 1980a).

The Americans did come, and on a scale Noto?i could scarcely have imagined, in the wake of the Japanese invasion three years later. The Guadalcanal compaign brought a need for Melanesian workers; and some 3,000 Malaitans volunteered to work with U.S. forces. Experience with American egalitarianism and largesse, and dialogue with Americans about collective bargaining and anticolonialism, helped to catalyze a more political confrontation than Noto?i's. The primary organization and theory of a movement that surfaced as Maasina Rule, "The Rule of Brotherhood,"[6] came from ?Are-?are (the southeast end of Malaita proper). But most of the Kwaio, and other Malaita peoples, joined the movement, which spread to neighboring islands as well. Although it was cloaked in religious symbols, Christian and traditional, and apparently acquired millenarian overtones (see Keesing 1978b), the movement was solidly anticolonial and political. Chiefs were appointed to confront the government, demanding jurisdiction in matters of custom and an end to prewar racism and exploitation. The conflict between Christians and non-Christians, and internecine conflict between kin groups, were seen as sources of weakness. A united front in which language groups, religious congregations, and traditionally feuding groups were joined, emerged; communal meeting villages and communal gardens were built (Keesing 1978b).

The British administration, initially sympathetic, eventually found the demands too brazen. Mass arrests, repression,

---

6. More properly "siblinghood": the ?Are?are label has no sexist overtones. On the movement, see Keesing (1978b) and Laracy (1976).

and gunboat diplomacy and intimidation were used to break the movement. Eventually, Maasina Rule was splintered and driven underground. But in the strongly traditional areas of Malaita where substantial bush populations remain (particularly Kwaio, ?Are?are, and Baegu), political activity that expresses a commitment to custom and autonomy has been a continuous theme for the last twenty-five years (Keesing 1978b, 1980c; Ross 1973).

Overtly, however, Malaita embarked from 1953 onward on a course toward decolonization British-style—the gradual creation of an elite educated in and committed to Western (and especially British) values and institutions, who could succeed the colonial masters. In 1978, this process culminated in the independence of the Solomon Islands, led by a prime minister from ?Are?are who had been trained as an SSEM teacher.

The breach between traditional and Christian communities in east Kwaio, closed only briefly in Maasina Rule, remains wide. We will return to this contemporary situation in chapter 5. For the moment, we need to narrow our view to the mountains above Uru, Sinalagu, and ?Oloburi where traditionalists remain dominant. Some of the changes in Kwaio life during the first fifty years of contact with the outside world have already been noted, particularly the impact of steel tools and firearms. The changes of the last fifty years since pacification call for a closer look.

1.4 Kwaio Society Since Pacification

The drastic thinning of ranks as a result of the 1927 punitive expedition changed the Kwaio social landscape sharply. The following figures show the populations resident within two zones of the central mountains of the east coast on the eve of the 1927 massacre compared with those of 1963–64 (the drop in interior population reflects moves to Christian villages on the coast):

	1927	1963–64
Coastal slope/plateau	459	288
Interior	384	225

Settlements are slightly smaller (mean population 8.9, compared to 9.95 as of 1927), and more widely scattered. With the danger of attack removed, it is more feasible for the sociologically marginal or disgruntled to live as solitary families.

A striking change that does not appear in census figures is an increase in spatial mobility, especially for young people. In days of blood feuding, children would be well into their teens before they were allowed to go to mortuary or marriage feasts, visit relatives in other areas, or travel freely to coastal markets. The danger of a sudden brawl, or of a child causing a quarrel, made parents prudent and restrictive; and a child's horizons and experience were narrowly confined.

Once the elders were disarmed by externally imposed peace, young people had less to fear from secret affairs with kin too close to date. Some affairs with first or second cousins, leading to marriage as the lesser evil, took place in the decade after pacification, but the statistical drift toward conventionally disapproved liaisons, and more free sexual relations among the young has been gradual. But by the 1970s most marriages were between couples too closely related to have dated openly; and sexual affairs were becoming commonplace among the young, sometimes leading to illegitimate births. By 1978, some descent groups seemed headed in the direction of statistical endogamy. Marriages between first and second cousins—however denounced by moralists—are becoming commonplace. For young people the pleasures and excitement of premarital adventuring are without heavy cost; it is usually their elders who must sort things out by paying compensation or financing a marriage.

Young men have also become more independent financially. The control strongmen and elders maintained over

goods brought back by recruits began eroding after pacification. Young men brought home money, tools, cloth, pipes,
tobacco, cooking pots, cigarette lighters, flashlights, hurri-
cane lamps, rice, and other goods. And, though under pressure to place these goods at the disposal of the parental generation, young men have achieved considerable economic
independence. This is a clue to some aspects of cultural conservatism. Adults substantially control *bata*, the traditional
shell valuables used in marriage financing and mortuary feasting. Maintaining a solid, relatively impermeable boundary
between the cash economy and the *bata* economy, and preserving the institutions where the latter prevails, is a vested
interest of the senior generation. Adults remain dependent
on the young for cash and the things it buys; juniors remain
dependent on their elders for the means to marry and advance
themselves in traditional ways.

Two economic changes of the fifty years since pacification, one occurring in the late 1950s and the second a phenomenon of the late 1960s and 1970s, bear note before we
begin to look at Kwaio religion. First, a major change in the
subsistence economy has been forced on the Kwaio by a taro
blight that virtually destroyed taro production. Sweet potatoes, introduced in the late nineteenth century, had been a
disvalued backup crop—something that could be planted in
a swidden after a taro crop had been harvested, or used to
tide a family over any gaps between taro crops. Since the
large-scale destruction of taro in the 1950s and 1960s, the surviving taro have been used for feasts, and daily subsistence
needs have been met mainly with sweet potatoes—a food
Kwaio eat only because they have to. With the decline of taro
production, rituals associated with taro have largely withered.
In the 1970s, taro production was on the upswing again (apparently hardy local varieties were evolving), but even now
sweet potatoes remain the dominant subsistence crop.

A second change is a shift in the nature and circumstances
of work for cash. With the growth of small urban centers in
Honiara and Auki, changes in plantation systems, and the

emergence of a Melanesian elite and class system, uneducated and culturally conservative Malaitans have become almost an anachronism in the cash sector. Surrounded by educated and westernized Melanesians doing remunerative work, on the very bottom of an indigenous class system (Keesing 1978c), and with buying power cut away by inflation, uncertain employment, and transportation costs, the young men from the bush areas are in a very different position than their fathers had been, although their work may be the same.

Walking through the interior, one is struck by conservatism. Visibly, the social landscape is not markedly different than it was in 1930; apart from the disappearance of firearms, it does not look radically different than it would have in 1890. Beneath these continuities, though, changes run deep: changes forced on the Kwaio by a British government committed to pacifying (if not "civilizing" or educating) them; changes deriving not from within these mountains but in the world beyond, which has moved from sailing ships to jet airplanes and transistors.

What remains the same, keeping Kwaio life on an ancient course, are the ancestors and their rules for human life.

Chapter Two

Encountering Ancestors

FOR AN ANTHROPOLOGIST, ancestors present themselves as triangles and circles on genealogies, and as imaginary entities in a theological scheme. But living in a Kwaio settlement brings home strikingly the way that, to those within the Kwaio world, ancestors have an immediacy as members of one's group and participants in the everyday life of the community. This immediacy is lost or distorted in taking a theological overview of "the religion." To begin to understand the subjective realities of this world, where humans talk daily with these unseen members of the group and nightly encounter them while their own bodies sleep, we can well begin to see it as Kwaio do: through the eyes of a child.

2.1 A World of Rules

A Kwaio child's first year is a time of indulgent human warmth and security, though not of uninterrupted gratification. Within weeks of birth, an infant is left for six or eight hours of the day with a caretaker—an older sister, a grandmother, a father—while the mother works in the gardens. So nursing is interrupted by long periods when no breast (or a dry grandmaternal substitute breast) is available. Although a child begins to get premasticated solid food in the second half of the first year, he or she may continue to nurse for two or three years. Birth of a subsequent sibling will substantially displace a nursing child and may lead to full weaning; but a more important transition, for a young boy, takes place around the age of one and a half, when he is no longer allowed to accompany his mother to the menstrual hut.

By the end of the second year, as linguistic competence begins to emerge and a child becomes 'sensible' (*manata?a*),[1] the paths of life for a girl and for a boy have begun to diverge. Gender of a *biibiu*, 'infant', is sociologically neutral; but a *wela wane*, 'boy child', and a *wela geni*, 'girl child', have very different roles and responsibilities that will progressively diverge.

For both e *abu*, 'it's taboo', is one of the most common utterances heard from adults and older siblings. Kwaio *abu* is the same word as *tabu* or *tapu* in other Oceanic languages.[2] In Kwaio, as in other Oceanic languages, (t)*abu* has an implication both of forbiddenness and sacredness—of ancestral power and ancestral proscription. The "forbiddenness" of acts, places, and things is, as we will see, contextual and relational, so that often a good gloss would be "off limits." What is off limits for you is appropriate, even enjoined, for someone else. I will often leave *abu* untranslated in the sections to follow, or will write it as (t)*abu*. Later I will return to analyze the semantics of the term more closely.

For a little girl, the ancestral prohibitions have a special urgency and bite. She is kept by her caretakers from the upper half of the clearing, the men's house and surrounding areas and shrines, and kept from taking any household items down into the *kaakaba*, 'women's taboo area'. But from the time she is deemed sufficiently 'sensible', certainly in her third year, she is verbally instructed in all those things which are *abu*. Some—her urinating in the house or clearing rather than the women's latrine—are matters that can be excused and

---

1. The Kwaio term *manata?a* implies both consciousness as a cultural being and some sense of responsibility.

2. The *t* phoneme dropped out, in most positions, during the evolution of Cristobal-Malaitan languages. Thus Oceanic *tama*, "father," is *ama* in Kwaio; Oceanic *mate*, "die," becomes *mae* in Kwaio.

even laughed at in a transitional period before a girl is fully continent, but they are soon to be a matter of life and death.

Seri, a bright little girl of five and a half, spoke confidently about the rules of the world in which she was growing up, in response to my questions.

> RMK: If Geninaatoo [her FBW] urinated in the house, what would happen?
> Seri: They would *siu* [purify] with a pig.
> RMK: What if Nanaua menstruated in the house, what would happen?
> Seri: Purification.
> RMK: Why?
> Seri: It's not to happen in the house. It is *abu* in the house.
> RMK: What about the men's house?
> Seri: It's *abu*, because men eat pig there. Women can't go there, even inside the boundary line. It's *abu*, because they [the men] eat pig there.
> RMK: Which pig?
> Seri: *Abu* pigs. Women can't eat them.
> RMK: Do men eat those pigs in the shrine or in the men's house?
> Seri: They eat them in the men's house. And in the shrine too.
> RMK: Do you drink men's water?
> Seri: No, only men drink men's water. They eat sacred pigs.
> RMK: And in the house, where do you sleep?
> Seri: In the house. The men's side is *abu*. [She goes on to explain how, when she was little, she could urinate in the house, like her one-and-a-half-year-old male cousin Efaa does; but now she has to go to the *kaakaba*.]
> RMK: Does Efaa go down to the menstrual hut with his mother?
> Seri: No, he's *abu* now. He's *abu* because he stays with men and goes inside the men's house.

A boy, when he is 'sensible' and has become *abu* in this sense, is increasingly incorporated into the world of men. He can go into the men's house, can go to shrines, and will be given pork when purificatory sacrifices are made. Things which are *abu* are less constraining for him than they are for a girl. He cannot go into the women's *kaakaba*, must treat sacred things and places with respect. Once he acquires linguistic competence, he can cause illness or misfortune with a stylized curse directed at an adult (although older children may curse one another in jest, and with impunity), just as a girl can. Acquiring sociolinguistic responsibility is part of becoming 'sensible'.

2.2 Unseen Presences

Except in rare cases adults proffer young children no meta-theory about these rules. *E abu* is sufficient explanation. But at least by the beginning of the third year, a child realizes that the social universe includes actors he or she cannot see or hear, and perceives that the things that are *abu* are prohibited not only by authoritarian parents, but by the unseen members of the community as well.

The evidence from which a child begins to construct a picture of unseen beings and forces is all around him. First of all, adults *talk* to these beings—to dead parents, grandparents, siblings, or children. A woman sits in a corner of the house whispering to a dead relative; a man addresses a clump of trees. Ancestors are whispered to by adults in performing magic. When an illness or misfortune occurs, a father or neighbor will break knotted strips of cordyline leaf, talking to the spirits to find out which one is causing trouble and why. The child learns that dead relatives encountered in dream are the 'shades' of the dead; other shades appear in the guise of living relatives, or unknown people. Adults' admonitions to children often refer to these shades as *adalo*, 'ancestral spirits'. A child learns that the bush around the clearing, the darkness of night, marginal places, are the abode of *adalo kwasi*, 'wild spirits', malevolent and dangerous; the clearing, the world of the familiar, is the realm of *adalo* proper, the spirits of the dead.

Adalo, a child learns early, are beings that help and punish: the source of success, gratification, and security, and the cause of illness, death, and misfortune; makers and enforcers of rules that must at first seem arbitrary. Subconsciously at least, a child must perceive that *adalo* are like parents; and to them, as to parents, a child's feelings must be deeply ambivalent.

Again, little Seri's perceptions are revealing:

RMK: Have you seen an *adalo*?
Seri: Yes.
RMK: Where?
Seri: In the bush. In the house. I dream them.
RMK: What does an *adalo* look like? Was it a male or female *adalo*?
Seri: A male *adalo*. It looked like a man, like our father Seda [who died when she was two]. And one who looked like [her living grandfather] Folofoʔu. And different *adalos* [i.e., ones she didn't know].
RMK: When you dream your father Seda, what does he say?
Seri: The *adalo* just throws pebbles. It says meaningless things. He's dead. It just throws pebbles at the bamboo [house walls]

RMK: Do you also dream Booriʔau [her living grandmother, in the absence of her mother her main attachment figure]?
Seri: Yes, all the time.
RMK: What about Kauboe [the family dog]?
Seri: No, only Bekileki [the ethnographer's dog, dead from a snakebite]. I dream its 'shade'. It barks at the *adalo* that come near him, like this [she yips].
RMK: Do you know about *adalo kwasi*? Have you ever seen one?
Seri: Yes. I recognized it. It threw things at me.
RMK: What kind of *adalo* causes affliction?
Seri: *Adalo matari* [malevolent outside spirits].
RMK: When Folofoʔu [her grandfather, a renowned diviner; see section 8.1] divines, what does he do?
Seri: He divines *adalo*. He sees the shades, the shades of the *adalo*. He sees them with his eyes . . .

Between the ages of five and ten, a child's understanding of this unseen realm of the spirits deepens and comes into more clear focus. Death of close attachment figures will almost certainly be experienced and worked through psychologically. In acquiring cultural competence a child will learn more of the rules that divide a clearing into invisible compartments, that prescribe what foods can and cannot be eaten, that specify who can sit where and drink from which water bamboo. Many rules must gradually fall into fairly coherent patterns, but others remain substantially arbitrary—as for instance the rule that one cannot weave a bag, or whistle, after dusk, or use a certain word (Keesing and Fifi?i 1969). Many rules apply to one's own descent group, even to one's own family, but not to the first cousins one plays with daily.

The child learns that the *adalo* send messages to the living in many forms. One's 'shade' (*nununa*)[3] wanders in dream; and one meets and talks to the spirits. Spirits also convey messages through living creatures: a firefly in the house is a harbinger of death; the cries of some birds are ancestral messages; a species of grasshopper, a variety of snake, are messengers for ancestors. A child comes to understand in a general sense that a realm of the invisible lies behind and parallel to the visible, material world. Young Fa?ani, when she was about ten, warned me to stop whistling as she guided me down a steep bush ravine: "This place is *adalo?a* [haunted] with dangerous spirits," she said. "Let them come, I'm not worried," I bantered, brandishing my walking stick. She patiently, and laughingly advised me that a cudgel was no defense against the spirits, who could capture one's 'shade' or inflict a mortal sickness.

A child's sociological map of the spirit world becomes progressively refined and differentiated. The malevolent spirits, generically referred to as *kwasi*, 'wild', are relatively undifferentiated. But to them are added special categories such as *funu*, small, hairy spirits about which little is known; *buru*, outside spirits that impersonate one's ancestors and mislead the living; and *fele*, malevolent spirits who are familiars of sorcerers, and vaguely thought to come from ?Are?are to the southeast. The unmarked (in the linguistic sense) category *adalo* proper is more sharply differentiated. A first axis is that

---

3. *Nununa* is the common term for "shadow," though an alternative term is often used for the shadow of an inanimate object. The *-na* suffix is the third person singular pronoun, directly affixed to indicate grammatically inalienable possession.

of closeness and remoteness (and, correspondingly, of lesser or greater power). 'Small *adalo*' are the spirits of dead attachment figures: parents, grandparents, and other recently dead (these are important, in general, only to those who knew them as living persons). 'Important *adalo*' are ancient and powerful spirits, properly designated as 'ancestors'. They are not spoken of by their real names, which are sacred, but by pseudonyms. We will see that these names are commonly used for pigs consecrated, in propiation or expiation, to particular ancestors. For children, who do a good deal of the work of feeding and tending pigs and who regard them as pets, the association between an ancient ancestor and the particular consecrated pigs that bear the ancestor's name is apparently strong. "La?aka," or "Amadia," or "Kwateta" is both an ancient, awesomely powerful, unseen spirit and a cranky old sow or frisky piglet in which that ancestral presence becomes tangible.

Another axis of differentiation is between one's own *adalo*, the ones a person is 'connected' to, and the *adalo*, small and big, that affect other people's lives, not one's own. There are general rules that all *adalo* impose and enforce. And you cannot ignore either these general rules or the special ones other people's *adalo* impose when you visit their settlements or territories. If you defile another person's shrine or clearing, curse against his family, use a word forbidden to them (Keesing and Fifi?i 1969), their ancestors will punish them; but you and your kin will be responsible. A child learns that his or her father is 'connected' to one set of *adalo*, and his or her mother to a different set. The two sets of ancestors, and the rights and relationships they come to represent (Keesing 1970), are physically represented in the pig herd jointly kept by father and mother.

From these two sets of ancestors, selectively cut down by circumstances of life experience and residence, a Kwaio child's own set of important ancestors will emerge. Many children, by the time they have reached ten or twelve, have come to feel a special bond with a particular ancient ancestor, expressed through prayer and propitiation. Such a bond will develop partly through the guidance of parents and other attachment figures, and partly through personal life experience (of illness and recovery, of delirium, or of dream) as given cultural definition through divination and the constructions placed by adults on events and fantasies. My data are not conclusive, but it is probable that through conventional dream interpretation a child associates such remote ancestors—who otherwise would be abstract and impersonal forces—with real (living or dead) or imagined persons encountered in dream: so that for a particular individual, one or several ancient ancestors acquire a human visage and personality. Thus little Seri's recurrent dream encounters with the grandparents who are raising her will probably become associated progressively with ancient spirits who guide her life.

A child, male or female, will from the age of three or four have begun to take part in the rituals staged by the family and descent group. Sacrifices, in propitiation or expiation, are common. These take a young boy into the shrine, where he hears the priest's prayers and undergoes *ribaŋa* (a rite where the priest spits on the chests of coparticipants) before sharing the sacred meal with the ancestors; and then into the men's house, to spend a night before returning to the house. Birth of a sibling takes the mother, and a young girl as attendant, into liminal isolation; and when they come back from the forest to the *kaakaba*, and later to the dwelling house, bespelled wood shavings are scattered in their path to purify them. Death of a ritually significant man or woman in one's group plunges the whole group into a sacredness that must be progressively removed in a series of rites in which men and women, boys and girls, play substantial though contrasting parts. Some boys and girls, by the age of ten or twelve, will have played a central role, as well as peripheral ones, in these rites: a girl perhaps by attending her mother or a neighbor in childbirth seclusion; a boy perhaps by being one of the 'buriers' when a sibling or relative dies, hence taking a leading part in the subsequent rites leading up to the mortuary feast.

In rituals, a child undoubtedly experiences the power and danger of immediate ancestral presence. These are times of special sacredness and special danger. They must make a strong emotional impact on a child and, whether deeper symbolism is understood or not, must reinforce and give order to a child's conceptions of the social order and cosmos.

For a girl the responsibilities to follow ancestral rules are particularly heavy, and Kwaio parents have no better safeguard over the lives of loved ones than to reiterate them unrelentingly. A girl of even seven or eight, should she urinate in her sleep, must report it to her parents; if the 'pollution violation'[4] were not purified she, her parents, or her siblings could die. When she reaches adolescence her menstruation will pose an added threat to the tiny community, so well before that her responsibilities must be deeply instilled.

By the time a Kwaio boy or girl reaches the early teens, then, the nature of the cosmos, its beings and powers, is fairly clearly defined. No child could escape constructing a cognitive world in which the spirits were ever-present participants in social life, on whom life and death, success or failure, depend. No child could fail to construct a world in which boundaries of sacredness and danger—male and female, living and dead, and their mapping out in space and expression in rules about substances and conduct—were clearly defined. Rules, ancient and unquestionable, govern the universe; and humans must follow them in thousands of everyday ways, or the ever-present and potentially punitive ancestors will bring disaster. But if everyday life orients a child to a world controlled by unseen beings and powers and governed by complex rules policed by the spirits, and if ritual experience heightens a sense of boundaries, categories, and transitions, there are few social pressures or cultural traditions that lead

---

4. *Siuŋa* and *naruŋa*, words that literally mean "washing," are used for pollution violations as well as the sacrifices that purify and expiate them. See section 5.2.

a child to seek to construct a coherent and global view of the cosmos and the symbolic system. What to a tidy-minded anthropologist seem to be crucial questions in orienting humans to the natural world they live in are left unasked and unanswered.

Chapter Three

The Spirit World

3.1 The Nature of *Adalo*

HOW DID KWAIO customs originate? How and why do ancestors control events? What are 'wild spirits'? Where do they
come from? A few individuals have found such questions in-
triguing and ventured to speculate about them; Kwaio culture
provided no answers.

But in those realms where Kwaio need to know how to
deal with their ancestors, their cultural tradition provides
guidelines for action. *Adalo* are in communication with one
another, and the living must take account of these connections, as well as the myriad rules they impose. A few elders
may know the genealogies and associated stories that explain
the rules; most people know only their practical entailments.
That ancestors desire pigs, shell valuables, taro puddings,
areca, coconuts, and other offerings—in a token or immaterial
form commensurate with the ethereal, invisible realm of the
spirits—is a fact of Kwaio life, and a guide to social action,
but not a puzzle to be solved, a contradiction to be resolved,
or a problem for explanation. Ancestors, as spirits, value what
humans value in life.

When Kwaio talk about origins—of the people of olden
times, of ancestral rules, of their way of life—they characteristically use an idiom of emergence from the earth (*wado*).

Thus

> The *adalo* originated from the earth (*eta mai naa wado*).
>
> The taboos we followed in olden times originated in the earth (*fa ʔaabuŋa fameru i na ʔo eta mai i wado*).

Wado, 'earth' or 'ground' or 'land', is in some contexts a key cultural symbol; but in these contexts concerning the ultimate origins of human ways, it is more a negative symbol of the unasked and unanswered than a keystone of cosmology, a bedrock of autochthonous origins. The rare folk philosopher may make of *wado*, as symbol of ancient origins, more than his or her fellows. Thus Oloiʔa, a gifted and knowledgeable woman, developed a simile in which humans sprouted from the earth, and all the bad things that befall them—illness and death—sprouted beside them:

> We sprouted from the earth like leaves: the land is like our mother. We sprouted from the earth—and death originated along with us humans. It's as though they put us here [the 'they' is impersonal and rhetorical] and they put dying here along with us. . . . All the things we die from sprouted, along with us, from the earth along with leaves and stones and trees. It's as though the earth created [lit., "gave"] death along with us humans.
>
> All the things we can die from—those are all things the earth put here with us. "You and the things you die from are to live here on the land." [Again, 'earth' is personified as a kind of abstract agent.] Everything that happens to us for the worse and everything that happens to us for the better sprouted with us from the earth. "Bad things are to sprout here with you. Good things are to sprout here with you. These things are to befall you; these are the things that will come to pass." So both good things and bad things stand with us here, with us who sprouted from the earth, with the leaves and trees and stones. . . . The earth is like our mother. It put everything here with us. If you do good things you will live well. If you do bad things, it's as though the earth itself will destroy you.

But 'earth' as abstract creative agent, as symbolic mother, and as source of human origins are not themes developed in Kwaio cosmology, ritual, or myth. Oloiʔa's view of beginnings in the earth, constructed from the symbolic resources of Kwaio cultural tradition, is best seen as a creative extrapolation from "Kwaio culture" rather than its canonical expression.

There are virtually no myths that explain how the world got to be the way it is. Most Kwaio accept the universe as it is, are unconcerned with how it might have become that way. Cultural competence demands that one be able to *operate in* this universe so as to enlist ancestral support and avoid ancestral wrath; it does not demand a coherent intellectual system.

Kwaio do, of course, seek explanations. One man plants a crop and it flourishes; another, with equal skill and effort, loses his crop. A wound heals, or it festers into crippling or fatal infection. A well-planned raid or theft succeeds or fails. A mortuary feast in which resources have been heavily invested may take place in clear weather, drawing guests from miles around, and guaranteeing financial success; or torrential rains may turn the feast into a wretched affair in a sea of mud, sparsely attended and financially ruinous. These successful or unsuccessful outcomes—not ultimate origins and systems—command Kwaio concern.

The *adalo*, Kwaio assume, can make things happen for better or for worse: the evidence of it is on every side. If a snake bites, or a tree falls on someone, it is because an *adalo* has willed it so. The *adalo* are all-seeing, all-knowing.

> We refer to the *adalo* as dead [*mae*]. But though they're dead, it is we who are alive who make the mistakes. The *adalo* see the slightest small things. Nothing is hidden from the *adalo*. It would be hidden from us [living people]. Even the slightest pollution. Someone urinates, someone menstruates, and tries to hide it. We can't see it: only the woman who does it will know about it. But still, the *adalo* will see it.

An *adalo* is everywhere, "like the wind," and thus can "see" events simultaneously in a dozen places, receive sacrifice in two or three shrines at once, communicate with the living in different places:

> Let's say that someone is sick. Well, there's a single *adalo*

[causing the sickness]. They'll *aria* [communicate with him through divination] at Larikeni's place that day. And they'll *aria* here [at Folofoʔu's]. They'll *aria* him at Batalamo's place, too. And they'll *aria* him at Tagiiʔau's place, and at Fuʔeamae's place, and at Fokaiʔa's place at Suriauo, too. Just on that one day they'll *aria* at all those places. If it was a living person [*wane moomoori*—that is, instead of an *adalo*] it would not be possible for him to get to all those places the same day. But the *adalo* can talk to all those places at once: "I'm angry with you, so-and-so." He can tell that to all of them, at six different places, or ten, on that same day.

The *adalo* can foresee, as well as control, future events—is unbound by the constraints of temporal sequence as well as space:

> An *adalo* has unlimited vision [*maana ka aga kwasi*, lit., "its eyes see wildly"]. Even if something hasn't happened yet, the *adalo* will see it. Something happens in secret, and [the *adalo*] sees it. Something hasn't happened yet, but [the *adalo*] sees it and tells us about it.

Such statements, which draw together the implications of Kwaio precept and practice and make explicit what is pragmatically assumed, are partly the creations of the few folk philosophers who reflect on such matters, and partly artifacts of the ethnographic context where one is trying to explain one's world to an alien interlocutor. I have virtually never recorded such statements of what is taken for granted in natural contexts.

Similarly implicit in Kwaio practice is a view of the world as bound together in vast skeins of causal connection. If one systematizes this view, one can say that this is a universe where virtually every event affecting human life for better or worse has a cause. Kwaio have an ultimately "open" conceptual system, rather than a totally determinate one, in that they recognize that something can 'just happen'. They sometimes distinguish between sickness or death visited by an ancestor and 'just sickness', without ancestral cause. (With introduced diseases, alien phenomena such as traffic accidents, and new solutions such as penicillin, this distinction has acquired greater salience in modern times.) But in practice misfortune, illness, or death is almost always *assumed to be* a result of ancestral displeasure; this assumption is abandoned only if divination and expiatory sacrifice over a long period yield no results (and even then, Kwaio are more likely to assume that the ancestral cause has remained hidden than that there is no such cause).

To construct from such a pragmatic philosophy a coherent cosmology in which events in the universe are interconnected in vast skeins, spun out by all-seeing and all-powerful spirits, would distort the subjective realities of this world. Kwaio do not know—or care—how ancestors cause things to happen. Kwaio have a self-centric perspective such that they are interested not in a global view of the total universe, but rather in ancestral interventions that affect *them*. (Indeed, a fundamental contrast between religions of classless tribal societies and religions of class-stratified societies seems to lie in this perspectival, as opposed to universal, view. The latter view has characteristically been a product of priestly classes devoted to systematizing a cosmology into a theology.) Here again, a folk philosopher will reflect on such matters in an ethnographic context. Folofoʔu observed that

It's as though the *adalo* were a man who was in charge of us. Even though we can't see him, he's our boss. If his mind is pleased with us then we won't get sick. If the *adalo* is looking after us, what can happen to us?

But if some pollution violation—urination or menstruation—happens and the woman doesn't report it, people will die from it. The *adalo* will afflict them. Our *adalo* will abandon us [lit., "give us up"] to an *adalo kwasi* to kill us, and we'll die. Or our *adalo* will abandon us so that a tree someone fells will fall on us. We'll die that very day we are abandoned, or the next day, or the next. Or a snake will bite us, or we'll fall down . . .

Anything you went out to do today could result in your death. You could die from a fall in your garden. The *adalo* might turn your mind so you would want some delicacy—a possum, say—in the top of a tree. You climb up and get to the top and you fall: that's the end of you. It's as though the *adalo* says to you, "Go and climb that tree." The *adalo* implants that idea in your mind so you'll have an irresistible urge for something up there. You say to yourself, "Oh, there's a possum on top of that tree." You climb up there, miss your handhold, and down you go to the ground.

Or if the *adalo* abandons you because of a pollution violation, it might visit a snake upon you [in the King James biblical sense] to intersect with you so it bites you and you die. The *adalo* doesn't give the snake instructions. It's as though it just draws you and the snake together [lit., "attaches the snake to you"], so it bites you. And even if we try to cure you, it won't succeed.

It is worth clarifying two points in this text, and pointing toward a third to which we will shortly return. The first is the notion of ancestors, if displeased with the living, 'giving them up' to death or misfortune (what I translated as "abandon"). The word used is the regular transitive verb "give."[1] Here, the idea of malevolent wild spirits hovering at the margins of the community is important. It is your own ancestors who envelop your group in a mantle of protection. If they withdraw this protection, you are left at the mercy of these inhuman, unsocial, and malevolent forces beyond human ken and influence.

Second, the verb *booŋeʔenia*, which I have glossed with the biblical "visit upon," needs explication. In its nonsupernatural senses, the verb base *boo-* refers to attaching, supporting, or levering; when the agent is an *adalo*, *boo-* refers to the joining of a misfortune—a falling tree, a biting snake—to a descendant, or the implanting of an idea in the mind. Kwaio have no developed conceptualization of how this happens. As Folofoʔu puts it, "It's not that we can see the *adalo* and say, '*adalo* so-and-so just jabbed that man'." It is in the nature of the *adalo* to visit misfortune upon the living or to protect them from it.

Third, when *adalo* protect the living from malevolent

---

1. Thus: *kwate-a bata fana*, 'give him shell money', and *kwate-gia*, 'abandon us' (to die). The *-gia* is the "us" pronoun, direct object of the verb; an *adalo* is agent of the verb.

forces, they *nanama* for them (or *nanama*-ize them). Since this is the Kwaio reflex of the old and anthropologically famous term *mana*, in an unfamiliar conceptual guise, we need to examine it more closely.

3.2 Mana

The uses Kwaio make of the ancient Oceanic concept of *mana* require careful analysis. One conceptual problem goes back to Codrington (1891), whose classic description of Melanesian *mana* led to much speculation about the evolution of primitive religion and introduced the word into the metalanguage of anthropology: as a *noun*, a "thing," a kind of spiritual power. ". . . Spirits, whether disembodied souls or supernatural beings, have it and can impart it" (Codrington 1891:191)—the "it" being "a power or influence, not physical, and in a way supernatural." But the basic form corresponding to *mana* in Kwaio, and in most other southeast Solomons languages, is a stative (a verb translatable with an English adjective: something *is mana*) and as a verb—an ancestor "*mana*-s" someone, some act or object *is mana*. Here we can only summarize briefly the Kwaio conceptualization of *nanamaŋaa* (*mana* in a metathesized, reduplicated, and nominalized form, which can be glossed as "*mana*-ization").

When the *adalo* are pleased with the living, they *nanama*-ize them (or *nanama* for them). When a priest sacrifices in a shrine and 'prays' to the spirits, he asks them to "*nanama*-ize us."[2]

> *Adalo* so-and-so, *nanama* for us, *nanama* for me. Give me good things. Look after me. Look after us, so nothing bad will happen in our [your and my] place. You stay there and protect us.

Kwaio do not know how the *adalo nanama*-ize them, or their

2. *Nanamaŋe?enia* is *nanama*-ize; *-ŋe?eni-* is a transitive verb ending, which takes "us" as direct object.

gardens and pigs.[3] It is not, they surmise, that *adalo* physically affect the taro or pigs, or in some quasi-physical way manipulate the lives of humans in a positive direction. Rather, it is the nature of taro plants, or pigs, or children to grow well and quickly to maturity unless some outside agent disrupts this natural process. The ancestors do not add some magical, mystical ingredient (*mana* as anthropologically conceived, an invisible agent of potency). Rather, by watching over humans and their efforts, the *adalo* allow their natural fulfillment.

Kwaio perceive that the *adalo* have *nanama*-ed for them when they see that natural processes have successfully run their course, that human efforts have been rewarded. As prominent feastgiver ʔElota put it,

> What we see is that something happens. Somebody recovers. The taro grows well. Unless the *adalo nanama* [using the term as a verb] the pig will die, the taro will grow badly. We don't see *how* it happens. What we see is the man who recovers. We see that he is alive. Or we see that the taro or pigs are good. Or that a man has won his court case. Then we know that the adalo has *nanama*-ed.

Kwaio also use *nanama* as a stative verb. If a magical spell works, it is *nanama*, 'efficacious'. If divination turns out to have yielded a correct answer, it is *nanama*, 'confirmed'.[4]

People say, of powerful magic, that "ʔola e toʔo, ʔola e nanama," "It's true, it's efficacious." The implication is that acts or processes have a natural potential or goal-state, a mode of realization. If this potential is fulfilled—whether it is the "working" of a magic spell or the confirmation of a divination—then "it" is *nanama*. (The "it" is often unspecified and abstract, as in "it came true.") The nominalized form *nanamaŋaa* is a verbal noun—not a substantive. We can best translate it as "*nanama*-ization": the process whereby *adalo* protect their descendants, and their efforts, from harmful forces.

---

3. When the direct object of *nanama*-ize is not a person but a herd of pigs or a garden, a different transitive suffix -*teʔeni*- is used.
4. There is not necessarily an implication of supernatural potentiation: if you try to start an outboard motor, and succeed, you can say: "It's *nanama*!"—it works.

In a forthcoming monograph (Keesing 1980e) I discuss the implications for comparative anthropology of this Malaita concept of *mana* as process and as state, not as a supernatural force or substance. I suggest that early scholars in Oceania may have falsely concretized *mana* as a "thing" because they sought to create a coherent and systematic theology out of a pragmatic philosophy. Kwaio, like many other Pacific peoples, are more concerned with acting in the world than creating an all-embracing metaphysical system. If we create one for them, we are prone to do so with a European, not a Melanesian, logic (cf. Needham 1977).

Perceiving *nanama*-ing as a kind of supernatural conferring of grace relieves Kwaio, apparently, of a need to speculate about how ancestors *nanama* the living and their efforts. Hogbin encountered a similar disinterest in metaphysics in Kaoka, Guadalcanal: "Nobody knows how *nanama* works, and I gathered the thought had never occurred to anyone before" (Hogbin 1936:245).

But for Kwaio, a kind of metaphysic is covertly expressed linguistically: an implicit conception of *adalo* as *nanama*-izing things and events by surrounding them with a kind of mantle of protection against destructive forces and malevolent beings. A key term is *ʔafuia*, which in its physical senses is 'around (the outside of)'. In nonphysical senses it carries a meaning 'on behalf of'. Thus *aga ʔafuia* is 'look out for, take responsibility for' (where *aga* is the common intransitive verb "look"). In many contexts of religious practice the subject of a verb is a human actor, but the agent through whom the act derives its efficacy is an ancestral spirit—so the 'on behalf of' implies either a mantle of protection or the active conveying of support:

> *naru ʔafuia* (sacrifice in expiation on behalf of)
>
> *rii ʔafuia* (consecrate a propitiatory pig to an ancestor on behalf of)
>
> *gama ʔafuia kaloŋa* (ritually eat a sacred taro pudding to ensure ancestral benefits for the land)

The "mantle" is metaphoric, not physical. It is protection of the kind a mother gives to her children, to keep them from harm. As Moruka, a young woman, expresses it,

> If the *adalo* is angry with you, and if some misfortune is about to strike you, your *adalo* will say, "If it strikes you, that's fine." The *adalo* isn't *nanama*-ing us, it is angry with us. And it visits some bad thing upon us. But if we carefully observe the things the *adalo* wants us to do, we won't be afflicted even in the midst of illness. . . . Let's take a taro garden. The *adalo* will watch over it. It keeps its attention on the garden to prevent anything bad happening to it.

Kwaio are more concerned with means than with meanings, with results than with reasons, with controlling than with explaining. The concept of *nanama*-ization gives a retrospective understanding of success and failure, good living and catastrophe; and it gives hope that by negotiating with ancestors, the living can enlist their powers and solicit their continuing protection.

Chapter Four

Magic

THE LINE BETWEEN magic and religion has been much debated in anthropological theory. So many variations have been encountered, so many exceptions found to every easy rule of thumb, that the general issue seems hardly worth debating. Rather, the main challenge is to describe indigenous conceptual systems in terms faithful to their own cultural logic, and only then to stand back and ask what the particular case might add to our understanding of *la pensée sauvage*, and *la pensée humaine*.

4.1 Magic as a Cultural Domain and Mode of Action

Kwaio do not conceptualize "religion" as a separate cultural domain. Nor, indeed, could they in a universe such as I have described; ancestors participate in every aspect of human life. But magic, as a form of human manipulation of the world that requires exact verbal formulae, is distinguished conceptually from other modes of action and forms of knowledge.

Magic is used to achieve a wide range of ends; it falls into a series of types or complexes; and it employs a wide range of substances and procedures. But common to all are, first, 'spells', which consist of conventional verbal formulae which must be uttered correctly to potentiate the magical procedure; and second, 'validations', lists of ancestral names, from the one who originally 'discovered' the magical procedure down through the list of the practitioners through whom the procedure was passed, to the present day.

The typical 'spell' consists of a list of objects or acts and goals, constructed in a verbal formula. Sometimes these are purely arbitrary: "two coconuts, two cordylines, two areca nuts, two pandanus," naming eight or ten or twenty pairs in a specified order. Other spells incorporate some description of the desired effect, and the list of objects is one on which the effect is supposed to operate. To 'bespell' the object or objects used in the procedure is to aru ?ia. Aru is the transitive verb base 'put'; to this the transitive suffix ?i has been added to create a special sense of "putting" the spell on the object to achieve the desired effect.[1] The names of the ancestors through whom the magic has been passed are then listed. (This is ruufa ?iŋa, 'validation', lit., "covering.")

Spitting or breathing on the object(s) bespelled is sometimes part of magical procedure, especially in curing magic (although Kwaio informants have never proffered a meta-theory about the potentiating powers of breath [see Hogbin 1936:263] or the efficacy of spittle). Such a conceptualization seems latent in the generic term for magical powers discovered by a particular ancestor: ŋisuna Kwateta, 'the spittle of ancestor Kwateta'.

Magic is conceptualized as falling in a series of complexes (according to the ends sought). A partial list will illustrate this:

gulaŋa (curing—of which there are many specific forms)
ribaŋa (protection from direct exposure to ancestral power)
oriŋa (protection against malevolent influences)
moo ?u (abundant yam and taro crops)
bibi (preservation of stable living)

Sometimes a single magical complex—buru or ?onifa—is used by one Kwaio descent group to protect fugitives, by another to soothe anger, by still another to secure vengeance or steal.

---

1. In the Cristobal-Malaita Kaoka language of Guadalcanal, aru is the term for 'spell', and also the generic term for magic (Hogbin 1936:254). In To'abaita, north Malaita, akaloa, "ancestor-ize," is used for 'bespell' (Hogbin 1936:263).

A term for magic may label a broad complex, of which a group commands various subvarieties; or a very specific single procedure, such as magic for bespelling additives to pigs' food to ensure their rapid growth and good health. A more broad conceptual grouping distinguishes between magic for 'living' (to?oruŋaa), including magic to preserve stability, achieve prosperity, maintain or restore health, grow gardens, raise pigs, purify, desacralize, and achieve other socially positive ends; and magic for 'destruction', ŋada?olaŋa, including powers to kill, to steal, to induce illicit passion, to ensorcell.

'Sorcery' (gelema, a term used for some kinds of love magic, as well as magic to kill) is particularly associated with outside origins and marginal areas (the Kwaio-?Are?are border zone, Kwara?ae). Within their own home areas, Kwaio are not particularly concerned with malevolent magic. But when you sponsor a feast or other sizeable gathering, you don't know who will come. Thus various kinds of magic are performed to ward off malevolent magic, destructive marginal spirits, the spirit-familiars of potential sorcerers, or other influences. A lack of concern with sorcery, in contrast to peoples both to the northwest and southeast, is reflected in the openness with which Kwaio eat together at feasts, and their lack of concern about exuviae. Kwaio were much more concerned, on the 'destruction' side of the magical ledger, with powers of fighting and stealing. Magical procedures to kill, to attain vengeance, to hide from vengeance, to steal pigs or valuables, or to protect or retaliate against theft, are all elaborated and are valued and envied (though now partly obsolete) resources.

Magic is conceived by Kwaio as, on the one hand, one of a number of kinds of interaction the living engage in with ancestors, a form of transaction. On the other hand, magic is viewed as one kind of technology, a form of pragmatic action distinct from more directly physical work (fencing or weeding a garden, cutting sago pith as food for pigs, plotting and executing a pig theft) which is added to such physical work to achieve success.

Magic has a kind of hierarchical relationship to sacrifice

Alefo bespells a bundle of cordyline to ward off malevolent agents from a feast.

and prayer as more generalized attempts to solicit *nanama-ization* from one's ancestors. Magic is relatively automatic in its operation (though Kwaio neither know nor care how it might actually "work"). If one knows the spell and a correct validation, the magic should normally "work" if it is correctly performed.[2] (The more theologically-minded concede that the ancestor who originated the magic may keep it from working properly).

But again, Kwaio take a pragmatic attitude—living as they do in an uncertain world. A curer may have considerable faith in his magic (which may include administering a poultice or spitting chewed leaves, hence sometimes having a pharmaceutical component). But he still must face the fact that it sometimes works and sometimes does not. As Folofoʔu puts it:

> If a person has a boil that is swollen, a curer bespells something and spits it on the boil. . . . If they spit that stuff on it, maybe it will burst and heal. We'll just wait and see. We try it. The thing we spit on the boil or the wound—if it is *nanama* [efficacious] we see that it succeeds, and the sore heals. If we try it and it isn't *nanama*—well it just doesn't work; the sore doesn't heal. I [a curer] bespell something. If it works I say, "Oh, the thing I did is really *nanama*! It's true!" If I bespell it and it isn't *nanama*—then some other curer will have to try. "Oh, I tried to cure that, but I couldn't. You [another curer] try . . ."

An important aspect of magical knowledge (*suaʔolaŋa*, lit., "naming things"[3]) is that it constitutes *property*, which can be bought and sold. This reflects the relatively automatic (if not always successful) operation of magic, in contrast to

---

2. Cf. Hogbin (1936) for cultural cousins of the Kwaio in Guadalcanal and north Malaita: "The spell is in some senses a prayer to the ancestors. . . . the natives regard magic, nevertheless, as practically automatic in action, although they do say that if the ancestors are displeased they may refuse to grant the request. They behave in practise as though the rite can always be depended upon to be effective . . . provided it has been properly carried out" (Kaoka, Guadalcanal, p. 256). "The spell is in theory again held to be a form of prayer to the spirits . . . in practise, nevertheless, magic is regarded as entirely automatic in action" (Toʔabaita, north Malaita, p. 263).
3. A term extended in modern times to education in a general sense.

the *nanama*-izing of descendants by their ancestors. You can buy knowledge of a particular magical procedure and spell originated by an *adalo* to whom you are not related. If the formula is used properly, the magic you have bought should "work."

But this does not mean that the raid, the theft, or the taro garden will turn out properly; it means simply that the desired influences will be exerted. Kwaio know that other influences are at work. These include other people's magic. For example, as you and your war party perform magic to enable you to surprise the enemy without warning, you know they are performing magic to protect them from attack. These influences also include more diffuse ancestral powers to *nanama*-ize human effort or withhold that influence. The destructive influences that threaten human enterprise may destroy your taro crop despite your careful and correct performances of garden magic unless prayer and propitiation have elicited a protective mantle of *nanama*-ization from the ancestor on whom you specially depend. This hierarchical conception of power, determinacy, and indeterminacy assumed by Malaitans is difficult for Westerners to grasp without reflection. An accused thief, for example, may be forced to undergo an ordeal to assert his or her innocence (e.g., picking up a hot stone without being burned). But a guilty thief may pray to a protective ancestor for the power to pass the test with impunity, hence successfully hide his guilt. Kwaio tell with delight of the two young Kwaio men who stole a bag of money from a Maramasike man on a recruiting ship; when they called at his home passage, the owner's kin forced the suspected thieves to swim a shark-infested estuary to prove their innocence. They prayed to their ancestors, jumped in, and swam safely to shore, falsely proclaiming—and demonstrating—their innocence.

Kwaio magical procedures resemble those found in other parts of the tribal world in using a logic of analogy and a logic of connectedness or contagion. To treat a broken bone, a Kwaio curer will prepare a bespelled poultice made from the bark of a tree with a tall, straight, unblemished trunk that resembles the way the limb is supposed to heal. To induce and facilitate a difficult birth, a magical potion is prepared of a highly slippery substance; the baby will slip through the birth canal. Magic to attract wealth characteristically uses highly scented aromatic herbs. These procedures draw on analogies with the desired end of the magic (what in classical writings is called the "law of sympathy" or "homeopathy"). Other procedures build on some physical or quasi-physical connection between the substance used and its target or goal. The exuvial magic common in Melanesian sorcery is only minimally developed in Kwaio (such magic employs the hair, fingernails, food leavings, etc., of the intended victim). But the logic of contagion is seen in the procedure whereby a pig owner cuts off a piece of a piglet's ear, tail, or skin and keeps it. Should the pig be stolen, he can use this remnant to perform magic against the thief and his kin, who have consumed the animal to which it was connected.

4.2 Magic and Religion

We can now pause to ask whether this special case illuminates more general questions about the relationship between magic and religion. A first point is that here they are on separate epistemological planes. Magic is a category of formulae and procedures Kwaio themselves distinguish from other kinds of knowledge and procedures. Religion is an analytical category distinguished by the observer; in the Kwaio case, I use it to include beliefs about and relations with ancestral and other spirits. Since magical procedures are communications with ancestors, they constitute one expression or mode of religious knowledge and action. Kwaio do not, indeed could not, distinguish their "religion" from their social structure, economics, customary law, or politics: in every realm of life ancestors, as the most powerful members of Kwaio society, play a central part.

Bataafuna of Gaʔenaafou consecrates a feasting platform with bespelled cordyline, ensuring that malevolent spirits will be magically kept away.

Kwaio magic interpenetrates other modes of religious expression. Magic is not strictly a private, individual concern, without a congregation.[4] The most sacred rites conducted by a descent group entail a whole series of magical acts; sacrifice itself requires the bespelling of the strangling vine and other magical procedures. As we will see, the most sacred rites in which members of a kin group collectively engage, lasting several months, cumulatively achieve both a generalized reinforcement of the group's relations with its ancestors (a quintessentially "religious" goal) and the attraction of wealth through *mamu* magic. What the Kwaio case can well teach us about the classic question about the difference between "magic" and "religion" is that it is the wrong question to ask.

4. The French sociologist Emile Durkheim contrasted magic with religion on this basis: religion has a "church," a congregation; magic does not (Durkheim 1912).

Chapter Five

Cosmological Structures

5.1 Kwaio Cosmology as a Cultural System

ALTHOUGH KWAIO SELDOM dwell upon ultimate questions of origins and meanings and explanations, they live in a world ordered by invisible lines, a world divided sharply by boundaries and categories that have a deep symbolic and pragmatic force. Preserving these boundaries, and following the rules for crossing them, is an imperative of everyday living, a matter of life and death.

The categories and symbolic structures expressed in these rules and boundaries of everyday life have a formal elegance that can be set out in a series of dyadic oppositions of the sort familiar from the work of Lévi-Strauss, Douglas, and Needham. These symbolic schemes are strikingly mapped out in the spatial organization of a Kwaio settlement. It will add to our understanding of Kwaio religion as experienced and enacted in everyday life to begin not with abstract symbolic categories but with the invisible lines that partition the red earth, lush vegetation, and thatch structures of Kwaio settlements.

Such an introduction may give a sense of the reality of these rules and categories, but perhaps it risks an empiricist myopia in which we see mud and bushes rather than underlying symbolic structure. We face again the conceptual problem on which I have touched several times. These symbolic systems clearly are collective and cultural, and clearly transcend the minds, and knowledge, of Kwaio individuals. The basic pattern of the Kwaio cosmological system is apparently many centuries old. Yet at the same time, the expression of this scheme in specific rules and ritual practices is changing continually in small ways; and individual participants place constructions on their cultural tradition that may cumulatively shape it.

One aspect of this theoretical problem needs to be considered at the outset. As I have noted, Kwaio share a common cultural heritage with other Malaita peoples, particularly those to the northwest. So close are these systems that I have no doubt a Kwaio priest could effectively assist in a To?abaita or Baegu sacrifice without him or his hosts feeling the slightest bit out of place, even though their languages are mutually unintelligible. The key religious concepts and practices are essentially the same; many labels for sacred plants and objects are cognate or identical. Yet this commonality of religious practice masks some important differences in the extent to which cosmology and mythology are developed in the contemporary cultures of the different areas. The saltwater peoples of Lau (Maranda and Maranda 1970) apparently have a much more developed system of cosmogony and cosmology than their bush neighbors and close cultural and linguistic cousins the Baegu (Ross 1973). ?Are?are to the southeast of Kwaio has been another center of cultural/cosmological elaboration. The Kwaio appear to have the least fully developed cosmological and mythic systems of Malaita (a fact consistent with the stereotype other Malaita peoples have of them as violent hillbillies). While the ancestral tradition common to all the northern peoples has been elaborated in some areas, particularly Lau, it appears to have atrophied, in the sense of cultural loss, in others, particularly Kwaio and Langalanga (Cooper 1972).

This pattern is fully consistent with differences in ecological orientation, economic position, and political organization. But it poses a theoretical problem in dealing with the Kwaio material. Can we use a symbolic equation that is systematically developed in Lau (Maranda and Maranda 1970) or

To?abaita (Hogbin 1936, 1939) to fill in apparently missing pieces of Kwaio "culture" which would make "the system" more coherent? Could Kwaio culture include symbolic structures which no Kwaio can articulate? If so, what is the epistemological status of a "culture," and its relation to the people whose lives it is supposed to infuse with meaning? The path ahead is strewn with pitfalls . . .

5.2　Realms, States, and Symbolic Oppositions

A Kwaio settlement consists of one, two, or sometimes three clearings, each an island of red clay, scraped bare of grass, in a sea of green. The orientation is inevitably sloping, in a steep and broken landscape.[1] At the upper margin of a clearing is a men's house (*tau* or *ta?ela*), where men and boys often sleep and eat. If there is an important priest[2] in the settlement, he will have a separate, sacred men's house (lit., "*adalo's* men's house") where consecrated objects are kept.[3] A sacred men's house is surrounded by medicinal, magical, and ritual cultigens: cordylines, crotons, evodia, coleus, ginger, etc. It is often above the clearing proper, sometimes in or on the margins of an adjacent shrine.

Below, in the middle part of the clearing, are one or more dwelling houses (*?ifi* or *ruma*). If a house stands by itself, it is ideally oriented so the uphill side is to the right of the door as one enters; but closely linked households often site their houses front-to-front. Below the houses are one or more menstrual huts (*bisi*), smaller than dwelling houses, usually rough in construction and thatched with wild leaves rather than the neat sago-leaf panels used for men's and dwelling houses.

1. Since each clearing replicates in full or in part the symbolic design I am describing, I shall not deal with the sociological complexities posed by multiple clearings (see Keesing 1980b and 1965). They may be separated by 200 yards or more of vegetation, or by only a few feet.
2. That is, a priest who sacrifices to an 'important *adalo*'. (See chapter 6.)
3. Foods such as possums and bananas, forbidden to women, cannot be eaten in a sacred men's house: hence the need for a secular one as well.

All the buildings are dark, with a single small door—a defensive measure as well as a means to stay warm in the mountain chill. Traditionally, men's houses were stoutly constructed for defense. Nowadays secular men's houses sometimes incorporate the fancies of young men cultivated by experience in Honiara, and are built on platforms or with verandas. More standardized, and more interesting, is the smoke-crusted interior of a dwelling house. The houses, rectangular in shape, are roofed with apselike extensions from the rear that allow smoke to escape, albeit slowly. (Magic is performed on a new house to keep it from being too smoky, but the results are not impressive.)

Along the downhill long wall, under the eaves, are pig-pens (tofi) where the pigs that forage during the day sleep. On the uphill side is a shelf overhead on which firewood is stacked, and on the hard-packed mud floor, along the long mid-axis of the house, are one or (usually) two fireplaces. The sitting and sleeping mats, water bamboos, and other contents of the house are not randomly placed, but are arranged to preserve invisible boundaries.

The central part of the clearing is the lalabata proper, in contrast to the men's uphill area (gula i laŋi, lit., "side above") and the women's downhill area (kaakaba).[4] In addition to the main paths out of the clearing, there is a path below the menstrual hut down to a women's latrine, and a path to the side to a men's latrine—each leading to a cliff edge or limestone sinkhole where excrement cannot be reached by foraging pigs. The invisible boundaries and their salience begin to emerge in the priest Louŋa's comments:

> When a new house is built, the opening is left for the door on one side, the 'women's side' [gula ni geni]. They can't put the door on the 'men's side' [gula ni wane]. When women go inside, they stay on the women's side. That side extends from the bottom margin of the fireplace downwards. A woman can enter the men's side, to sweep the house, or to get something;

4. The entire cleared area is in some contexts referred to as lalabata (that is, the destinction between lalabata in the narrow sense and kaakaba is neutralized).

but she can't sit or sleep there. She can't sit at the lower edge of the fire, or by the middle . . .

Within the house, women's sleeping mats are taboo. They can't put them up above [on the roofs or firewood racks]; they can't put them on the men's side. If a woman stepped over the fire, or stepped over men's things, it could cause a death: it's *abu*.

Men's sleeping mats are forbidden for women to sit on. They can put the top part of their bodies across them when they sleep; but a woman must keep the lower part of her body on a 'woman's bark mat'.

Men's bamboos of water, when they are brought to the house, are stood up on the men's side. Women's water bamboos are put on the women's side . . . . Women can't go [to the part of the clearing] above the house. It's *abu*. That "side above" within the clearing—it's all right for women to go up there to scrape [the ground clean].

And they can come to just beneath the men's house, and go back down [e.g., to bring cooked food to the men's house]. But they can't go above the men's house, or in the entrance . . .

. . . There is a separate place where pig shit is thrown away, and a separate place for young children's shit.[5] Both these places are near the "fire-lighting place" [*furiʔi lalauelena*].[6]

The men's house has its own rubbish pile, next to the men's house, because the remains of consecrated pigs are thrown out there, and leaves from above the men's house, they have to be thrown out. The grease from consecrated pigs that has been spilled in the men's house is thrown out there. That rubbish pile has to be separate. . . . If the drainage channel [for rainwater] from the men's house emptied down into the house area of the clearing, and if the drainage from there emptied down into the menstrual area, that would cause a death. Because the dust and trash from the men's house would be carried down to the house, and then to the menstrual area. It's all right for the runoff from the men's house to join the runoff from the house; but they have to divert that water off to the side. . .

The rules for fire, enacted routinely in a Kwaio settlement,

5. This is in addition to the *tafu*, the main rubbish pile for household trash.
6. The dividing line between menstrual area and household area, above which males—other than infants—must stay.

maintain the invisible boundaries. A burning coal cannot be taken from dwelling house to menstrual hut. Rather, it must be used to kindle a neutral stick at the border of the *kaakaba* (the "fire-lighting place"), which is then taken into the menstrual hut to light a fire there.[7] No other household objects or personal possessions (tools, pipes, betel lime, bag, skirt) can be taken by a woman into the *kaakaba*. Only personal jewelry, cane belt, and (for a married woman) pubic apron— items intimately associated with her person—can cross the boundary back and forth.

At this point, we can deduce certain underlying symbolic structures. As Louŋa's text clearly reveals, an important categorical opposition is between

| FEMALE | : | MALE |

spatially represented as

| DOWN | : | UP |

The men's house, associated with ancestors, sacrifice, and mortuary ritual, and the menstrual hut, are categorically opposed both directly and in a more abstract sense:

MENSTRUAL HUT	:	MEN'S HOUSE
REALM OF FEMALE REPRODUCTIVE POWERS	:	REALM OF ANCESTRAL POWERS
CHILDBIRTH	:	DEATH

This latter opposition will be more evident upon examination of rituals when women give birth and when, after the death of a priest, men symbolically give birth to an ancestor.

Note that the lower half of the clearing and the upper, the menstrual hut and the men's house, the women's realm and the men's, in their communion with ancestors, are in a mirror image relationship—one mapped out in spatial ar-

---

7. Similarly, a coal from the menstrual hut can only be used to ignite a fire in a childbirth hut by means of a mediating piece of wood.

rangements and dramatized in ritual. In this scheme, as represented in Kwaio, there is no explicit development (as reported for Lau; Maranda and Maranda 1970) of a conceptual opposition between UTERUS, as locus of dangerous female power, and SKULL as locus of dangerous ancestral power. It may be significant that the afterbirth is buried in the ground during childbirth seclusion and the skulls of the dead are exhumed as sacred relics. There is a more general opposition between FLESH and BONE, of which the pelvic area and skull are focal points; and a parallel opposition (in contexts involving the living) between BODY and HEAD.

(UTERUS)	:	(SKULL)
FLESH	:	BONE
BODY	:	HEAD

The list can be extended by parallel distinctions operative in other contexts, some of which we will encounter in this chapter and those that follow.

BLOOD OF MENSTRUATION	:	BLOOD OF WAR/ SACRIFICE
DEATH IN CHILDBIRTH	:	DEATH IN BATTLE
SMOKE OF MENSTRUAL GARDEN	:	SMOKE OF SACRIFICE

The structures as we have set them out are dyadic. Yet the middle area of a clearing is (although internally divided, as with the inside of a dwelling house) open to both men and women. Whereas the menstrual area is *abu* for men and the men's house is *abu* for women, the middle area is *mola*, 'non-abu'. So we have two analytical problems: first, the conceptual system has two polar terms and a middle term; and second, each polar term is marked as *abu*.

A closer look at the terms *abu* and *mola* is needed. We have seen that *abu* is Oceanic *tabu* or *tapu*; *mola* corresponds to (though it is not cognate with) the Polynesian *noa*(see, e.g.,

Salmond 1978:13–15 for Maori). Recall that I glossed *abu* as 'off-limits', which indicates its relational and perspectival nature. It is not an absolute state: a person is not *abu* in and of himself or herself, but only in relation to other people who stand contextually in a different position. A place is not *abu* in and of itself, but only from the perspective of someone who is in a contrasting, *mola*, position. This is one reason why a gloss such as 'sacred' would be misleading. We imagine that (or talk as if) sanctity is a quality that inheres in a place or an act or an object. Kwaio *abu*-ness has no such implication. A Kwaio men's house or shrine is *abu* from the point of view of those—women, infants, Christians—who are excluded from it; but it is not *abu* in and of itself. A woman giving birth is *abu*, and so is the women's latrine, the menstrual hut, the childbirth shelter—but only *in relation to* those who cannot enter them. When *abu* is used of an *act*, rather than a place or person, it carries an implication of forbiddenness because of ancestral rules. But again, what is *abu* for one person is *mola*, 'permitted', for another: it may be enjoined. It is *abu* for a senior man to use a woman's pipe or betel lime, but *mola* for a young man. It is *abu* for anyone other than a mother in childbirth and her attendant to sleep in the childbirth hut; it is *abu* for *them* to sleep anywhere else. The menstrual area is *abu* for them (because they would 'defile' it); the menstrual area is *abu* for men because it would 'defile' them.

Mola is similarly contextually and relationally defined. In various contexts, it can be glossed as 'ordinary', 'permissible', 'profane', or simply non-*abu*. We have seen that the central part of the clearing and dwelling houses are *mola* in contrast to the menstrual huts and latrine area below, which are *abu*. And the central part of the clearing is also *mola* in contrast to the men's house and shrine area above, which are also *abu*. But note that in depicting an area or state as *abu*, we are taking a sort of sociocentric, neutral, canonically *mola* point of view. We situate ourselves, as observers, in the middle part of the clearing. If instead we situated ourselves in the position of a menstruating woman, it is *mola* for her to be there, and *abu* for her to be in the dwelling house. Similarly, if we situate ourselves in the position of a priest who has returned from sacrificing a pig in a shrine, it is *mola* for him to be in his men's house, and *abu* for him to be in the dwelling house.

Being *abu* does have, in a sense, a positive and negative valence. A man who is *abu* by virtue of acting as priest for his group might be thought of as "sacred"; a woman who is *abu* to confine the dangerous blood of childbirth in the forest might be thought of as "polluted." But Kwaio make no such terminological distinction, and I believe it is dangerous and unwarranted to impute one to them: it not only depicts femaleness in negative terms, but it distorts the relational nature of out-of-placeness. "Pollution" does not, as we will see, inhere in substances or places—any more than "sacredness" does. It is *relational*, an invasion of category boundaries. In the formal language of semiotics, we can simply treat *abu* as the *marked* term of the pair, and *mola* as unmarked (Maranda and Maranda 1970).[8]

We can return to the layout of the Kwaio settlement to see the expression of this subtle conceptual scheme in dyadic and triadic structures:

REALM OF WOMEN	:	REALM OF MEN
DOWN	:	UP
LEFT	:	RIGHT
ABU FOR CONTAINMENT OF FEMALE POWERS	:	*ABU* FOR CONTAINMENT OF ANCESTRAL POWERS

The *mola* realm, the center of domestic life, is the middle

8. However, the Kwaio categorical system does *not* correspond to the one reported for Lau by the Marandas, in which two senses of *abu*—one 'sacred' (*mamanaa*) and the other 'polluted' (*sua*)—are contrasted. *Mamanaa* is cognate with Kwaio *nanamaŋaa*, '*nanama*-ization', which is not used by Kwaio in the sense of 'sacred'; *sua* is used in Kwaio, but always and only in relation to an act of *defilement*, an invasion of category boundaries. The bark mats in a menstrual hut are not *sua* (although they are, from the perspective of the dwelling house, *abu*): they are just where they are supposed to be.

term in space, and symbolically:

ABU (♀)	MOLA	ABU (♂)
WOMEN	FAMILY	MEN
DOWN	MIDDLE	UP
WOMEN'S AREA	LALABATA	MEN'S AREA
MENSTRUAL HUT	DWELLING HOUSES	MEN'S HOUSE

These triadic symbolic structures perhaps call for a more general theoretical comment. First, in setting out a list of parallel symbolic oppositions of the sort familiar from the work of Needham,

moon	:	sun
female	:	male
dark	:	light
left	:	right
death	:	life
down	:	up, etc.

we do not imply that all the terms in the left column are associated with one another (women are not always symbolically dark, and they are certainly not all dead). The contrasts are posed in particular ritual or spatial contexts, and not necessarily together. Moreover, there is no necessary contradiction between dyadic and triadic symbolic schemes. The middle category may serve as a mediating or liminal term. Thus the opposition FEMALE : MALE is mediated in some contexts by the essential genderlessness of infants (who enter the women's area with their mothers); and the partial acquisition by some women (mainly postmenopausal) of an *abu*-ness through association with ancestors, to which the *abu*-ness of menstruating women is inimical.

Moreover, as with *abu* (♀)/*mola*/*abu* (♂), a triadic distinction and a binary one may be closely linked. The triadic opposition may *become* a dyadic contrast by the neutralization of one of the oppositions. Thus:

MOLA	:	ABU (♂)
ABU (♀)	:	MOLA

The mirror image relationship between POWERS OF WOMEN and POWERS OF ANCESTORS is expressed vividly in the isolation of MENSTRUATION and SACRIFICE. During her menses a girl or woman must sleep in the menstrual hut. After the flow has finished, she spends a final night there, then washes to purify herself, and (after spending the day in the clearing) finally enters the house. The men and boys who partake of a sacrifice sleep in the men's house, wash ritually in the morning, and only after doing so can enter the dwelling house. Such transitions from *abu* to *mola*—upwards or downwards—are always ritualized, if only by washing to remove traces of menstrual blood or the grease of sacrificial pork.

The mirror-imaging is more striking (and the transition more elaborately dramatized ritually) in the case of childbirth and its symbolic converse, the isolation of *suruʔai*, the 'taboo-keeper', after a crematory sacrifice or death of a priest. Before childbirth the pregnant woman builds a 'childbirth hut' (*fale ni lafiŋa*) out of sight in the forest below the *kaakaba*; and when childbirth is imminent, she withdraws there, remaining out of sight of men for fifteen days after the birth. In this period of isolation, she remains (except for necessary bodily functions) on her bed. An unmarried girl attends her (*ʔokoeʔenia*, lit., "carries bundles"), bringing her water and food from a special plot in the 'menstrual garden'. After elaborate rites of purification, including shaving the head and washing, the mother, neonate, and attendant come up to the *kaakaba* and can be seen by men, but cannot enter the domestic realm for a further period of seclusion. In the symbolic converse of this procedure, a man retires into a sacred men's house[9] and remains in a partitioned-off area, entering and leaving by a special door, and staying out of sight of women. When not participating in rites, he is supposed to stay on his bed. He is attended by a young man who *ʔokoeʔenia*, bringing water and food from a special sacred plot. Eventually, before

---

9. Traditionally, in the forest in or beside the group's main shrine, but nowadays often at the upper margin of the clearing. See section 6.4.

he is seen by women at the upper margins of the clearing, he undergoes purificatory rites (including washing and head-shaving). These sequences not only dramatize the symbolic mirroring of WOMEN'S POWER and ANCESTRAL POWER; they express the parallel mirror-imaging of CHILDBIRTH and DEATH: the 'taboo-keeper' is symbolically giving birth to a new ancestor (see Maranda 1976).

The complexities of these symbolic polarities are illustrated in another context where the operant contrast is between CHILDBIRTH and WAR: a warrior wounded in combat retires to a lean-to in the forest, helped by an attendant. That shelter, like the childbirth hut, is a *fale*.[10]

At this point, the terms "pollution" and "polluted" need further clarification. The Marandas (1970) describe the realm of women in Lau as *sua*, 'polluted'; and in earlier publications I did the same for Kwaio. But Kwaio do not refer to the *kaakaba* area as *sua*, or to a woman who is there as *sua* (see Hogbin 1939:114–15). From the standpoint of the community, she is *abu*, in the sense of being ritually isolated. But while she is in the menstrual area she is exactly where she is supposed to be: it is *mola* for her to be there, it would be *abu* for her to be in the clearing. Women's bodies are not spoken of, or thought of, apparently, as inherently unclean. Rather, the dangerous substances that emanate from women's bodies must be *kept within their proper bounds*. When they go outside these bounds, the transgression against ancestral rules is called a *siuŋa* or *naluŋa* (lit., a "washing," i.e., something that requires purification). The pigs sacrificed in atonement/purification are *boo ni siuŋa* (lit., "pigs for washing"). We can, I think, reasonably gloss such a violation as 'pollution', and gloss such sacrifice as 'purification'. The ancestral rules requiring containment of the bodily emissions of women within strict bounds can be glossed as 'pollution taboos'. But it is more faithful to the Kwaio conceptual world simply to refer

---

10. Oceanists will recognize an old Eastern Oceanic term for "house" (as in Samoan *fale*; and Maori *whare*), derived from Proto-Austronesian *balay*, "structure."

to them as *fa?aabuŋa naa ta?a geni*, 'women's rules'. These emissions are part of women's essential nature, the concomitants of women's power. Women are potentially polluting, but they are not polluted.

The potentially polluting substances include the blood of childbirth and menstruation, canonical manifestations of women's reproductive power. But they include feces and urine, and even vomit. A woman who urinates or defecates in house or clearing massively pollutes (*binua* or *fa?agenia*)[11] it; the place where the pollution occurred becomes 'defiled' (*sua* or *kwa?a*), unless or until it can be purified. But the Kwaio data also exemplify Meigs' (1978) point that polluting substances out of place need not be exclusively associated with women. If a man or boy should defecate or vomit in a sacred men's house, this is a pollution violation (*siuŋa*) against the ancestors, and must be purified.

All this leaves us with a slightly awkward labelling problem, but better that than distortion. When men become *abu* from sacrifice, or the whole kin group (men and women) become *abu* because of death of the priest, we can perhaps gloss *abu* as SACRED and speak of the state as SACREDNESS (with the reservation expressed earlier that *abu*-ness always expresses a relationship, not an inherent quality). But the converse state of liminal isolation women enter during menstruation and childbirth cannot adequately be glossed as "polluted"; it is, in Kwaio terms, simply *abu*. We can specify this state only by circumlocution, as (according to context) *ABU* TO PREVENT POLLUTION, *ABU* FOR CONTAINMENT OF WOMEN'S POWER, or simply *ABU* (♀).

Another symbolic complex builds on center-periphery polarities. Thus *kaloŋa*, 'forest', is contrasted in different contexts with settlements, clearings, gardens, and territories, conceived as nexuses of human occupation. We find symbolic

---

11. The latter term is analytically interesting because morphologically it is CAUSE— BE FEMALE, i.e., "female-ize" (Keesing 1979a:19, 21).

oppositions between

| FOREST | : | SETTLEMENT |
| FOREST | : | GARDEN |

These contrasts serve as more general vehicles for expressing a polarity of

| NATURE | : | CULTURE |

Again, this operates through middle terms and transitional zones and categories; and the symbolic structures are complex and contextually expressed. The NATURE : CULTURE contrast may pair (as suggested less formally in chapter 2) with

| WILD SPIRITS | : | ANCESTORS |

which is expressed through contrasts between

FOREIGN	:	DOMESTIC
UNCONTROLLED	:	CONTROLLED
PERIPHERY	:	CENTER
NONHUMAN	:	HUMAN
ANTISOCIAL	:	SOCIAL

If water is an agent of purification, the forest—outside the realm of CULTURE—is an agent of insulation, and of purification through *naturalization*. A strip of vegetation between clearings insulates against pollution by menstruation or urination. The forest as purifying medium is brought into play should a consecrated pig be contaminated by eating human excrement. Young people can eat a contaminated pig, but if they are to do so, it must be killed, cooked, and consumed in the forest far from human settlement (and near to a stream where purificatory washing will be possible).

The forest as decontaminating agent, through naturalization, is also used when a mother dies in childbirth. Here, two cultural principles come squarely into conflict: the principle that burying the dead is a task for men; and the awesome contaminating power of the blood of childbirth, here compounded by the mother's death. The usual solution is for one or two men to descend to the childbirth hut, bury the mother, and then withdraw to the forest near the clearing for a prolonged period of isolation and progressive purification. (Death of a woman, in other circumstances, removes her dangerous powers: the association of *ABU*/FLESH/LIFE/WOMEN and *ABU*/BONE/DEATH/MEN permits a construction in which death is purifying and sacralizing. As we will see, many powerful spirits are ancestresses; and senior or respected women commonly are buried in shrines from which they were excluded in life. An interesting expression of this symbolic complex is the old rule, now in abeyance, whereby a man could not become a priest as long as his mother was alive: the aperture through which he was born was still potentially polluting flesh, but would be neutralized in death.

The Kwaio conception of a

| NATURE | : | CULTURE |
| FOREST | : | SETTLEMENT/GARDEN |

polarity, and the importance of such categories in structuring Kwaio behavior, are illustrated by rules about menstrual blood. Pollution is caused by menstrual blood *out of place* (see Douglas 1966, 1970), that is, within the realm of CULTURE, and outside of the proper boundaries. A menstruating woman cannot enter the main clearing, and cannot go into a garden, without causing massive pollution. But in the FOREST, the realm of NATURE, she walks freely on the paths, stepping aside off the path—but not far—when a man comes past. The man is unconcerned that she may have spilled menstrual blood on the path he is walking on, for the path, though partly cleared, is in the realm of NATURE, not CULTURE. The relative autonomy of the categorical scheme from actual fears of bodily substances militates against the sorts of deep anxiety about sexual relationships and male-female interpersonal relations reported for some New Guinea societies (such as Wogeo; see

Hogbin 1970).[12] It also has promoted the development of magical and other ancestral means for circumventing normal rules. Thus some groups command magic that partly protects them against the massive contamination caused by maternal death in childbirth; and some groups command magic that allows men to enter the *kaakaba* (women's latrine area) to steal pigs.

In contrast to their life-and-death concerns with preserving boundaries and following ancestral rules, Kwaio are as uninterested in explaining the ultimate nature of the universe as they are with explaining origins. The religious system I have described, of course, draws a distinction between the spirits and living members of the community:

LIVING : ANCESTORS

And implicit in this, and in ritual practice, is a distinction between the realm of the tangible and visible and the realm of invisible beings and powers, the forces that activate and guide the course of events. We can distinguish these realms as

PHENOMENAL : NOUMENAL[13]

Kwaio experiences in dream, the perception of shadows and reflections, and the unpredictability of events despite human effort to control them confirm the presence of shades and essences. So, too, do the visible state transitions of tangible substances into smoke, and liquids into steam.

But this distinction between the visible and invisible implies no transcendance, no ultimate separation between the ancestral realm and the human. Nor does it imply any conceptual systematization regarding the noumenal realm. Kwaio are, by and large, interested only in this realm insofar as it

12. Although it is *abu* for a man to have intercourse with his menstruating wife, even in the forest.
13. The terms are derived from Kantian philosophy. Noumenal refers to the realm not perceivable through the senses, phenomenal to what is visible and tangible.

intersects with and affects the outcome of human endeavor, hence with pragmatic manipulations and ad hoc rather than systematic explanations.

It is in keeping with this pragmatic concern with the immediacies of life—with success in feasting and feuding, gardening and stealing—that Kwaio have left conceptions of the nature of the natural world—the phenomena of space and the cycling of sun, moon, tides, and time—undeveloped. In the northern Malaita cosmological pattern, a conception of a hierarchy of "heavens," associated with stages or cycles of creation, is developed in varying degrees: most strongly, apparently, in Lau, with its outward and maritime orientation (Maranda and Maranda 1970), less fully in the bush areas (e.g., Ross 1973:118). In Kwaio, this scheme is scarcely developed at all (or perhaps, has withered away, since there are terminological reflexes of this scheme in, for example, the use of the same word for stars and fireflies; see Ross 1973:110).

There are no developed folk theories of sun and moon. Folofo?u observed, when I told him about the Lau conceptualization of the heavens, that "maybe people here knew about that in olden times, but we don't. A person is born and sees the moon. And he learns that it is *siŋari*. And we know the sun and call it *sina*. But we don't know how they originated." Kwaio have no elaborated conceptions about the heavens, or the stars. A distinction is made between SKY (*laŋi*) and EARTH (*wado*), with AIR (*lalo*) as a middle term. The model of the universe, to the extent it is developed at all, is one of continuities and cycles, without beginnings and creations.

In the chapters to follow, I will demonstrate expressions of Kwaio symbolic structures in Kwaio ritual and in everyday life, and situate them in the political processes in Kwaio society and in its ongoing history.

Chapter Six

Ancestors in Kwaio Social Structure

6.1 *Adalo*, Descent, and Descent Groups

KWAIO PRESERVE KNOWLEDGE of an ancient past when men and women discovered (or brought from abroad) the powers and procedures on which life as it is known today depends. In the next chapter, I will examine the stories and epic chants in which these events and personages are recounted. Here, however, it seems best to begin with a time, placed by tradition some twelve to twenty generations ago, when great ancestors lived, fought, gave feasts, and founded shrines: Amadia, Kwateta, ʔIgiʔigi, Laʔaka, Teʔealo, Nunufa . . . (names which Kwaio use as pseudonyms in everyday life). These ancestors do not necessarily represent the starting points of the deepest genealogies. (Amadia, founding the ancient shrine of Gwagwaʔemanu, is known to have come from the interior peak of Iofana, and to have sacrificed to a dimly known line of ancestors.) But they represent the known founders of modern Kwaio life, the source of the powers on which the living depend.

In this age of great ancestors, the remembered powerful forebears were connected to one another by intermarriage, alliance, and feud; their descendants spread and founded new shrines and territories. Thus the spatial system of territories and shrines is conceptualized in genealogical terms.

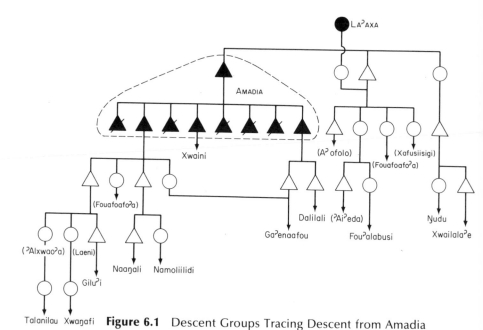

Figure 6.1 Descent Groups Tracing Descent from Amadia

NOTE: Those in parentheses trace descent tie but do not sacrifice to Amadia, in some cases due to a competing ancestor, e.g., La?aka. Sacrifices to Amadia are for the father and his eight sons. (From Keesing 1970, courtesy of *American Anthropologist*.)

The landscape of the Kwaio interior appears, to the alien eye, as a sea of green, a dense forest broken periodically by gardens and recent secondary growth, and an occasional tiny settlement. Steep slopes and small peaks, limestone outcroppings and sinkholes, slippery red clay, rain-fed streams, form a broken physical world. To the Kwaio eye, this landscape is not only divided by invisible lines into named land tracts and settlement sites; it is seen as structured by history. Many of the small peaks are crowned by shrines, the old ones marked by towering old trees; and these shrines and other sacred places are viewed as connected with one another in hierarchies as branches and offshoots, centers of the same ancestor's presence and power.

To understand how descent groups and their shrines are tied together in complex networks of traditional genealogical connection, and how processes of lateral fission and segmentation lead to proliferation of groups and hierarchies of shrines would take us into unnecessary detail (see Keesing 1970 for a partial account). Figure 6.1, showing the descent groups tracing connection to the ancient ancestor Amadia, illustrates these genealogical linkages; figure 6.2 shows a larger network of connections between ancient and powerful ancestors, and how descent groups are interlinked by sacrifice to them.

We can see from these diagrams that a wide range of Kwaio in different descent groups trace relationships to and propitiate the same ancient ancestors. Thus the congregation united by common relatedness to Amadia or La?aka is large and dispersed. (We will see that individuals propitiate a half-dozen or more of these ancient ancestors, so that there is substantial overlap between a category of descendants of Amadia and of descendants of La?aka or Kwateta.) These broad categories have limited significance. La?aka as sacrificed at A?ofolo is regarded as a sort of different manifestation of the *adalo* than La?aka as sacrificed at Fouafoafo?a, using a different complex of magic. But there are contexts, as we will see, where all ritually senior males related to La?aka can partake of sacrifice together; or where all relatives of La?aka comprise a temporarily relevant social category.[1]

The genealogies maintained by descent group priests and other knowledgeable men and women are generally similar in structure. They begin with a founding ancestor, some ten to fifteen generations back from the senior generation of the living; and they usually continue with a single line of agnatic descendants (son and grandson of the founder). Sometimes collaterals, male and/or female, occur in these upper levels.[2]

---

1. These involve blood feud. Until La?aka and other relatives of a slain person are paid 'ancestral atonement' (*firiadaloŋaa*), no one related to any of these *adalo* can enter the clearings or house of the killer's group without risk of supernatural punishment of the latter (see Keesing 1978a, ch. 12 for a purported violation thought to have caused many deaths).

2. "Upper" and "lower" refer to the way anthropologists draw genealogies, not to the way Kwaio conceptualize them (the Kwaio are more likely to use vegetative metaphors, with ancient ancestors at the base and their successors as branches).

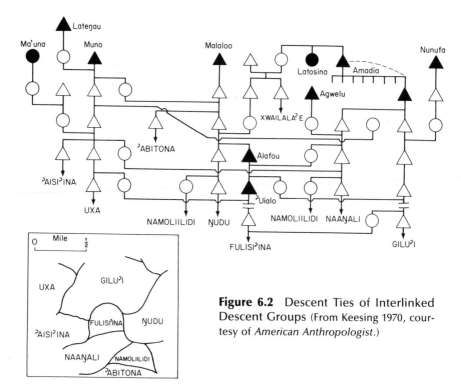

Figure 6.2 Descent Ties of Interlinked Descent Groups (From Keesing 1970, courtesy of *American Anthropologist*.)

Key to Figure 6.2
Descent Group Abbreviations

ʔAISIʔINA	A	NAMOLIILIDI	Na	UKA	U
GILUʔI	G	NAA꬞ALI	N	ʔABITONA	Ab
FULISIʔINA	F	꬞UDU	Ng		

Patterns of Sacrifice

By Giluʔi Priest
  G to Amadia
  G to Nunufa
  G to Latosina
  G to Agwelu
  F to Amadia
  F to Nunufa
  N to Latosina
  U to Amadia
  Ng to Latosina
  Ab to Amadia
  U to Agwelu

By Fulisiʔina Priest
  F to Agwelu
  F to Alafou
  F to ʔUialo
  F to Malalou

  U to Agwelu
  A to Agwelu
  Ng to ʔUialo

By ꬞udu Priest
  Ng to Malaloo
  Ng to Amadia
  Ng to Muno
  Ng to Alafou
  G to Malaloo
  Na to Malaloo

By Uka Priest
  U to Lateŋau
  U to Maʔuna
  U to Muno
  F to Lateŋau
  F to Maʔuna

By Naaŋali Priest
  N to Amadia
  N to Nunufa
  N to Agwelu

By ʔAbitona Priest
  Ab to Muno
  Ab to Malaloo

By ʔAisiʔina Priest
  A to Maʔuna
  A to Lateŋau
  A to Muno
  N to Maʔuna

By Namoliilidi Priest
  Na to Amadia
  Na to Agwelu

(If so, it is because they have moved or married to different areas, and serve as connecting links to other groups.) The single line of agnates usually continues down to the last five or six generations; at that point the genealogy branches to show several collateral lines, the individuals clearly remembered by the living.[3]

But the most powerful ancestor(s) propitiated by the descent group may not be the founder(s). For 28.4 percent of the groups I studied they are; but for 19.4 percent they are more remote agnatic ancestors of the founders; and for 52.2 percent they are more remote ancestors to which nonagnatic ties are traced (e.g., through the wife, mother, or grandmother of the founder; see Keesing 1970, table 3). Such linkages are shown in figures 6.1 and 6.2. Thus Amadia is the principal ancestor of (among other groups) Giruʔi, Naaŋari, and Darilari; and Laʔaka is the principal ancestor of (among other groups) Aʔofolo, Fouafoafoʔa, and Kafusiisigi. By traditional ties of intermarriage, members of a descent group will not only sacrifice to their own focal ancestor(s) through their own priest (e.g., Dudu to Malaloo in figure 6.2), but will propitiate the powerful ancestors of other groups, through the priests of those groups (e.g., Furisiʔina members sacrificing to Amadia and Nunufa through the Giruʔi priest, in figure 6.2).

Pairs of descent groups with contiguous lands represent the outcome of segmentation and concurrent ritual segmentation. In such a case, one is regarded as senior, the other junior (Darilari and Gaʔenaafou). These relationships are expressed ritually in procedures of sacrifice, through coparticipation of both priests.

6.2   The *Foʔota* System

The names by which ancient ancestors are commonly known are pseudonyms, *foʔota* or 'offering' names. A *foʔota* (from

3. Genealogical charters with this structure are common in New Guinea and other parts of the tribal world, so they reflect quite general cognitive and sociological processes.

fo?a, 'invoke an ancestor') is a pig consecrated to one's ancestor, and referred to by the ancestor's pseudonym (Amadia,
La?aka, etc., are such pseudonyms; the actual names such
sacred ancestors bore in life are too sacred to be used except
in prayer or invocation in a shrine). Kwaio 'consecrate'[4] a
fo?ota pig, usually as a piglet, and raise it to full maturity as
a visible offering to the ancestor. Should it die or be stolen,
a replacement will be consecrated, as soon as possible. Fo?ota
pigs are raised to solicit ancestral support in human ventures:
to induce one's powerful ancestors to nanama-ize one's life
and work, to maintain a protective mantle.

Eventually fo?ota pigs are usually sacrificed; but sometimes they are fed until they die, beyond full growth and
maturity. The ideal circumstance for sacrificing one's mature
fo?ota pigs is a mortuary feast. These fo?ota pigs comprise
part of the total array of pigs for the feast. Their sacrifice at
the time of the feast serves to elicit special nanama-ization
(and hence attract guests, prevent inclement weather, and
prevent fights or mishaps). The fo?ota pigs sacrificed for the
feast can be eaten only by ritually senior (see section 6.4) men
related to the particular adalo to which they are consecrated.
"Amadia is here," "La?aka is over there," the feastgiver an-
nounces; those who eat a particular fo?ota partake together,
and then must stay—temporarily sacralized—in the men's
house.

How many fo?ota a man or woman will be raising at a
given time will depend on his or her prosperity and the vicissitudes of pig-rearing cycles. When one's sow bears a large
litter, a number of piglets may be consecrated. Those families
which are prosperous and industrious in pig-rearing (and necessarily, then, in gardening) are able to keep a half-dozen to
a dozen fo?ota pigs for husband's and wife's sides at one time.
Their prosperity is seen as result of ancestral support, so a
positive feedback loop connects wealth, industriousness,
fo?ota pigs, and the inferred flow of ancestral support.

---

4. Riŋe?enia, from rii, 'call out', is the transitive verb 'consecrate'.

For the Kwaio family, a critical strategic decision is how many of their pigs to consecrate as *fo?ota*. There are two other main categories of pigs: 'purificatory pigs' and 'ordinary pigs'. Kwaio need both recurrently; and the latter, especially, are economic assets in that they can be sold or deployed strategically in the prestige economy. But it is dangerous to raise many 'ordinary' pigs which one could have consecrated: one risks ancestral displeasure, and hence the withholding of the support on which all enterprises, and life itself, depend. Purificatory pigs are required whenever a violation of ancestral rules must be expiated—pollution or a curse that must be purified. Most pollution violations can be expiated by sacrificing a piglet or smallish pig—one that is on hand, or can be bought when needed (sometimes on credit of an expected litter).[5] Ordinary pigs, used for mortuary feasts and presented by the bride's side in marriage feasts, are nowadays usually bought from coastal Christians. This avoids the danger of jealous ancestors coveting a big, fat, secular pig, and of potential thieves, for whom secular pigs are particularly tempting (and safe) targets. Sometimes Kwaio use a middle strategy, by consecrating a pig to a 'minor' *adalo*, the spirit of a dead parent or grandparent. It could not, then, be coveted by a more distant and powerful ancestor (one's dead parent often acts as intermediary to distant *adalo*, and they are assumed to be on friendly terms); but should the pig then be needed for some other purpose (either purificatory sacrifice or secular use) it can be diverted, with promise of a replacement piglet when circumstances permit.

An adult man will normally "keep" from eight to fifteen *fo?ota*. (That is, he maintains an active relationship with these ancestors and periodically consecrates pigs to them. As will be discussed in section 6.4, he does not necessarily partake of pigs sacrificed to them.) A woman can never eat a *fo?ota* pig, but will normally 'keep' (and periodically raise) from three

---

5. Some important *adalo*, such as Kwateta, have special pseudonyms for purificatory pigs, which may be raised for months or years, like *fo?ota* pigs, and are sacrificed before a mortuary feast to purify any violations that may not have come to light.

to ten (which are sacrificed by the priest of her natal descent group, and priests of other groups to which her father and brothers give pigs for sacrifice). Thus a family's pens contain pigs consecrated to the husband's and wife's ancestors. These constitute a set from which their children will eventually select a reduced set, particularly powerful or salient in terms of residence or life experience. A person will often 'hide from' one or more powerful ancestors. These will be ancestors associated with kin groups other than one's own, from whom one can safely "hide" by virtue of spatial and social separation. A fo?ota name may denote not one ancestor, but a cluster of them. Thus (figure 6.1) Amadia designates a father and eight brothers. A pig sacrificed to Amadia goes to, and solicits power from all of them. But even where a fo?ota name designates a single ancestor, a sacrifice enlists support not only from that ancestor but from a "group" of associated ancestors. When a descent group sacrifices to its founding ancestor, the sacrifice goes to all deceased members of the group. In this sense, ancestors comprise a kind of supernatural analogue of a Melanesian "big man" system, with the ancestors to which fo?ota are consecrated as foci of power. The same is true, for example, when members of Darilari sacrifice to Amadia (figure 6.1): the 'shade' of the pig is thought to be divided by Amadia among Darilari descendants, including its founding ancestor, grandson of the senior Amadia.

6.3 Sociology of the Living, Sociology of the Dead

Such parallels between the Kwaio system of ancestors and sacrifice and the social structure of the living call for closer examination. I have suggested (1970, 1976) ways in which the sociology of the dead, and the relations of sacrifice to them, form a kind of analogue to the sociology of the living. It is worth briefly summarizing the argument, although to go further would require a much more detailed analysis of Kwaio descent groups than is possible here.

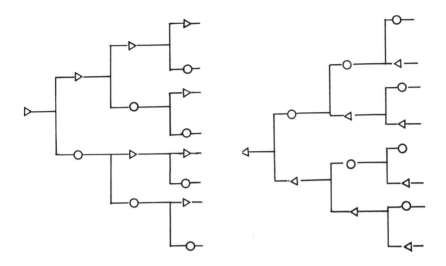

Perhaps it is simplest to say that the system looked at from the perspective of the living is a kind of inversion of the system looked at from the perspective of the dead. Looking from the standpoint of a particular living person, he or she has many ancestors; a person represents the conjunction of a number of lines of descent (the Kwaio talk about this in terms of "returning from" a series of ancestors). From the standpoint of an important ancestor such as the senior Amadia, a series of ramifying lines of descent "return" outward. Although genealogical diagrams distort somewhat the Kwaio conception of "returning" or metaphors in which ancestors are like the base of a tree from which descendants ramify, they illustrate the perspectival mirroring. These perspectival focuses are oriented by the ancestors' exclusive concern with their own descendants, and ego's concern with his or her own ancestors. An adult Kwaio man or woman raises pigs for sacrifice at a number of different shrines, to different ancestors; an ancestor receives pigs at a number of shrines from different descendants. The force of agnatic and nonagnatic descent emerges in this mirroring as well:

Nonagnatic affiliants to a descent group are included among its ancestors when they die and receive sacrifice along with agnatic ancestors. Just as in life ideally they do not succeed to the priesthood [see section 6.4] or secular primacy ahead of agnates . . . , so they would not assume primacy in the "ancestral kin group." An ancestor who had a dual descent group membership in life can receive sacrifice . . . from those with whose descent group he affiliated as a nonagnate. This reflects, on an eschatological plane, the possibility of dual membership. Among the living, such a possibility is expressed in ritual when the same person, at the same event, undergoes the *ribaŋa* sacrament twice, once as a member of each group. (Keesing 1970:761)

Ancestors serve as crucial points of reference in terms of which the living trace their relationships to one another and to land. People who participate (directly or indirectly) in sacrifice together through a particular priest at a particular shrine comprise a single ritual community; one validates land rights in a descent group's territory by participation in this ritual community. Two people who don't know their genealogical relationship can establish their kinship with reference to such a ritual community—that is, by virtue of common descent from the ancestors of the same *fanua*, even if for each it is a remote tie. (For example, if my father's mother's father was from Giruʔi, and your mother's mother's mother was from Giruʔi, we know we share common descent: the Giruʔi priest is supposed to be able to establish our precise connection. When a purificatory pig is sacrificed at Giruʔi, we—or our brothers, if we are women—could partake of the communion.) I have suggested that it is in ritual contexts (such as those following the death of a priest; see sections 10.3 and 11.1) that those who have a primary affiliation to a place such as Giruʔi are most clearly crystallized into a "descent group," as the core of a ritual community: in everyday life, the edges of the group may be blurred, and its members physically dispersed by out-marriage and shifting patterns of residence (Keesing 1971).

The more ancient and powerful ancestors like Amadia also serve as crucial points of sociological reference: any two people related to Amadia are *futa suria adalo*, 'related because of a [common] ancestor', and have minimal kinship obligations to one another (Keesing 1980b). Within a neighborhood such as that shown in figure 6.2, common ancestors such as Amadia, and linkage between shrines and their priests, define in religious terms the close social relations among groups long linked by intermarriage and alliance in feuds.

The procedures of sacrifice and ritual relations between priests further express social relationships, cast in genealogical terms. The complex of magic for sacrifice (*kwalo*, "vine," referring to the vine used to throttle pigs) will be shared by the priests of a set of interlinked shrines; thus the priests from Giruʔi, Dudu, Naaŋari, and Namoriiridi (figure 6.2) use the same sacrificial magic for sacrifice to Amadia, and so constitute a single *maaʔekwalo*, 'ritual section'. The priests of shrines closely linked (commonly by agnatic descent from the same ancestor), such as Giruʔi and Naaŋari or Darilari and Gaʔenaafou (figure 6.1), are coparticipants in one another's sacrifices. Whereas normally only the priest who sacrifices can eat the head, liver, and other sacred parts of a pig he has sacrificed, the priest of a linked shrine can partake of these portions, in specified ways. The shrines have a specified primacy (Giruʔi as prior to Naaŋari, Darilari as prior to Gaʔenaafou), and the priests for each have a senior-junior relationship, ritually expressed. The Giruʔi priest can eat the head, as well as other sacred parts, of a pig sacrificed by the Naaŋari priest; the Naaŋari priest can eat the sacred parts, but not the head, of a pig sacrificed by his Giruʔi counterpart.

Shrines and sacrifice, and the propitiation of ancient ancestors, thus provide a kind of mapping of the history of social relationships, an enactment of the past as it continues in the present, through the invisible but ubiquitous presence and powers of the *taʔa baʔita*, 'people of olden times' (lit., "big people"), who watch over their descendants.

6.4 Shrines

Most shrines (*baʔe*) are used for propitiatory and purificatory sacrifice (they are called 'strangling shrines', referring to the way pigs are throttled with a vine tied around the snout). Some of these shrines are also used for 'crematory sacrifice'. These *baʔe ni suuŋa* are particularly sacred. Other shrines, or portions of shrines, are used for burial and as skull repositories. As we have noted, a *fanua*, 'shrine-territory', has a traditional founding shrine and a series of branch shrines at subsequent settlement sites. Old shrines may have been closed as a result of dangerous sacredness or defilement (especially by the 1927 punitive expedition), or simply disuse (the latter are classed as 'cold').

Some branch shrines within a *fanua* are not venues for sacrifice to "local" ancestors. In Gaʔenaafou, for example, a shrine has been established where the priest from Fouʔalabusi (five hours away in the interior) comes to sacrifice. A Fouʔalabusi woman named Faʔaoria, now in her fifties, married a Gaʔenaafou man, and she and her children raise pigs to her ancestors. The local shrine obviates the need to carry pigs a long distance. In a generation or two, Faʔaoria's descendants might be authorized to sacrifice separately, with one of them serving as priest. Through such processes, branch shrines at which local priests sacrifice to nonlocal ancestors are dotted throughout the landscape.

Focal points of sacredness are the *umu*, 'ovenstones', on which sacrificial pigs are cooked. They are not "altars" in a strict sense, but they have the same aura of sanctity. A single ancestor to which pigs are sacrificed will have one *umu* for propitiatory sacrifice, another for purificatory sacrifice. But the sociology of ancestors, as reflected in ovenstones, is exceedingly complex. Some ancestors receive sacrifice on the same ovenstones, others are strictly separated. Some *umu* are used for both *foʔota* and purificatory pigs, some ancestors have separate *umu* for each purpose—all governed by complicated rules. Thus the physical arrangement of the piles of ovenstones in a shrine—Amadia here; Agweru six feet away over there; La?aka on this side; ?Igi?igi on that side—constitutes a kind of physical map of the ancestral universe of a particular descent group. The founding of a significant branch shrine is ritualized by transfer of one ovenstone from the original shrine to the new one. As foci of ancestral sacredness, the ovenstones can become targets of curses. To speak of defecating on *umu* is to defile an ancestor. In taking an oath (Keesing 1979a) to deny a theft, a suspect may be requested to say "I shit on the ovenstones of [ancestors] Q, R, S . . . and stole so-and-so's pig"; if the suspect is guilty, he will massively defile the stones and call down ancestral wrath. Drastic purification to "throw away the curse" by sacrifice will be required to make amends.

Most settlements will have at least a small secondary shrine immediately above the men's house; it and the sacred area next to the men's house serve as settings where the spirits can be addressed by a priest or other spokesman. These secondary shrines often serve as burial places for men. Important women are usually buried at their outer margins, or beside men's houses.

Some descent groups maintain a 'sacred men's house' in or near their principal shrine. There is some evidence that this was the traditional pattern, where this men's house—out of sight of women in the forest above the clearing—was the symbolic converse of the childbirth hut below the *kaakaba*.

6.5   Priests and Other Officiants

Each descent group normally has one 'priest', *wane naa ba?e* ("shrine-man"), who acts as officiant when the group sacrifices to its principal ancestors; he *tania ba?e*, "holds the shrine," on their behalf.[6] In ideal circumstances he is a senior

---

6. Rarely, two or more priests may have divided ritual duties on behalf of the descent group, but this usually happens only when the descent group has two separate clusters of ancestors, associated with different lands and propitiated at separate shrines.

man agnatically descended from the founding ancestors. But in modern times, especially with numbers in the mountains thinned by Christianization and the depredations of the 1927 punitive expedition, there may be no senior agnates available; hence many nonagnates, and young men scarcely into their twenties, have been pressed into service.

A priest is not a full-time ritual specialist: in everyday life he works and lives in ways scarcely different from his fellows. Some special rules of sacredness restrict his contact with women's things, extensions of the rules that apply to any ritually senior man. But when he acts as officiant in important rites, he enters into sacred and dangerous communion with the ancestors, requiring special isolation and sacredness. Many men find these rules, particularly those enjoining chastity, onerous; hence succession to the responsibilities a priest carries is not always eagerly sought.

The senior men of a descent group (or, if it has dwindled, the cognatic descendants with the strongest interests and greatest knowledge) bear a collective responsibility to learn, and hence preserve across the generations, the sacrificial magic and genealogical knowledge on which the group's ritual survival depends. In sacrifice, one or more of them will act as assistants. They will also provide guidance for a new and young priest.[7] In some cases, a young man has had to succeed to a priesthood without learning the needed magic and sacrificial procedures, with no other kin knowledgeable enough to instruct him. The solution is for the young priest to ask his dead predecessor (as a 'minor' *adalo*) to perform those procedures he does not know, and fix things up with the "big" *adalo* concerned.

In theory, it is the ancestors themselves who choose a successor to become priest, through divination (section 7.1). But where a man has been thoroughly trained by an aging

---

7. An ideal pattern of succession to the job of priest would be for the oldest son of the oldest of a set of brothers to succeed his father, and for the dead father's brothers to serve as assistants and ensure continuity of ritual knowledge.

priest (ideally, his father) to succeed him, the outcome would be a foregone conclusion (if it were put to divination at all). I have recorded cases where the outcome was not only very much at issue, but became a matter of concern, local politics, and confusion (see section 11.7).

The death of the priest, who serves as spokesman in dealing with the ancestors, plunges the descent group into dangerous sacredness. When the priest joins the ancestors to whom he has sacrificed pigs, a door has been opened between living and dead; it must be ritually closed again in a prescribed sequence. The group goes temporarily into liminal isolation from outsiders, augmented by a cluster of close cognatic descendants and affines whose primary affiliation is outside. This ritual community must command all the knowledge its members need to stage a demanding and elaborate sequence of rites of desacralization (chapter 10); correct procedure is a matter of life and death. (In 1979, the old priest and craft specialist Sulafanamae used earnings from sale of plaited ornamental combs to buy a cassette tape recorder so he could record magical spells for his children and leave instructions on the ritual procedures to be followed after his death: a good deployment of twentieth century technology for ancient purposes.)

Many descent groups (about half) periodically *suu*, cremate a piglet in sacrifice at times when the mantle of ancestral support is in doubt or jeopardy, to persuade the spirits to *nanama*-ize their living.[8] Such a 'crematory sacrifice' (lit., "burning"), like the death of a priest, plunges the group into liminal isolation and special sacredness which must be removed in a sequence of desacralization rites (chapter 10). A priest who performs crematory sacrifices is subject to some further restrictions of sacredness to which other priests are not.

---

8. Those that do not have given up crematory sacrifice because of the dangers involved or because of the desecration of the sacred shrine by the 1927 punitive expedition.

A second regular ritual officiant is a man who *tania kwalo ni geni* (lit., "holds the women's [strangling] vine")—that is who ritually kills 'women's pigs' for mortuary feasts. This man is ideally junior to the priest, often a younger brother. He serves as a ritual assistant in many contexts of sacrifice and desacralization, in addition to killing the women's pigs. Whenever in the course of the desacralization rites after death of a priest or crematory sacrifice, the women of the group undergo *ribaŋa* desacralization or take some other active part in the rite, it is he who acts as officiant. This is one of many respects in which women serve as important links in the ritual life of the group, symbolically and sociologically. Because this priest for women's pigs has been a co-officiant in the whole series of crucial rites, he may well be the most knowledgeable and best qualified successor to a dead priest; in any case, he is likely to be an important link in the transfer of ritual knowledge.

When a priest dies and the ritual community is plunged into sacred isolation, one man *abuŋe ʔenia be ʔu*, 'keeps taboos for the dead', on behalf of the group. We have seen (section 4.1) how this taboo-keeper[9] retires to his bed in the sacred men's house, attended by a young man. He is symbolically giving birth to an *adalo*, the inverse of childbirth. In the sequence of desacralization rites after death of the priest, the taboo-keeper forms, with the new priest and the women's priest, a triumvirate enacting the key ritual roles.[10] The taboo-keeper serves as such only for a single cycle of death and desacralization. He is chosen from the available range of unmarried men on the basis of circumstance, including willingness and responsibility in taking on a demanding and dangerous task on behalf of the group.

Other male members of a descent group may serve as

---

9. The taboo-keeper's name cannot be spoken: he is referred to as *suru ʔai*. His mirror image, a mother in childbirth seclusion, is referred to as *geni*, 'woman'.

10. Other important participants are the *maa ʔelaee*, "section of the dead," the several males who buried the dead, and a ritually senior woman who *ribaeteeta*, "undergoes desacralization first." See section 6.6 and chapter 8.

priests for "outside" ancestors. A man may sacrifice to the ancestors of his mother's, father's mother's, or mother's mother's descent group (often, at a local shrine)—either because there is no active descent group left there (so he is serving as officiant for a remnant, dispersed ritual community), or because he and his family are living so far from the territory to whose ancestors they raise pigs that he has been authorized to sacrifice separately at a branch shrine. Such a "secondary" priest does not carry the heavy burden of sacredness of a man who serves as the main priest sacrificing to the powerful ancestors of a *fanua*. A similar minimal sacredness applies to a man who sacrifices 'minor' *fo?ota* pigs to the spirits of his dead parents or grandparents.

6.6   Steps to Sacredness in the Life Cycle

As we saw in section 2.1, the paths of male and female begin to diverge importantly when, in the second year of life, a male infant is (although still nursing sporadically) sufficiently weaned from his mother that he need not accompany her into menstrual isolation. At this point he can go into the men's house and into shrines. He can begin, although at first in a limited way, to take part in the ritual life open only to males. By his third or fourth year, he can begin to partake of purificatory sacrifices.

From this age until he is in his twenties or beyond, he is in a kind of halfway stage of ritual maturity. He is not highly vulnerable to pollution by women. He can share cooked food with women, can use their betel lime, puff their pipes, can go to the margins of the *kaakaba*, can go into a 'menstrual garden'. A young man in this stage of ritual juniority cannot yet partake of *fo?ota* pigs consecrated to important ancestors, even those he himself may have raised.

At some stage when he is in his twenties or beyond, he will be invited by the priest to partake of a *fo?ota* pig sacrificed to one of his important ancestors. This transition is not ritualized in any dramatic way. But once a young man has crossed the threshold for one *fo?ota*, he enters a new ritual status, of full seniority. This status seriously restricts interaction with women; being more sacred, a man is more vulnerable to pollution. He cannot eat cooked food from a container from which women have eaten (hence men eat from separate bamboos of steamed vegetables); he cannot drink 'women's water', or use a woman's pipe or betel lime; cannot divide a betel kernel with a woman. And he can no longer be in close proximity to *kaakaba* or menstrual garden.

A man who has partaken of one *fo?ota* will not necessarily begin to partake of all the other *fo?ota* he keeps. Partaking of propitiatory sacrifice means sharing a sacred meal with ancient and powerful ancestors, and an induction into both greater sacredness and greater danger. It is a step to be taken separately, and cautiously, with each ancestor. A man in middle age may still have one or two important *fo?ota* he raises for sacrifice but does not eat. Apparently, the rule (section 4.1) that formerly prohibited a man whose mother was still alive from becoming a priest applied to eating *fo?ota* as well. (Recall the rationale that the man is polluted by the continued existence of the vagina through which he was born.)

The taboos of sacredness applying to a priest, and those added restrictions applying to a priest who 'cremates' sacrificial pigs, are extensions of those that apply to any ritually mature man. They concern both separation of men (by virtue of their sacredness) from women and women's things, and the increasing sacredness of their own person. A ritually mature man's head, teeth, and knees (symbolic foci of sexuality, displaced from the genitals?) are particularly sacred, so that he can make binding injunctions with reference to them ("By my head you can visit so-and-so!"), which—if violated—demand purification. These restrictions become more binding, and the dangers of pollution more extreme, for a priest. Thus a priest who cremates pigs will avoid being in a house with an infant girl for fear of being polluted by her urine or feces— although for others, an incontinent female infant poses no dangers.

Now I will turn to the life cycle for women. I have shown (section 2.1) that a teenaged girl acquires greater potentially polluting power when she begins to menstruate. Throughout her active reproductive years, until she reaches menopause, her powers to create life are symbolically defined as actively dangerous.

Women do not act as ritual officiants (although many senior women are highly knowledgeable about ritual procedures, and senior women perform some important roles in the ritual life of the group). They do have close and direct communication with spirits of dead parents and powerful ancestors. They pray to them, talk to them, meet and communicate with them in dream. There is no contradiction between contact of this personal kind and the symbolic opposition of men's and women's realms. It is emanations of women's bodies *out of place* that violate ancestral rules. A woman in the menstrual hut is virtuous, not offensive; and successful childbirth is as dependent on *nanama*-ization as successful war or feasting.

However, a woman may become marked by special sacredness. An ancestor may *fa?aabua*, 'sacralize', her.[11] Whereas in many tribal societies women move into a liminal category between male and female when they reach menopause, this association is indirect in Kwaio. A woman may become *abu* well before she reaches menopause (in rare individual cases, before her childbearing has begun); and not all postmenopausal women are *abu*. A woman becomes *abu* because of some special communication from the particular ancestor or ancestress with whom she has a specially close bond. This may happen when this ancestor saves her from an illness or she has some other experience, in dream or waking life, which she and others construe as a message instructing her to follow the rules of an *abu* woman.

A woman who is *abu* must avoid contact with menstruating women, and childbirth. If she has a menstrual hut, she must have one of her own; she cannot enter the huts other

11. *Fa?a-* is a causative prefix attached to stative verbs and instransitive verbs to create (with the addition of the object pronoun -a) transitive verbs meaning "cause to be X" or "cause to X." *Fa?aabua* is CAUSE-BE *ABU* (*fa?aabunau*, 'cause me to be *abu*').

women use, and cannot eat food from their menstrual gardens. Although other women of the community can go down to the childbirth hut when birth is taking place, or afterwards, without being polluted, she cannot.

Any women who lives long enough to be one of the sole survivors of her generation, or the mother of a man who has attained prominence, will certainly have become *abu* (although a postmenopausal woman in her fifties may well not be). When an important woman dies, particularly the one who *ribaeteeta* (undergoes desacralization first), the mortuary rites will parallel those for the death of a ritually mature man who is not the descent group priest: the group will become *abu*, though less so than for a priest's death, and will go through a scaled down and temporally condensed series of desacralization rites.

Chapter Seven

Adalo: The Powers and Precepts of the Dead

IN SECTION 3.1 the nature of *adalo*, their powers, and their interaction with the living were briefly introduced. In the sections to follow, I will look more closely at *adalo* as Kwaio conceive of them—at categories of *adalo* and ancestral powers, at the knowledge about them as ancient living beings, at the rules and special power attributed to them, at concepts of the soul, and at the processes whereby *adalo* rise from "minor" status to eventual sacred prominence.

7.1 Kinds of *Adalo*, Kinds of Powers

Those Kwaio who reflect about such things perceive that *adalo* are powerful because of powers they exercised in life. Thus Amadia is supposed to have discovered—and used in life—the powers he now confers on descendants to grow taro, as *adalo na ʔinoi* ('*adalo* for taro shoots'). Many of the major *adalo* are *adalonimae*, 'war spirits', who were *lamo* (warriors) in life and who now convey powers to kill: Kwateta, ʔIgiʔigi, Gilogilo, Nunufa, Akalo. . . . Some are sources of other destructive powers, particularly for stealing pigs and valuables (a matter of prestige as well as predation).

Other powers are associated with ancestresses, most notably LaʔaKa (who is propitiated by some 78 percent of the adults in my sample). La?aka, often simply referred to as ?afe, 'wife', is a kind of protective maternal figure who conveys refuge for fugitives, saves the comatose, and otherwise sustains life in times of crisis. (She also, as we will shortly see in a myth, commands powers to kill.) La?aka, although ancient, is not an impersonal and dangerous presence, but a close and protective one. Other ancestors are specially propitiated because of their powers of *mamu* (magic for attracting wealth), their powers to protect people from malevolent spirits or false accusations, or their powers to purify and guard against pollution.

The kinship traced between *adalo* sometimes is associated with complementary powers. Thus Gilogilo was a feared *lamo* and conveys powers to fight; his father Imekwai conveys powers of feastgiving and gardening. As we will see, a parallel complementarity of power is also reflected in the fact that many of the powerful ancestors whose origin lies in the central Kwaio mountains convey powers of stability, wealth, and good living; and many of the dangerous, destructive powers to kill, steal, and magically afflict derive from abroad, brought by ancestors who drifted or wandered as refugees expelled by their own people. This same close or peripheral contrast is expressed in terms of time as well as space: powers of war and destruction often derive from ancestors more ancient than those who play an active part in everyday life and who are propitiated as *fo?ota*.

Here we must keep in mind the distinction between the general power of an ancestor who *nanama*-izes those descendants who raise propitiatory pigs, and the special magic formulae discovered and passed down by the *adalo*. The *fo?ota* pigs people raise are consecrated to those principal ancestors who *nanama*-ize their gardening, feasting, pig-raising, and fighting; the special magical powers people command derive from *adalo* to which they may be unrelated. (The only exceptions to the general principle that *adalo* only concern themselves with the lives, well-being, prosperity, and proper conduct of their own living relatives are several 'war spirits' who have, in effect, abandoned their own descendants as insufficiently warlike, and have "recruited" stronger congregations to which they were not related.)

To go further, we must look—necessarily briefly—at the stories about the ancient past that give shape to Kwaio ideas about the spirit world.

7.2   Stories of Ancestors

Two main genres of oral tradition preserve and transmit Kwaio knowledge about the ancient past. One comprises stories told in narrative form; the other comprises epics sung to chanted accompaniment at feasts. The stories concern the lives of ancestors, the origins of their powers. There are no formal contexts for their recitation. Senior men, and sometimes women, tend to be repositories of these stories. The epics are predominantly stories of old blood feuds, sieges, and battles. They include exploits of powerful *adalo*, but tend to concentrate on a more recent past, five to ten generations ago.

Most of the stories about *adalo* are naturalistic in the sense that they describe events contemporary Kwaio would regard as possible in the everyday world (although they may represent prodigious feats of fighting, feasting, or gardening, and human powers of formidable magic). These naturalistic stories depict ancestors planting taro, giving feasts, collecting blood bounties, quarreling, and living in kin groups and settlements, as contemporary Kwaio do. They do not fit comfortably into the category of "myth" as usually conceived by anthropologists. A story of the powerful *adalo* Agweru will illustrate.

> Agweru began as a boy in the mountains of Kwara?ae [northwest of Kwaio]. One day his grandfather told him to go out and shoot a pigeon. He went out, shot one with his bow and arrow, and brought the feathers back to his grandfather. His grandfather showed him how to press the feathers into his hand, beside his fingers.[1]

1. Agweru, whose real name is said to have been "Bird Beak," is associated with birds in various magical or ritual contexts.

From that day onward, he could not stay in peace. He began to kill people—visitors who chanced to come along, anyone. And pigs too. So his people drove him into exile.

He came down to the coast, made a raft, and drifted down to Kwaio, to Ɖariesi. He came up on the shore. He saw a giant Tridacna [bivalve]—the kind that is forbidden as food now. He wanted it to eat, but he couldn't get out to where it was. At last, unshaven and long-haired, he went to sleep there on the beach.

Two girls from Ɖariesi came down to the beach and saw him sleeping there. They went back and told the men. So the men came down. They asked him who he was and where he had come from.

"From Tolo [Kwaraʔae bush]. They drove me out."

"What were you looking for here?"

"I want that Tridacna over there."

They dove and pried it off and brought it for him, and together they took it to Ɖariesi. They gave him that shell. And they shaved him and cut his hair. And they gave him a girl from there to marry.

They produced eight sons.[2] Four of them died in the [ocean] pool at Bulakaniburu. One of them jumped in and sank. He didn't come up, so a second one jumped in, and sank. And then the third, and the fourth. So there were only four who lived. Those are the ones we're descended from.

The power of Agweru began when the eight feathers of the pigeon were taken by his grandfather and pressed in beside his fingers. The power that came from his grandfather pressing the feathers is power to kill a man, or to steal taro, or to seduce a girl, or to steal a pig. You can turn that power one way or the other, to achieve different ends.

This story illustrates several points. First, there is nothing in it that is strikingly superempirical or "mythical," apart from the conventional use of the number eight. Second, the story explains the source of *ŋisuna* Agweru, the magical powers passed down by his successors. Third, it explains food and other taboos associated with the *adalo*. Fourth, it illustrates the pattern, already noted, whereby powers of destruction were brought to Kwaio from the outside by exiled wanderers.

---

2. Eight is a sacred number and a symbolic way of expressing plurality in north Malaita. Sibling sets of eight are common in stories of *adalo*.

There are some stories which cross the boundary into the realm of superempirical events. Thus, in one otherwise na-turalistic account, a young boy left by his relative, *adalo* Gil-ogilo, on Leli Island near the Kwaio coast was rescued and brought to the market place at Sinalagu by a sea turtle. There is nothing surprising about finding such events in the oral traditions of a Malaita people. Myths about superempirical events—snakes and sharks as talking, sentient beings; hu-mans assuming animal form, etc.—are common among East-ern Oceanic-speaking peoples of the southeast Solomons, and through most of island Melanesia. They were apparently a part of the early culture of northern Malaita, so it is their relative rarity and peripherality among the Kwaio that is strik-ing. The distribution of mythic accounts, especially those about ultimate origins, is mainly around the margins of Kwaio territory, the Kwaio-Kwaraʔae border zone inland from Uru and the Kwaio-ʔAreʔare border zone to the southeast.

Two stories recorded from different parts of the moun-tains behind Uru will illustrate a spectrum of the more "mythic" accounts of the origins of ancient powers.

The Origins of *Mooʔu* Magic

A man named Orinaaʔoko founded the lands at Ofana and ʔAdaʔada and Ageʔeriufa. . . . He bore sons, the oldest named ʔAbaalata. Then Orinaaʔoko died. His sons prepared to give a mortuary feast for his death—all but ʔAbaalata, who had no pigs, no taro, no money. His brothers made fun of him for being so poor, as they cleared their taro garden and raised their pig herds for the feast.

ʔAbaalata cleared a small taro garden, only the size of a house floor. He went out into the bush to hunt, with his dog. The dog barked at a snake, in a crevice at K. The man came, saw it, and started to run away. But the snake spoke to him. "Don't run away. Stay here and talk! You'll die if you run away after seeing me!"

So ʔAbaalata came back. The snake asked him who he was and what he was doing. He told it about how he had nothing for the mortuary feast for his father's death.

"Do you have any pigs?" asked the snake.

"Only one boar."

"Bring it and tether it for me."

So the man brought his boar.

"Now listen to what I tell you. Moo?u [that is, a magical spell], for money and pigs and taro. You listen to the spell. Then go back and fence in an enclosure."

"But I don't have any pigs—I've just brought you my only one."

The snake told him what to do. "When the feast is ready, your taro plot will be big enough. And the pen will be filled with pigs, even though you have none left. What you do is this: when the pigs are being tethered, come up here. Take a green cordyline and recite over it what I just told you [as a spell]. Then beckon with it, and that will summon pigs into your pen. You are to give the last one to me."

So when his brothers had tethered their pigs, thirty of them, ?Abaalata told them to get ready to tether his pigs. His brothers just laughed. But he went as he had been told, bespelled the cordyline, and waved it, beckoning pigs. And they came—filled the pen to overflowing. He put the last one out for the snake, as he had been told. His brothers came and were amazed to find his forty pigs. After they were tethered, he took his brothers out to his little taro plot. And, lo and behold, they dug up ten thousand corms.

That's the moo?u we have passed on. We still know how to recite it for plenty of taro and yams; we still know how to bespell evodia with it for mamu, to earn money. But that way of calling pigs with cordyline has been lost. We don't know how to do that anymore . . .

The Origins of Lamo?a Powers from La?aka

The beginnings of our fighting power, we descendants of adalo La?aka, didn't come from a man, but from a sun. This sun manifested itself [lit., "rose up"] in a banyan tree at K. It started when the people at Molo?ani were preparing to give a mortuary feast, raising a lot of pigs. This sun[3] came up into the banyan tree, amid crashing of thunder, flashing of lightning, and pouring rain. The sun's rays ["fingers"] reached into the pigpens and took pigs and ate them. The men from Molo?ani, not knowing what had happened, tried to track the pig thieves—but found nothing. The next day the sun took

---

3. "Sun" here is conceived as a miniature sun-manifestation: the word for "sun" is preceded, in the Kwaio story, by the numerical classifier used for fruit and fruitlike objects—a kind of "sun-fruit," an animate being.

more pigs, and ate more the day after. The sun ate all the pigs for their feast—then started to eat their children. The people tracked after the secret killers, but couldn't find any.

One of them, Takole?emae, decided to keep watch for the culprits. He stayed up all night—but instead of finding a man, he saw the sun, coming down to take a child up to the banyan. In the morning he told his people it was the sun, not a man, who had been killing them and their pigs. So the eight men from Molo?ani decided to cut down the banyan tree. They cut and cut with their adzes, all day, but the tree would not fall. The next day the trunk had become whole again. They tried for several days, but the tree could not be felled. So they announced a bounty to be paid to whoever could fell the banyan.

Kin groups came from far and near, and tried to fell the tree—but none of them could do it. Finally [the man who is now] *adalo* Abuloiasi, whose real name was Fuigela, heard about it. He and his seven brothers from Gule?ekafu brought down their strong magic—their *burumae*, their *noo*, their *nafa*. They used it to cut down the banyan. When they cut into the tree, it started to bleed. They felled the tree. They cut the eight fingers from the sun, the eight wristlets, the eight woven necklaces, the eight lime containers.[4] The eight brothers from Gule?ekafu cut eight pieces [of rattan] closed at the ends, and eight pieces open at the ends. They spread the two sets out. "Who is going to take them?"

The *adalo* from Kafu strode forward. "I'll take the eight closed pieces."

So he took them back to Kafu. The eight open pieces were taken back to Gule?ekafu. That was where the people from Gule?ekafu, the descendants of Abuloiasi, got their powers of vengeance magic. The pieces taken to Kafu were the powers of Lamo?a, powers to kill. But these powers were too dangerous, they made the Kafu people wild killers. And eventually all the men from Kafu were killed.

But when only a woman was left—that was [*adalo*] La?aka—the power passed to her. That's what made her strong, for killing and for protection from vengeance. The people descended from La?aka have passed down that power, and have been strong with it. They kill with this Lamo?a, and then she protects them afterwards.

---

4. These were rattan creepers festooned on the banyan tree.

I'd like to pause here to reflect on the concerns with which Kwaio deal in myth. They are, above all, concerns with magical powers and their origins. Ultimate human origins are not viewed as problematic. The more mythic, as well as less mythic, stories of the ancient past assume a world where humans gave feasts, raised pigs, grew taro, and fought blood feuds. The problem with which they deal is the origin of superhuman *powers* in this human world. The great ancestors were those who *incorporated* these powers into Kwaio life, whether by bringing from outside magic taught by a human agent (Agweru) or acquiring magical power from a nonhuman agent. The myth of the origin of *moo?u* magic is ambiguous on this point. In a subsequent comment on his story of how the snake taught the spell to ?Abaalata, the priest said, "It was his [?Abaalata's] father that taught him that magic, through a snake that talked."

Stories about ancestors not only describe the origins of their magical powers, but describe their relationships with one another. Recall the story in which a sea turtle rescued a boy from the island where he had been abandoned by Gilogilo. The boy, after rescue, became the *adalo* Koufo. The story explains why the propitiation of Gilogilo and the propitiation of Koufo are mutually incompatible—because of the residual enmity between their shades. Gilogilo, supposed to have been a short-tempered warrior, drove his younger brother (*adalo* Kwisi, also a powerful spirit) into exile. And although when Kwisi died Gilogilo exhumed the bones and revered them, the propitiation of both *adalo* is again avoided. Friendship between *adalo*, explained in stories, also is used to explain ritual practices. Thus Muno and Malaloo, supposed to have been friends and allies in life, receive propitiatory pigs separately; but a purificatory pig sacrified to one is shared by both.

Here we must remember that the shades of *adalo* are participants in everyday social life. The ancient spirits, with their great powers, may or may not have been contemporaries in life; but they are contemporaries, as it were, in death.

Hence a Kwaio priest's generalization may not strictly be true: "If two people were related or were friends when they were alive, their shades would be friends when they were dead. It's impossible for them to be related in death in ways they were not in life."

But in practice, *adalo* are seen to have ongoing social relations, based on friendship, jealousy, rivalry, and kinship, as humans do in life. Ancestors may intercede with one another; the spirits of dead attachment figures may serve as intermediaries to distant and powerful ancestors. Thus, the son of a man living with his maternal kin became seriously ill when his father was away. Divination by the men they lived with indicated that the ancestor who was causing the illness was an agnatic ancestor of the sick boy to which others in the local group were not related; and there was no one at hand to act as intermediary in expiatory sacrifice. The local priest's solution was to solicit his own ancestors to intercede: to approach the *adalo* who was causing the illness, and urge the spirit to allow the boy to recover temporarily pending the return of his father, who would then sacrifice an expiatory pig. Human motives, of greed, jealousy, and forebearance, are attributed to *adalo* when humans seek, through divination and other means, to find reason in their misfortune.

A pig, consecrated to Laʔaka, was stolen from an elderly priest. He suggested to his kinsman who was seeking the cause through divination that ancestor Gorogoru might have caused Laʔaka's pig to be stolen because he wanted a pig himself. The answer, through divination (see section 8.1) was affirmative—it was in response to this question, one of many put to the test, that the *adalo* "spoke." "I'm the original ancestor for this place, and Laʔaka just came—but she got a pig and I didn't. So I had it stolen." Once this message was attributed to Gorugoru, the priest managed to obtain a piglet and consecrate it to his jealous ancestor. When the piglet began to look sickly, another divination was held. This time the message was from Laʔaka: "If you don't consecrate another pig to me to replace the one that was stolen, I'll keep his [Gorugoru's] from growing properly." In such webs of interpretation, Kwaio attribute meaning and motive to the events of an uncertain world.

7.3 Shades of the Living, Shades of the Dead

Kwaio evince little concern about, or interest in, their own future state of being as a *nunuiʔola*, 'shade' (lit., "shadow thing"). There is some sense of continuity between a person's personality and experiences in life and concerns and social relations as an ancestor—particularly since a recently dead person will continue to be a presence in his or her own local group, and vis-à-vis children or other close kin. For example, "If we've said bad things to a person when he was alive, or done bad things to him, when he dies he will get his revenge, and afflict[5] us [Louŋa]."

Like other peoples who view their ancestors as punitive (see Fortes 1960), Kwaio seem not to take as problematic the fact that a parent or grandparent or sibling who was loving and protective in life becomes, after death, a zealous and vengeful guardian of virtue who brings illness and death to close relatives, even young children. How and why are loving and protective humans transformed in death to punitive agents? The rare folk philosopher, such as Oloiʔa, may articulate the contradiction, but offers no resolution:

> It was our ancestors who originated with the earth. And it is these ancestors who bring affliction on us—our ancestors, down to our great-grandparents, down to our grandparents, down to our fathers and mothers, and our brothers. Even if it is my own brother who has died—he will cause me to get terribly sick. If he wants me to die I'll die—even though we are born of the same parents. Even the mother and father who brought me into the world: if they want to bring mortal af-

---

5. The Kwaio term *daua*, and its intransitive form *kwaidau*, literally meaning "take hold of," are ambiguous in reference to *adalo*, in that they can be glossed as 'afflict' or 'destroy/kill'. I translate them throughout as 'afflict'.

fliction on me, then I'll die. They no longer care about [in the sense of having love and sympathy for] me. When they were alive they'd say "my child" to me, and love me: they wouldn't harm me. But when they're dead it's different.

But that, for Oloi?a (and—less reflectively—for her fellows) is simply the nature of the world, of life, of the spirits. Again, there are no myths, no explanations—and scarcely a developed perspective on what one's own situation will be when one is transmuted by death into ancestorhood.

A living person has a 'shade' (*nunu*); and it is this noumenal manifestation of the person's being that remains, after death, a presence in the community. A shade comes into being, Kwaio think, with the birth of an infant (there is no standardized folk theory of why or how this might happen). The shade of a newborn infant is thought to be precariously bonded, as it were, with its physical body. When mother and childbirth attendant come up to the menstrual hut, the mother calls to the shade of her infant lest it be left behind; and when a mother travels with her infant in its first months of life, she may go through ritual procedures to prevent malevolent spirits from capturing the child's soul.

Most Malaita peoples conceive of two soul components, one of which goes to a Land of the Dead, while the other remains as an ancestral spirit in the community. These soul components are variously associated with shadow, reflection, and breath. Notions about the Land of the Dead and two soul components have clearly been elements in the pool of ideas in Kwaio communities for many centuries. But given the pragmatic concern of the living with rules and ways of everyday life, rather than metaphysical theories, ideas about the soul and about the Land of the Dead, Anogwa?u (which I will examine in section 7.5), seem to be of marginal interest, and hence inconsistent, contradictory, and variable among individuals. It is almost as though these ideas are continually evaporating from the pool of knowledge but being renewed by the trickle of ideas coming in from surrounding peoples.

Some Kwaio knowledgeable about sacred lore believe

that the 'breath' that "talks," seen as a life force that vanishes with a dying gasp, goes to the Land of the Dead, while the *nunui?ola*, "shadow thing," which is seen in life as shadow on the ground or reflection, remains in the community as *adalo*. The old priest Talauŋa'i said, for instance, in response to my question about whether the *adalo* who affect everyday social life were different from the shades that go to the Land of the Dead, that:

> The shade that talks goes to Anogwa?u. The one that afflicts us stays here, in our home country. There are two. The one we see with the sun stays here. Our breath goes to Anogwa?u when we die, our breath that we speak with. Our shade, what you see as a shadow in the sunlight, stays here as an *adalo*.

Others have different and idiosyncratic ideas about two soul components, and many assume there is only one "shadow thing" which remains as *adalo* in the community. For some, the idea of Anogwa?u, the Land of the Dead, is so remote that no contradiction is perceived. Others assume that the 'shade' visits or stays temporarily in the Land of the Dead, then comes back; or that the 'shade', able anyway to be in many places at once "like the wind," can be in Anogwa?u and around the communities of his or her kin. Thus, from an elderly woman: "When we die, our shade goes to Anogwa?u. It doesn't stay there long. It comes back and afflicts us as an *adalo*." Another woman, highly respected for her ritual knowledge, told me that:

> The shade that afflicts us is the same one that goes to Anogwa?u. When we die our shades go to Anogwa?u; but even so, they stay here with us. There's only one *nunui?ola*. Even though Anogwa?u is across the sea, the shade goes there. . . . It goes there to Anogwa?u, comes back and stays here in Kwaio.

The respected and knowledgeable priest Louŋa told me in 1977 that:

> The *nunui?ola* goes to Anogwa?u, and it afflicts as well. . . . The *nunui?ola* doesn't stay at Anogwa?u. When a person first dies, maybe it goes to Anogwa?u, but it comes back and moves all over the place, seeing everything.

But seven years earlier, Louŋa had given a different account:

> A man dies and his shade becomes an *adalo*. . . . When
> we die, our flesh just rots. But our shades, what we see as
> shadows moving around on the ground, are transmuted into
> *adalo*. The shade of a dead person goes to Anogwaʔu. But even
> though the shade is there it afflicts us here. . . . Even though
> it is far away, its voice is heard here, causing us to be sick. . . .

Others—not just young people—knew and cared only about
the *adalo* that directly affect human life. Thus a woman in her
seventies, widow of a sacred priest, told me:

> I don't know anything about that. We unimportant people
> don't know about those things, about Anogwaʔu. All I know
> about is the *adalo* that afflict us. We divine the reason and
> straighten it out, and we're saved.

The shade of a person who has been killed must be given
compensation, in the form of a pig and token shell money,
as 'consolation', lest vengeance be taken. After the death of
an important man or woman, particular care is taken, through
divination, to comply with the wishes of the decedent, about
burial, ritual procedures, the exhumation of the skull, and so
on.

Here questions come into view about how some shades
are attributed power and rise progressively toward important
ancestor status, while most, after being propitiated by children and grandchildren, fade into limbo.

7.4. An Ancestor's Rise to Power

It takes several generations before an *adalo* passes from
'minor' status into the relative obscurity of "rank-and-file"
membership among the ancestors of a *fanua*, then eventually
disappears from ritual memory; and it is across this period
that a few *adalo* progressively rise to greater prominence.
Eventually a very few are attributed great powers and are
widely propitiated. How these procedures work—why a few
rise to power and the rest fade—can only be inferred by extrapolation.

A person who was weak in life could never become strong as a spirit:

> A man who was strong when he was alive—a man who killed, who talked strongly, who was an important priest—when he dies, his shade will be strong. His shade says something is to happen and it happens. . . . If a weak man dies, how could his shade be strong? . . . If you dig up a yam tuber and it is fat and sound, and you replant a cutting from it, the yam that grows from it will grow fat and sound the way the original one was. In the same way, the shade of a person will be the way the person was when he was alive. . . . The things he did when he was alive are the things he will do when he is dead. [Louŋa]

The death of an 'important decedent' (be ʔu ba ʔita) plunges the descent group into sacred isolation, and calls for an elaborate sequence of desacralization rites (chapter 10) culminating in a large mortuary feast. In this period the decedent will have ample "opportunity" to make a mark on community life by imposing demands, causing illness, or otherwise causing disruption. All this, being discovered through divination, represents the interaction of random chance with the expectations and inferences of the group (that is, only those questions are put to the test which people conceive as relevant, and as plausible answers; which one receives a "yes" answer is a matter of chance, but the outcome will affect the questions put forth in subsequent divinations). A newly deceased shade who intervenes early in the daily life of the community (as discovered through divination) is likely to do so again and again . . .

Some adalo rise quite quickly to become major adalo; fo ʔota pigs sacrificed to them are sacred (thus can be eaten only by ritually mature adult men, and cannot be diverted to secular purposes). This usually reflects some special contact a very sacred man had, in life, with the ancestors. He was kakaru, 'insane' (in a sense that implies visions, possession, or other 'sacred' fantasy states, as distinguished from idiocy or senile incompetence), or had some other special rapport of a shamanistic sort with the spirits. (There is no culturally defined role for a person with "shamanistic" powers, but the

rare man with such psychic bent—such as Fuamae of Tofu—
is attributed special sacredness in life, and then in death.) The
most striking case of a genealogically recent 'major' adalo is
Fataŋuruŋuru of Kwailala?e: the fo?ota name of the great-
grandfather of the Kwailala?e priest ?Aika (Keesing 1976:395,
plate), who died in 1966. Fataŋuruŋuru was a kakaru in life,
and in death his powers are formidable. Anyone who sat on
?Aika's bed in the men's house is said have been thrown to
the floor, and ?Aika himself reported being shaken and
dumped periodically.

For most decedents, the transition to 'major' adalo status—or limbo in the category of adalo not singled out for
special sacrifice—is more slow, and follows (at least in theory)
a prescribed path (Keesing and Fifi?i 1969). A descent group
priest becomes sacred to his grandchildren (that is, a pig consecrated to his spirit is sacred and cannot be diverted); a
ritually adult man becomes sacred to his great-grandchildren;
others become sacred, if at all, to their great-great-grand-
children. It is at this stage that an adalo moves into the kinship
category walafu-, 'ancestor'.[6] Kwaio refer collectively to their
'ancestors' as walafui?ola (lit., "ancestral things"), or as faia-
late?ewane, 'people four (or more) generations removed'. In
precise rendering, then, adalo in its generic sense means 'spirits of the dead'; only those classed as walafu- are 'ancestors'.[7]

In practice, the rise of a shade to power as an ancestor

6. To the Kwaio, there is nothing strange about classifying dead people with kin
terms—even if they died a hundred years ago—or, for that matter, about using a kin
term vocatively, in addressing an ancient ancestor (in theory the term is self-recip-
rocal, and means 'descendant' as well; I will leave to philosophers the question of
whether such a usage actually exists).

7. A further semantic complication is worth noting, for the sake of sociological pre-
cision. Kwaio distinguish between 'cognatic kinship' and 'descent' (Keesing 1970). A
person's cognates, living and dead, are those he is tooŋa?i, 'connected to'. These
include collaterals in ascending generations and their spouses (Keesing 1968). An
individual may propitiate, and seek power from, any adalo to whom he or she is
"connected," i.e., any dead kinsman or woman. A person is descended from (or-
iolitana, lit., "returns from") only his or her lineal relatives in ascending generations;
and only such a relationship to an ancestor confers rights over land initially cleared
by that ancestor. "Descendant" is thus only loosely the reciprocal of "ancestor" in
this sense of dead relatives in ascending generations to whom ego is 'connected',
but no alternative term is available.

must depend heavily on the worldly success of his or her descendants in gardening, feasting, and (in olden times) fighting. Powers manifest by living Kwaio are attributed to their ancestors and their ancestrally conferred magic. The most powerful ancestors are, apart from their powers in life, distinguished by both the success and the proliferation of their descendants.

I would like now to return briefly to the Land of the Dead.

7.5   Anogwaʔu

Like most north Malaita peoples, Kwaio associate Anogwaʔu with Ramos Island, between Malaita and Santa Ysabel. In pre-European times, Kwaio would have heard stories of the place through the saltwater people, but not seen it; nowadays many men have seen the island at a distance. But this remoteness of the supposed physical locus seems associated with the conceptual remoteness of Anogwaʔu to most Kwaio. Ideas about the Land of the Dead seem more important to their cultural cousins further to the north: in some versions, Anogwaʔu is a kind of spiritual transformation of the economic relations of the living, with the dead souls holding markets on the beach where taro and fish are bartered.

Those Kwaio who profess any knowledge of Anogwaʔu envision it as a realm where the dead lead a life much like that of living humans: they live in villages, raise taro and pigs. The most fully developed accounts of Anogwaʔu I recorded (both from women) were similar in two respects. First, the village was depicted as having separate entrance paths: one, flanked with green cordyline, was the entry for souls of people who had died of natural causes; the other, flanked with red cordyline, for souls of people who had been killed. (One of the two added a third path, for those who had committed suicide.) Second, when a person is 'dead', his or her shade is (or may be) encountered by the shade of his or her father and/or mother. If the shade of a deceased parent intercepts your shade after death, but before your shade has actually entered the village of the dead and been seen by the shades of more remote spirits, then your shade can be (if the parents so choose) returned to life. Sometimes another, ancient, ancestor may intervene and restore the shade to life. Here, recall that such intervention that restores a woman to "life" is taken as a message that she is to become sacred (section 6.5). Kwaio define states of coma as "death," viewed as a liminal (betwixt-and-between) state that can become terminal. A few Kwaio men and women report having 'died' and found themselves in the Land of the Dead.

The note of scepticism about Anogwaʔu expressed by the great Kwaio feastgiver ʔElota (Keesing 1978a) provides an apt final perspective on the Land of the Dead:

> Anogwaʔu . . . I've heard the talk about that, but I don't know if it's really true. People who have actually gone there, like Bita Saetana, say the dead live there as we do here. . . . All I know is what people say. The old people from the bush used to talk about that—about how the shades of the dead go to Anogwaʔu. Is the adalo that stays here different from the shade that goes to Anogwaʔu? Who knows?

After this brief excursion into eschatalogy, we need to come back to the world of the living; and to look at the complex transactions with their ancestors which are a focus of individual and group life.

Chapter Eight

Communications and Transactions with Ancestors

IT WOULD TAKE volumes to describe the complicated sequences and procedures of Kwaio ritual in full detail. One of the seeming contradictions in Kwaio religion, at least in terms of anthropological theory, is this elaboration of ritual procedure without mythic explanation or rationale, without an elaborated view of the cosmos, and without an accompanying exegetic tradition. A people so uninterested in the origins and ultimate nature of their world, so uninterested in the origins of their customs and way of life, nonetheless have attributed to their ancestors detailed rules and procedures, which must be followed if the living are to prosper; to err in these procedures, to break these rules, invites disaster.

In the next three chapters, I will sketch the main outlines of these ritual procedures and ways of communicating with ancestors. This will not only fill in needed ethnographic substance, but will provide a needed background to the theoretical questions that have been raised but not answered.

First, it is worth trying to evoke again the phenomenological realities of this world in which the living and the dead are coparticipants in everyday life. A substantial proportion of the conversations that take place in a Kwaio settlement are not between living humans but between the living and the dead. My neighbor Folofo?u and his family will illustrate. Almost every day, Folofo?u will be seen, often in early morning or at dusk, carrying on a lengthy conversation with his oldest son, whose skull overlooks the clearing. His wife Booriʔau, in the house or garden, will converse silently with her mother and father, long dead, or her grandfather; and through them, to more remote ancestors. Folofoʔu is a diviner of high repute, and his kin and neighbors, and more distant "clients," engage him several times a week in divination sessions in front of his house. Their sons and daughter pray to their ancestors for guidance and help. In nightly dreams their wandering shades encounter and communicate with ancestors, often in the guise of living humans. This is not a world where ancestral shades are remote presences, creations of theological imagination. They are part of the daily social life of Kwaio communities.

8.1   Divination

Everyday divination of the sort Folofoʔu does can be performed by many men and some women. The standard Kwaio procedure, *ariŋa*, uses cordyline leaves. Green cordyline leaves are brought (usually gathered by the client), dried over the fire, stripped from the midrib into half-widths, knotted, then bespelled. These leaves are called *felo*. The client and/or diviner, after discussing the problem (illness or theft of a pig, illness of a child, etc.), its possible ancestral agent (one of an array of *adalo* related to the afflicted person),[1] and the possible cause of that ancestor's displeasure (urination or menstruation in house or clearing, an error in ritual procedure, a curse, an ancestor's desire for a pig, etc.), begins to put questions to the test. Each leaf is pulled by the diviner until it breaks. Folofoʔu explains:

> If I break [the *felo*] and the knot isn't on this side [the side being held in the left hand and wrapped around the left index finger]; if it comes off on this side, then it is *fuu* [which implies that the knot is unbroken, and the answer still hidden].[2] I pull

1. That is, the sick person, or the owner of the stolen pig, etc.
2. The stative verb root *fuu* in other contexts carries meanings of 'to be stable, steadfast, unmoved'.

Folofoʔu holds knotted divining leaves as he and his wife Booriʔau ponder possible causes of a grandchild's illness.

the *felo*; I twist it round my finger; I break it, and the knot is still there [he demonstrates]. So the *adalo* isn't speaking. The *adalo* isn't speaking with that knot.

If the next one I pull, for another question, doesn't break [with the knot] intact, then that's the *adalo* speaking. It speaks in confirmation. It breaks quickly. I pull it, not very hard, and it breaks—that's the *adalo* speaking.

Most of the time—90 percent of the time or more, depending on the condition of the leaves—the knot remains intact or the *felo* cannot be broken. When the *adalo* "speaks," a second, confirmatory, answer is sought—using a remaining length of the same leaf or breaking several more, putting forth the same question. First, the ancestor is identified; then the cause of the trouble is identified. (Sometimes multiple ancestors, and/ or multiple causes, are turned up.) Finally, it is ascertained through divination what is needed to restore the favor of the aggrieved spirit—usually it is sacrifice of a pig, occasionally payment of token valuables, sometimes some act, such as exhumation of the dead person's skull, which the spirit is demanding.

When divination reveals which *adalo* are causing the trouble, and why, the living take corrective action. Kwaio take a pragmatic attitude toward divination. As Folofo?u put it,

It's not as though we see what is causing the trouble the way we see something with our eyes. We find out in divination which *adalo* is afflicting us. We raise a pig to that *adalo* and we find out whether that was really true. . . . If we see that a child is sick, unable to eat, it's as though the *adalo* is saying something to us. We divine and then we sacrifice a pig. If the child gets better, eats and plays, then we know it was true. That's the way we verify [the cause]: "Oh, it's true that that *adalo* was afflicting the child. My child is playing and eating now." When we find something in divination, we act accordingly and see what happens.

Moruka, a knowledgeable young woman, further clarifies:

If it's not really that *adalo* [discovered in divination] that asked for a pig, in order that our pigs or taro grow well, then even though we sacrifice it, nothing will happen. If the *adalo* [we discovered in divination] really is asking for a pig, we'll see things get better. But if I raise a pig to an ancestor, and it isn't the right one, how can that make my taro grow well? It can't. We say, "Maybe [the *adalo*] just deceived us. We did what they asked and nothing happened. It's something else that is afflicting us, something hidden." If we divine something and it is true, and we raise up a pig to that ancestor, our taro and our pigs and our living will be good.

Divination is used to determine who the ancestors want as successor to a priesthood, when a mortuary feast should be held, and so on—that is, as a source of ancestral guidance. In these sessions, the diviner and/or client phrases the possible answers as statements by the ancestor involved: "Keep the taboos for my death for sixty days," or "Dig up my skull in ten days."

However, some diviners, such as Folofoʔu, are deemed to have powers beyond simply transmitting questions and getting answers. They have powers to see what is hidden to others (*maatoʔo*, lit., "eye-true"). The physical agency may be cordyline leaves, it may be powdered lime, it may be sensations in the divine's body: but the powers of perception are the diviner's. He is able to visualize a scene—thus identify a thief or discover a missing person. In 1970, when two boys were lost in the flooding following a cyclone, Folofoʔu divined that they had been buried by a landslide; digging where he told them to dig, searchers found the bodies. In 1976 Folofoʔu divined to find the whereabouts of a young man missing for months, who was thought by his kin to have gone off to a plantation after a quarrel. He discovered the young man had hanged himself in the forest near his settlement; searchers found the bones, beneath a vine tied into a noose.

Like other elements of Kwaio custom, divination is viewed as having been handed down from olden times, when the Big People (*taʔa baʔita*) fought, gave feasts, raised pigs, planted gardens, and lived in harmony with their ancestors as the living today cannot. Like other elements of Kwaio custom, the ultimate origin of divination is shrouded in an obscurity of disinterest, as something that "began with the earth" (*wado*).

8.2 Curing

'Curing', *gulaŋa*, bears brief mention in its own right and to clarify Kwaio ideas about disease, hence about ancestors. Curing comprises many varieties of treatment for many kinds of ailments—snake bites, fungal infections, secondary infections of wounds, and so on. They combine physical procedures with magical spells. In many cases we would want to say that the effects are purely magical (as in the treatment of a broken limb by tying to the break a poultice made from shavings of a tree with a straight and unblemished trunk).[3] In others, pharmacological research might reveal a beneficial kind of folk medicine, or a new drug (the plant juices used to treat fungal infections seem at least as effective as most drugs in the Western pharmacopoeia). In many, psychological effects play an important part in achieving the desired effects. Thus I have fairly solid evidence that the "medicine" used to induce lactation in a substitute mother when a nursing mother has died, leaving a very young infant, is successful in some cases. A woman who has not borne a child can produce milk if she undergoes the needed hormonal changes; and apparently that can be psychologically induced by rubbing the breasts with a substance made from the tree *Alstonia scholaris*, which exudes a white milky sap: sympathetic magic that works, at least some of the time.

A man or woman who performs curing will, if not a close relative of the patient, be rewarded by a small payment of shell valuables or, in the case of protracted treatment of a serious ailment, by a small feast as well. In the period when the patient is being treated, she or he may be placed by the

---

3. At least, if there were any beneficial effect, it would come equally from any other kind of tree shavings, unbespelled.

A curer performs extraction magic. He will produce a foreign object "extracted" from the patient's sore back.

curer into a kind of liminal (marginal or separated) state in which food taboos and other restrictions are imposed. The taboos are then lifted in a feast at which the ancestors receive a token first portion of the special foods, through the medium of smoke, and patient and curer then eat together.

Curing, like other magic, draws on ancestral powers and is ultimately subject to ancestral will and whim. As Folofo?u put it, "we try it and see if it works." This then leads us into Kwaio ideas about illness. Let us look at a case where a person chopping with an axe is wounded on the leg when the blade glances off the wood. Kwaio know perfectly well that the axe blade, and the person swinging the axe, have directly inflicted the wound. But why did it glance off this time, when five thousand previous blows by the axe-wielder, and countless blows by others, have struck home? It was an ancestor that turned the blade—and Kwaio will divine to find out why.

At the same time, they will treat the gash, tying it up,

cauterizing it, or otherwise treating the wound with the best available combinations of folk medicine and magic. Though the symptoms have been treated, the cause of the ancestor's displeasure must still be dealt with. If not, the same person or a close relative may be punished in another way—by illness, by snakebite, by other misfortune. Or the wound may fester; it may turn into fatal gangrene (always a danger in a tropical climate where house posts take root and grow, a paradise for bacteria). Curing, in other words, treats the *symptoms* of illness and injury; only sacrifice or other atonement can treat the *causes*.

8.3   First Fruits

The *adalo* who first cleared the forest and established territories and the land tracts that comprise them are still the owners of the land. When taro and yams are cultivated, the ancestral owners must partake of first fruits from the garden, with the priest as intermediary, before the living owner of the garden can partake of the food. The procedures vary with yams and taro. Yams are planted and harvested on a seasonal cycle; taro is planted and harvested continuously through the year. (Taro was by far the more important crop for subsistence in the mountains). With taro growing stricken by blight, and the coastal zones where yams were most important in the hands of Christians, both modes of first-fruit ritual are less central than they were several decades ago. I will demonstrate in chapter 15 that ancestors' ownership of the land, and their rights to first fruits, are important political instruments in the struggle by traditionalists to prevent Christian invasion of the mountains.

For taro, we may distinguish between two broad categories of gardens—ordinary subsistence gardens, and special sacred ones used for important mortuary feasts and other special purposes. The ordinary gardens call for two separate presentations to the spirits. In the first, the owner of the garden presents entire taro plants and coconuts to the senior member of his immediate kin group (often his older brother). This man, the one who has invoked their ancestors in performing garden magic, *gama ʔulasi* ('opens with sacred food') the garden by making a pudding of taro and grated coconut.[4] If the garden owner has performed the magic himself, he and his ancestors eat the pudding.

The second presentation, *niunikaloŋa,* "coconut of the land," goes to the main ancestors of the *fanua* through its priest, who eats a taro and coconut cream pudding (a meal symbolically shared with the ancestors, who partake of its spiritual essence). This, then, becomes an important ritual expression of social relations, since it dramatizes the unity of the *fanua* as a whole, the descent group's collective relationship to its ancient ancestors, and the mediation of this relationship through the priest as custodian. Who eats *niunikaloŋa* for particular land tracts defines which group exercises primary land rights.[5]

For a sacred taro garden, a more elaborate first-fruits rite involving the entire descent group was usually performed (this rite is not now practiced in the face of taro blight). In this rite a special shrine, *ba ʔe ni fafi ʔialo,* 'taro-baking shrine', is used. The garden owner, after keeping special taboos during maturation of the taro, takes coconuts and taro to this shrine. The priest takes one of the taro corms and breaks it in half. He tells the *adalo* (Amadia, or whatever other ancestor the group looks to for powers of taro cultivation) that one half is for the *adalo,* the other half for the priest's pudding. The *adalo*'s half is burned. The priest's half is cooked, in a customary oven (heated stones, covered with leaves), with the rest of the taro. In a small separate oven, other taro are baked for the *niunikaloŋa.* The priest eats his half-taro, then a taro

---

4. This is the less important of the two major categories of taro and coconut puddings, a *gwasu* (*fousuu*), in contrast to a *lakeno,* made of taro dough and coconut cream. There are several subvarieties of each, used in different ritual contexts.
5. If a gardener discovers a cuscus opossum or kills a bird in a garden, that belongs to the *adalo* and must be given, like *niunikaloŋa,* to the priest.

and coconut pudding. Then the rest of the baked taro are divided, along with fish or grasshoppers, among the men of the descent group. The leaf oven, now too sacred to be dismantled and discarded, is rebuilt and left in place.

The women, excluded from this rite, still cannot eat from the garden. They stage a separate rite, ʔutaʔulasi, which desacralizes the garden and opens it for women. In this rite taro corms are wrapped in leaf, baked in a leaf oven, then pounded with stones. A packet is presented to the priest. After he eats, the women do so, and the garden is open.

First-fruit rites for yams, telefaʔiŋa, reflect a regional ordering unusual among the politically fragmented Kwaio. Yams and the magic for growing them are traditionally associated with the coastal zone, and in particular with the shrine and ancestors of Takwaʔi, near the mouth of Sinalagu Harbor. The Takwaʔi priest opens the yam harvest season first; other groups follow, in an order at least notionally specified for the whole region.

The word telefaʔi is derived from tele, one of two equivalent forms for talking to an ancestor in prayer. The priest takes the first yam to the shrine, with the first harvest of canarium almond nuts. Calling the ancestors in order, from the founder through the priest he succeeded, the priest presents the yam and nuts to them. He returns, chews bespelled betel mix at his men's house, then eats a sacred pudding. Only after the ancestors have received their due can the living members of the group begin to eat yams.

8.4 Childbirth Ritual

In section 5.2, some of the elements of childbirth procedure were touched on briefly, to illustrate the mirror-image relationship between ritual isolation in the domain of ancestral power and ritual isolation in the domain of female power. There are strong reasons, theoretical as well as empirical, for expanding briefly on the procedures of childbirth isolation and return from abu to mola.

As Bell (1980a, 1980b) has pointed out, what men do in liminal isolation has been viewed as religious ritual; what women do in liminal isolation has very often been cast in other terms—as private rather than social, as (if anything) magical rather than religious. We risk a similar distortion if we depict Kwaio childbirth isolation (as I have done in previous publications) in terms of pollution and purification, in contrast to the sacredness of male ritual. Both are matters of collective concern to the community; both entail complex procedures for moving in stages from an *abu* to a *mola* state. Nevertheless, there is an asymmetry between isolation in the realm of women's power and isolation in the realm of ancestral power with which we must come to terms. The blood of childbirth poses a danger to the community in a way the blood of sacrifice does not. The mother and her attendant potentially bring with them contaminating essences that could render the settlement *sua*, 'defiled'. After sacred isolation a priest could be contaminated by premature contact with women in their *mola* state which, because of his communion with ancestors, would invade their sacredness. It is this asymmetry I seek to capture in glossing the two sequences of *abu* to *mola* as *desacralization* in the case of a priest, and *purification* in the case of a mother, infant, and attendant. Both are equally "religious." The sequence of isolation and return is well summarized in the account by Fenaaori, a senior woman to whom men defer in knowledge of the sacred.

> First of all, we take off our [married woman's] belt and apron and put them in the menstrual hut. Then we go down to the 'childbirth area' [*lafiŋa*, from *lafi*, 'give birth']. While she's in labor, women from the clearing can touch her. But once she has given birth, she is *abu*. Only her attendant can touch her. The women from the clearing can rub her neck and massage her while she is in labor; but they leave and go back to the clearing when she has given birth. Two shelters have been built down there.[6] The attendant can't go into the

6. For most kin groups, there is a single lean-to, divided down the middle, with a separate door for each.

mother's hut. It's very *abu*. Even things from the menstrual hut, like fire, can't be taken into the 'childbirth hut' [*falegwari*, lit., "cold isolation house"].[7]

A fire is supposed to be taken down only once, when they first go into the childbirth area; and the fire must be kindled outside the childbirth hut, not inside. All the things from the menstrual hut, like tools and tobacco, are *abu* and can't be taken into the childbirth hut.[8]

The mother just stays in [the childbirth hut] with the baby. Only one bamboo of water is supposed to be given to the mother, at the start; she has to use it for the full ten days. The mother and attendant can't eat from the same tray. The mother's bed is on top of the afterbirth [which has been buried there]; and if the attendant were to go inside, she would become *biibiila* [not *sua*: *biibiila* refers to a slimy viscosity]. The mother's one bamboo of water can be refilled, but there must be only one.

After ten days in the childbirth hut[9] the mother washes. She washes the baby, then gives her to the attendant; the attendant shaves the mother's head. Then the mother dismantles her childbirth hut and piles stones or logs over it [to keep foraging *fo?ota* pigs from getting to the afterbirth]. After that she can go into the attendant's hut, the day before they are to 'ascend' [*fane*]. They can then eat food cooked on the same fire; but that fire must not be taken back to the menstrual hut. The next morning they dismantle the attendant's house, and pile things on top to keep *fo?ota* pigs from going inside. If an *abu* pig went in there, and was later sacrificed in the shrine, the *adalo* could kill someone because of it. They can't take anything from down there up to the menstrual hut.

Fa?afataa, another woman respected for her knowledge, takes up the account, beginning with the purification of mother and attendant before they 'ascend' to the menstrual hut:

We have to stay there for fifteen days. The day we are to go up, my attendant takes a razor blade [in the olden days, a piece of chert] and shaves my head. I wash my body; I wash my newborn child. The attendant gathers all the things she has

7. The "coldness" is, of course, symbolic.
8. Note the relational nature of *abu* here and in the previous usage.
9. Fifteen days in the procedures used by most Kwaio groups.

A childbirth attendant sprinkles wood shavings to purify her first entry to the father's house.

A childbirth attendant holds the baby and a packet of wood shavings as she leads the mother—with shaven head—to the menstrual hut.

used; I, the mother, gather all the things I have used. I go into her [half of the] hut down there. We sleep together and in the morning we wash. The attendant has her own bamboo of water to wash with and I have filled my own, to wash with in the morning. I left my [married woman's belt] in the menstrual hut. I put on a belt made of fiber from the forest, with leaves tucked into it.

They [the men] have prepared wood shavings and we throw them out as we come up [the attendant, holding the baby, comes first and throws out the wood chips on the path and around the door of the menstrual hut]. When I come up, no man can see me. Even my own husband can't talk with me that day—it's *abu*. That's the first day, the day we come up. My attendant can be seen, and can talk, but not me—not until the next day, when they can see me and talk to me.

Folofoʔu bespells wood shavings to purify entry of a newborn grandson into the clearing.

For six days we stay in the *kaakaba* [menstrual area]. On the sixth day, my attendant washes herself and the baby. She holds the baby up against her neck and she throws out the wood shavings they have put on the pathway. She and the baby go up to the house. She goes only into my husband's and my house, and the first day nothing she touches can be eaten by men. Only the husband can eat the things she has touched. She cooks for him, who begot the child. She stays there with the father, and goes out and gets sweet potatoes for him, and firewood.

Then, late the next afternoon, she takes wood shavings they have bespelled and goes back to her own house. She has to throw them out before she can go into her place. Otherwise, it would be a [pollution] violation.

Although the focus is on isolation of mother and attendant, the whole process is a community affair. The women of the group accompany the mother during childbirth and can freely visit the margins of her hut (unless they are *abu*); for them, no purification is required. The men of the community keep abreast of developments in labor and childbirth at a distance, performing magic (including preparing bespelled infusions of *biibiila*, an evodia that produces a slimy, viscous liquid, to induce the birth through a slippery canal by sympathetic magic) if labor is prolonged and difficult. Should the mother die in childbirth—far from rare under these conditions—they swing into action to resolve the crisis of burial (recall section 5.2). And when the purification is required, it is the priest or some other man with requisite magic and expertise who prepares the wood chips.

I will return to the complementarity of male and female roles in ritual, and to the cultural conceptualizations of birth, death, and life trajectory implied in the sequences of 'ascending' and 'descending'. First though, we need to look closely at crucial ritual events on which the well-being of the community depends: first, sacrifice; and then, the sequence set into motion by death of a priest.

Chapter Nine

Sacrifice

ADALO, LIKE THE LIVING, crave pork. By feeding them pork, or promising to do so by consecrating pigs, humans can induce their ancestors to *nanama* for them and elicit forgiveness for their mistakes. Sacrifice of pigs is a central part of Kwaio religion, and the pursuits of everyday life.

9.1 Purificatory and Expiatory Pigs

The most common sacrifices are for purification/expiation (*siuŋa* or *naruŋa*, both terms that literally mean "washing"). Every few days, within a Kwaio neighborhood, a small pig or a piglet will be sacrificed to purify an offense—most commonly, urination or menstruation in a house or clearing. The offenses may be reported by the girl or woman responsible, or may be discovered in divination. When Kwaio discover in divination that a pig is demanded by an ancestor as compensation for a violation, or a violation is reported, they may immediately sacrifice one they have on hand—a relatively small one, or sometimes a relatively large one that has been raised for secular purposes, a *boo mola* ('secular pig'). An alternative to immediate sacrifice is consecration of a small pig for expiatory "washing," with an explanation to the *adalo* that the pig that has been given will be raised and fattened for subsequent sacrifice. A few *adalo* for whom this is regularly done have special pseudonyms used for such consecrated "washing" pigs. One reason Kwaio are reluctant to raise pigs to maturity while leaving them as secular is that should a pollution violation occur, it will be difficult for them to explain to the aggrieved ancestor(s) why they are sacrificing a small pig in expiation, rather than this large one. If they have no large secular pigs in their herd, they can sacrifice a small one they have, buy a small one for sacrifice, or dedicate a small one for eventual sacrifice (which can then be done at some appropriate occasion, such as a mortuary feast, when resources in pigs are being mobilized in pursuit of prestige).

The group participating in an expiatory sacrifice will depend on the size of the pig, and the occasion. All men and boys, regardless of whether or not they are related to the *adalo* to which sacrifice is made, can take part. In practice, males of an immediate neighborhood are likely to take part; when the pig is large, others may join in, or may be sent pieces of pork.

The priest sets off, either carrying the pig himself or having it carried by a helper. He and other participants leave their bags at the edge of the shrine. A coal from a men's house fire is taken to kindle a fire in the shrine; firewood is cut by young men. When the priest goes into the shrine he addresses the spirits by name—their real names, not pseudonyms. He explains to them whose pig is being sacrificed, and which *adalo* is to be the recipient (which the *adalo* involved knows perfectly well, having watched over the pig since it was consecrated as a piglet); or explains what violation is being purified, and by whom. Then the priest, usually with the help of an assistant, suffocates the pig by wrapping the snout with a bespelled vine, and then closing off its windpipe. (One Kwaio woman of metaphysical bent suggested that the shade of the ancestor suffocates the shade of the pig.) The pig, once dead, is butchered. The blood is collected in bamboo tubes and cooked, with pieces of seared intestine, into blood pudding. The sacred parts (head, liver, base of spine) are carefully set aside and kept track of as the carcass and joints are seared on red hot ovenstones—those of the *umu* of the ancestor to

The old priest ʔAika kills a purificatory pig in Foumalo shrine.

A young priest addresses his ancestors in the shrine before throwing them a token valuable.

whom sacrifice is made. The carcass and joints are then baked on the stones in a leaf-covered oven. The pork and roasted taro corms are set out. The priest performs *ribaŋa*, a common rite through which those about to partake of a sacred meal become protected from the dangers of the ancestors with whom they will share food. The officiant chews betel and a bespelled sprig of the aromatic shrub evodia, and goes down the line of participants, counting magically over each, then spitting on his chest. He then recites over the food, and spits on it, rendering it *mola* enough to be shared by living and dead. In the procedure of sacrifice, the allocation of a share to the spirits has already been expressed by the burning of a hair, an ear, or a token piece of pork.

Before sacrificing a purificatory pig, the priest may take a tiny length of shell beads and throw it into the shrine. He refers to it as a major valuable; Kwaio recognize that the ancestors can make use only of the invisible essence of the valuable, so the physical shell beads given are only a material token of an immaterial gift. The occasional Kwaio cynic may chuckle about this as 'lying' to the spirits. But it is part of a much wider pattern Kwaio take for granted, in which physical representations of invisible gifts to the spirits serve to enlist ancestral support.

The tone of behavior during sacrifice is generally serious; the priest himself, when he speaks to the ancestors (*kwaialasi* or *tele*), often goes into a quavering voice and may be virtually possessed, weeping and suffering fits of shaking. However the other participants, particularly young ones, may banter and play while inside the shrine. There is no tone of reverence in the face of the sacred, of a sort I naïvely felt should be appropriate.

This most common form of expiatory sacrifice is only one of several categories of purificatory sacrifice. First, within the category of "washing" there are sacrifices that purify the way for a mortuary feast, a fight, or other event, or purify the way for a more sacred sacrifice. Major and hence dangerous forms of sacrifice and other ritual cannot safely be carried out unless the ancestors are favorably disposed toward the living; and there is always a possibility that some as yet undiscovered violation could have incurred their displeasure. Sacrifice of a purificatory pig as a precautionary measure similarly allows a feastgiving group to push ahead with confidence in ancestral support. (Heavy rains before a feast will send the feastgiving group into a flurry of divination and purificatory sacrifice to ensure clearing weather.)

Other forms of expiatory/purificatory sacrifice, often preceded by sacrifice of a purificatory pig as described above, are made to cleanse and expiate drastic offenses or ritual errors. The most important of these is *to ʔositaataaŋa*, "throwing out of a curse," where a very sacred shrine for crematory sacrifice has been massively defiled by a curse. More than a dozen other categories of specific sacrifices—for instance, to clear the way so that *foʔota* pigs to two or more separate ancestors can be sacrificed using the same ovenstones—entail detailed procedures and magic which must be part of a descent group's repertoire should the need arise. Another crucial mode of expiatory sacrifice entails giving pigs to the important ancestors of a person who has been killed in a fight or feud. The pigs, presented as compensation by relatives of the decedent and/or the killer, are classed as *firiaadaloŋaa*, 'atonement to the ancestors'. Until these pigs have been given, any interaction between relatives of the killer and the killed may be punished, by the offended ancestors, by death (see Keesing 1978a: ch. 12).

Having glimpsed this complexity, we can turn to the sacrifice of pigs consecrated to named ancestors.

9.2 *Fo?ota* Pigs

Procedures for sacrifice of *fo?ota* pigs are generally similar to those for sacrifice of "washing" pigs. There are a few key differences. First, although other males can be (and sometimes are) present, the male group actually partaking of *ribaŋa* and the sacrificial meal is clearly limited and defined. Only men who are 'connected' to the *adalo* to whom the pig is consecrated can partake of the communion. For sacrifice of a *fo?ota*, then, there is a defined *congregation*. The men included in it normally comprise those cognatic kin of the *adalo* who fall within the same *maa?ekwalo*, or 'ritual section' (that is, members of the descent group by whom the sacrifice is made and those in other ritually-linked descent groups—such as Giru?i, Naaŋari, Ɖudu, and Namoriiridi, as shown in figure 6.2 and described in section 6.3), who have attained ritual maturity by partaking of this *fo?ota* (section 6.6). Members of such a congregation who are not present at the sacrifice will be sent portions, if this is feasible, which must be consumed in men's houses. Where a *fo?ota* pig is sacrificed for a mortuary feast, the congregation is expanded to include any cognatic relative of the *adalo* who has partaken of this *fo?ota*, whatever his *maa?ekwalo* (see section 6.3).

A second distinguishing feature is the sacredness of the

communion. Those who partake of a *fo ?ota* sacrifice must go into temporary ritual isolation in a men's house. Not until the next day can they reenter the *mola* realm of the domestic house and central clearing, and then only after washing to remove the grease of the sacrificial meal. Note here the symbolic inversion of women's menstrual isolation, which similarly entails—after the menstrual flow ends—a final night in seclusion and ritual washing before entering the *mola* realm.

We can turn now to the most dramatic and dangerous form of Kwaio sacrifice.

9.3 *Suuŋa*

When relations between the living members of a descent group and its ancestral members[1] are disrupted or are seen to have deteriorated, the priest may resort to a dangerous step to induce ancestral support: the cremation (*suuŋa*, lit., "burning") of a pig.

The shrines where cremation is performed are particularly sacred, and supposed to be ancient. They are distinguished by the fact that an ancestor who is the group's primary source of *nanama*-ization is buried there. Often this is an ancestor more remote than the founder; as we will see in chapter 11, relations between priests who perform *suuŋa* express in the rites of sacrifice connections in the ancient past which manifest themselves in present-day social relations.

The priest Louŋa describes how a hypothetical crematory sacrifice is initiated and performed:

> If a man's pigs grow badly, if his taro is no good, if he can't earn any money, he will divine to find out what is wrong. He finds that the *adalo naa gofuŋa* [the *adalo* to which they cremate pigs; *gofuŋa* is an alternative term for "burning"] is causing the trouble, because he wants a pig. The man reports this to his group: "Let's make a crematory sacrifice." A crematory sacrifice is for getting pigs, for earning money.

1. Who in this context include ancestors from whom the descent group founders are descended.

First, the priest of that group takes a big pig and sacrifices it [as *siuŋa*] to clear the way for the crematory sacrifice. . . . The pig is sacrificed; then they schedule the cremation in four days.[2] "I'll come to you in four days" [the priest says to the ancient ancestor buried there].

In late afternoon of the day before the sacrifice the group [of males] which will go [with the priest] to the shrine gathers. Everyone else stays in the dwelling house, but they go up to the men's house. We talk and the *adalo* comes to us. [The priest] yawns [a sign the *adalo* has come to him].

"You be quiet, I'm going to bite my areca nut: the *adalo* is here." He yawns and yawns and then bites into his areca nut. And then he talks to the *adalo* in prayer [*kwaialasi*]: "We are sleeping here; tomorrow awaits me, I will stay awake."

After that, no one can say a word. At dawn [the priest] takes the piglet; they bring a lighted coal and they set off. When they get near the shrine, they put on their ornaments. They bundle sticks [*uruuru*] up in leaves; they put on cowrie shell ornaments and fighting belts. They take up their old weapons, clubs, and spears.

They get to the waiting place [*furiʔi lamaŋa*], and the accompanying party waits there. Each one has carried a bundle of sticks, and they put them all in one place. The priest takes two cordyline clumps and two crotons and two shoots of bamboo [which he has brought with him]. Holding one set of each in each hand, he sweeps clear the path. He sweeps, sweeps, sweeps . . . until he gets to the place where they ready the pig. He counts over the firesite [above the skull of the ancestor]: "Two, four, five, six, seven, eight." Then he leaves the cuttings [of cordyline, etc.] there and goes back [to the others]. The man down there [who is giving the sacrificial pig] gives him [the priest] the coal. [The priest] takes the coal up and gathers wood and starts a fire. Then he goes back a second time. He gets down there and [the man] gives that pig to him—the man who is sacrificing [here, literally "destroying"] it on our behalf, giving that pig for [the benefit of] the taro, for earning money, for giving feasts. . . .

The priest takes that pig and takes it back to the fire. He calls out: "Yooooooo. This thing is always pressing upon us, causing pigs to die, causing people to die, keeping us from earning any money. That's what I've come about, to give a pig for our taro, for porpoise teeth and red money."[3]

2. Three days by our method of counting.
3. Valuables used in important prestations.

He prays to all the ancestors, then calls out their names one by one. The last ancestor he doesn't call; he is still holding on to the pig [which by this time he has throttled]. The first time he goes all the way down [the chain of former priests] until he gets to his father [or predecessor]: "This is the pig so-and-so asked for, this is the pig so-and-so asked for, this is the pig. . . ." He gets down to his father and starts again from the beginning. The second time he goes all the way through the names; and then he puts the body of the pig in the fire and cremates it. He doesn't take off the vine he has throttled the pig with, doesn't let go of it until it is in the fire.

The priest continues to face the cremation fire, picks up his bundles [of cuttings], and begins to back up, holding them. He steps backwards to where the cordylines have been planted [after previous crematory sacrifices], glancing sideways to see where they are. He gets to that place and crouches down, pressing the two cordylines down into the ground. Then he goes backwards to where the crotons have been planted, crouches down, and plants one [cutting] with each hand. Then he backs up and does the same with the bamboo shoots. Then he turns around. He closes it with the "closing ancestor" [that is, the ancestor they invoke to "close" the shrine again]. And he goes back. He goes back and gets to his men's house and husks his coconut.

The rest of us who have gone with him eat taro too. He breaks open his coconut and makes a *fousuu* [taro and grated coconut pudding]. From that time, when he goes into the men's house after eating his pudding, it is closed with a piece of wood. Who will see him? Women can't see him—only us men. Only we people who are *abu* can be at that settlement.

The taboos [*abuŋa*] are like those for the death of an important person.[4] Only the man who attends to him[5] can feed him. They stake off two or three sections of taro for him—no one else can eat from those.

On the second day [after the sacrifice], the priest eats another pudding, and a piglet. That is *lau ʔulasiŋa* ["take hold-opening"]. People who are keeping the taboos partially [e.g., husbands and children of women of the group making the sacrifice] are then *mola*. The priest eats his pudding and pork, then stays on in the men's house. In the old days, he'd have

---

4. See chapter 10.
5. The word is the same as that for a childbirth attendant.

been taboo for a hundred days.[6] After forty days, they schedule the "feast of the dead" [fonulaanimae]. That's part of the series of partial liftings of taboos. Ten days and some taboos are lifted, ten days more and others are lifted, ten days more. . . . They schedule the fonulaanimae in ten days. On the tenth day they take a fo?ota pig to the shrine and sacrifice it. And then a big secular pig is killed and cooked. The group divides that and that community is mola again.

Some of the taboos are different [from those when a priest dies]. The stick they put across to partition off part of the men's house for suru?ai [the term used for the taboo-keeper, whose name is not used] is taken to the shrine [and put there]. Once they give the fonulaanimae, the suru?ai is not abu by himself any longer. He can eat food cooked on the main fire in the men's house, and women can see him. The rest of the men can go down and eat in the house; but he himself must stay on in the men's house after the fonulaanimae.

After forty days more, they schedule the fa?asafiŋa ["making supernaturally powerful"] to take place in ten days. He is to ?uimousia ["break to finish it"] in the shrine. The day before, he eats a lakeno [taro pudding]. There are two pigs for that. One the priest will eat himself, a pig sacrificed in the shrine. The other, a pig for fa?asafiŋa, is a secular pig, one women can eat. [The men] build a taualea [feasting shelter] with fronds of fishtail palm. The man who sacrifices women's pigs goes with the priest. . . . They "take hold of the adalo," and come . . . to the taualea. They go around inside the taualea where the women's pig is tethered, and each time they get around full circle, they count: "Two"—then around again. "Four." Then around. "Six." Then "eight." Then they break open a coconut. Then they go into the men's house and the priest makes a lakeno pudding. That ?uimousia ["breaks to finish"—that is, closes] the shrine: "I ?uimousia the shrine; I ribamousia" [perform sacrament to close it]. He blesses and eats the pudding. Then he goes and sacrifices the piglet in the shrine, to clear the path for the women's pig. The next morning, the women's pig is killed. The women line up and undergo the sacrament [ribaŋa]. They eat their shares of pork, and that closes the shrine.

After that the kin group is freed from all the taboos. They can go to other people's feasts. After that, their pigs will grow well, their taro will grow well; they'll earn money; they'll live

6. Usually in fact fifty days; days and nights are double-counted as separate "days."

in good health. He [the priest] has climbed the path of the ancient shrine.

This sequence calls for some comment. First, the full length sequence of fifty (supposedly one hundred) days takes place only the first time a particular priest performs *suuŋa*. The length of the taboo period is subsequently reduced by half, or more. Second, the mirroring of childbirth ritual—with the *suru ʔai* taking to his bed, attended by an unmarried young man—is fairly transparent. So is the symbolism of continuity back to ancient ancestors in the planting of cuttings by the priest after sacrifice.[7] (We will return to such symbolic themes in chapter 12.) Third, the isolation of the descent group as ritual community has important implications for Kwaio social organization (which will be touched upon in chapter 11). And finally, Louŋa's reference to the parallels between the liminal isolation and sequence of desacralization after crematory sacrifice and the sequence following the death of a priest suggests that a clearer understanding of symbolism and procedures will emerge after we examine this mortuary sequence. I will get to that momentarily. But first, some more general reflections on the meaning of Kwaio sacrifice are in order.

9.4   Meanings in Kwaio Sacrifice

In sacrificing, Kwaio are engaging in a transaction—a prestation in Mauss' sense—modelled on those between the living (in particular, those from subordinates to superiors): a valued commodity is given to solicit intangible support, or to compensate for an offense. Because the superiors to whom the presentation is given are invisible shades, what must be conveyed to them are the shades of the pigs, transmuted from physical form by fire. This is the way Kwaio explicitly view sacrifice. Why ancestors should want pigs is not problematic:

---

7. McKinley (n.d.) suggests that the planting of cuttings by the priest may represent a symbolic inverse of the throwing out of wood chips by mother and attendant.

living humans do. (As Leach [1976:83] points out, what the ancestors are claiming is not simply the shades of pigs—which presumably they could take themselves—but expressions of *submission* by mortal humans.)

One can ask deeper symbolic questions. One can view sacrifice as analogous to a funeral, as a rite that transforms material substance into immaterial essence. Through identification of the sacrificed pig with its owner, it transforms the donor, by analogy with an initiation rite:

> The procedures . . . *separate* the "initiate" (i.e., the sacrificial animal of the donor) into two parts—one pure, the other impure. The impure part can then be left behind, while the pure part can be aggregated to the initiate's new status. In the case of sacrifice the sacrificial victim plays the part of the initiate, but since the victim has first been identified with the donor of the sacrifice, the donor is, by vicarious association, likewise purified and initiated into a new ritual status. (Leach 1976:84)

There is a problem in applying Leach's conception to the sacrifice of Kwaio *foʔota*—named as they are for the ancestors to whom they are given. Are they identified with the donor or with the recipient? The transfer of a *foʔota* pig to the ancestor takes place not when it is killed, but when it is consecrated. The ancestor at that point "owns" (the shade of) the pig. Whether it is eventually sacrificed or allowed to die of old age, and—if sacrificed—whether at a mortuary feast or at some other time is deemed to be a matter of the will of the ancestral "owner," as revealed in divination. It is this ancestral "ownership" that allows Kwaio to substitute a replacement pig should a *foʔota* be stolen, or should it die prematurely, be defiled, or have to be diverted for another purpose (a procedure which is rare and difficult, if the pig is consecrated to an important ancestor). The position of the person who is raising the *foʔota*, vis-à-vis the ancestor to whom it is consecrated, parallels that of a person who is feeding and caring for a pig on behalf of a relative. The conceptual model for the consecration of the pig to the *adalo* for whom it is then named is a gift based on kinship connection that solicits support—

the presentation of a pig for a feast in support of the "big man" as feastgiver (Keesing 1978a), for instance. The feast-giving leader reciprocates with patronage and protection; the *adalo* reciprocates by *nanama*-ing for the donor and his or her kin.

Expiatory pigs, and the token presentations of shell valuables that characteristically accompany them, are modelled not on the solicitation of patronage, but on the payment of compensation. (Kwaio have many categories of compensation payments. Some of them reflect an explicit parallel with expiatory sacrifice, as when one "washes" (*siufia*) a man one has sullied with a curse, or a husband one has cuckolded; or when one 'pays atonement' (*firisia*) to the living relatives of a person one has killed, and to their dead relatives (*firisia adalo*, in *firiadaloŋaa*; see section 9.1).

But why *kill* an animal in sacrifice? Why this sacrament of blood? In Kwaio terms this may not be problematic: one presents cooked pork in many forms of prestation, so presenting (the shade of) a cooked pig to an ancestor is a logical expression of a conventional pattern. But the deeper symbolism of sacrificial communion is less simply explained anyway.

In view of the long anthropological interest in sacrifice—from Robertson Smith (1889) through Hubert and Mauss (1897–98) and such modern social anthropologists as Evans-Pritchard (1956), Firth (1963), and Leach (1976)—it would be foolhardy to seek here to construct a general theory from the Kwaio case. Death, in Kwaio cosmology, is a door between the impermanent earthly world and the world of the spirits, unbounded in time and space. Sacrifice carries powerful and deep emotional meanings for the Kwaio, I think, because the pig in its death throes or immolation opens death's doors, brings the priest and the tiny community with him face to face with the powers of the infinite. In this sense, Leach is right: the pig's life is substituted for those of the sacrificers. It is in this context of death—as in the context of human death, as we will shortly see—that the ancestors communicate most directly with the living, and the living with them. It is a dialogue through the doors of death.

There are other questions we can well ask of Kwaio sacrifice, questions rooted in the material world, not the realm of the spirits. Pigs—all pigs—represent the cumulated embodiment of the labor of the women who tend, feed, and nurture them. Yet somewhere on the order of three quarters of the pigs raised in the mountain communities I have studied are killed and eaten in sacrifice, hence consumed by males. This figure cannot be taken either as a rough baseline for "traditional" Kwaio culture[8] or as a simple economic fact. The pigs women eat are increasingly obtained by purchase from Christians, either for shell valuables or for cash—the latter derived almost entirely, and the former partly, from men's labor. Nonetheless, it is clear that men get much of the tangible benefit of pigs women feed. By consecrating a pig—a pig she will not then be able to partake of—a woman induces her ancestor to *nanama* for her, enabling her efforts and earnings to prosper. She also willingly feeds her husband's *fo?ota* pigs and those that will be used to "wash" violations: by doing so, she helps to secure the health, prosperity, and stability of the tiny community into which she has married. Even where she works to feed secular pigs, they very often are used as prestations in marriage transactions or mortuary feasts—more often than not, presentations made by her husband. Only indirectly, through similar prestations of pigs raised by other women, does she get a return of pork, and even then her portion is likely to be a small strip of belly fat for which she has had to give shell valuables. The religious ideology in terms of which males eat pigs they do not raise and do not pay for

8. Economic patterns have changed radically in recent decades because of the encapsulation of Kwaio traditionalists within their mountain enclave. Ironically, the consequence for the economics of pig husbandry has not been a greater self-containedness, but a separation in which pigs for secular uses—in the contexts where women can eat them—increasingly come from Christian communities along the coasts. In pre-European times total pig production may well have been higher, but a higher proportion must have been consigned to secular uses.

can be looked at as—among other things—a mechanism for the appropriation of women's labor. It is a perspective to which we shall return, in seeking to understand Kwaio religion both as a system of meanings and as an ideology rooted in earthly economics and politics. We need first to turn to the ritual sequences set into motion by a death in the community, and then to examine the sociology and symbolism of Kwaio ritual.

Chapter Ten

Death and Desacralization

ANY DEATH PLUNGES a Kwaio community into the shock of collective bereavement. How deep the shock, how dramatic the subsequent events, depend on the age and identity of the decedent, and the circumstances of death. We shall first look at these axes of variation, then turn to their outcomes.

10.1 Kinds of Decedents, Modes of Death

Death in infancy or early childhood is commonplace in the mountain communities I have studied, which are largely cut off from Western medical care[1] and situated in a climate and setting where disease and infection take a heavy toll. Death of a young child deeply grieves the family and close kin, but its sociological and religious consequences are relatively limited. Most families have experienced such bereavement. Death of a child after the early years, when the child has acquired a more full social personality, is more deeply disruptive; by the time adolescence has been reached, the death is a major loss to the local community well beyond the confines of family and immediate kin.

Death of an adult profoundly disrupts the community: it usually leaves a spouse and children, as well as natal kin,

1. Now they remain cut off partly by choice, since Kwaio non-Christians could—but seldom do—make use of the well-equipped and professionally staffed Atoifi Adventist Hospital on the coast (see chapter 15).

bereaved. Unless it has been preceded by a long, wasting illness, it has usually left them unprepared for the shock of loss. Introduced respiratory diseases—tuberculosis, pneumonia, influenza—take a heavy toll of Kwaio (most often men, it would seem from my data) in their middle years. Those who survive epidemics and degenerative illnesses of middle age, and do not succumb to cancers induced by pipe smoking and betel chewing, are incredibly tough physically, and often live into their late seventies or eighties (two men I knew died at about ninety-four). When a man or woman becomes aged and feeble, death is accepted as natural and often recognized as imminent, so death itself is not a critical bereavement in terms of emotional shock.

But if the shock of premature loss lessens as a life runs full course, the sociological and religious impact of death may increase with age. An old man often is surrounded by extreme sanctity as channel to the ancestors, repository of lore, and center of the religious life of the community. An old woman, especially one who is *oleoleta*, 'last survivor' (lit., "leftover"), of her generation, has also become a focus of sanctity, having for years taken the lead woman's part in descent group rites. (She *ribaeteeta*, undergoes the sacrament first; she *ʔoiʔulasi*, presents an initial valuable in desacralization rites; hers is the "senior" pig among those given by *ino rumaʔa*, out-married women of the descent group.) Concurrent with the sanctity of a very old person, who begins in some respects to border on a kind of living ancestorhood, is the substantial probability that one or more sons, having reached middle age, will be men of substance and prestige who have taken over a mantle of secular leadership. (Here one must remember that Kwaio descent groups are tiny, usually including only a handful of men in their middle years). The death of an aged father or mother is likely to be both an occasion to mark ritually the sanctity of the decedent and to assert the power and largesse of those who will honor the dead.

The circumstances of death determine the action taken by the community. The most important distinction Kwaio draw is between a person who has been killed—murdered or killed in a fight—and a person who has "died." A *lalamua*, 'killed person', becomes the focus not for burial, mourning, and desacralization, but for vengeance. The attendant rituals (in abeyance since the Pax Britannica) entailed the victim specifying a desired target for vengeance, and eventual putting up of blood money (*sikwa*) if vengeance could not be claimed directly. I shall focus my attention on a *be?u*, 'dead person'.

As I have noted, an unexpected death is more disruptive than a death prefigured by wasting illness or senility. For a very old man, a men's house may constitute a kind of death-bed setting for many months until death comes. Recall that the Kwaio category *mae*, to 'be dead', includes states of coma; so that death is viewed as liminality that may become terminal with the final passing of breath and vital functions, not as an abrupt end to life. When this passing of the dying person's breath (*maŋona*) occurs, the community is plunged into mourning.

Rather than describe the variant modes of mourning, preparation of the body for burial, interment, and exhumation of the skull, I will look in some detail at the sequence in its most ritually elaborated form, following the death of a descent group's priest. We can usefully pause to glimpse the sequence in which kin of the bereaved family come together, in the weeks to follow, to mourn the loss.

10.2 'Wakes'

On the tenth day after a death, relatives and neighbors of the bereaved family gather for a *boni*, 'wake'. The scale of the gathering, and of the contributions of food (in the form of taro puddings, fish, and other valued items) that accompany it, depends on the importance of the decedent. For the death of a child, only a fairly small circle will gather. They stay up all night with the bereaved family, often listening to the recitation of epic chants by a bard and chorus of accompanists, singing and clacking bamboo sticks until the light of dawn.

A second *boni* is held ten days later, another ten days after that; a *boni* is held every ten days[2] until on the hundredth day an *ʔisileʔeboni*, 'finishing-off wake', is held—with a larger-scale presentation of puddings, fish, and often other prestations by kin of the bereaved family. They will remain publicly in mourning—a state which includes a dishevelment where men allow facial and head hair to grow, and people are generally unkempt—until, months later, a mortuary feast is given.

This period entails a partial separation and liminality of the bereaved group. Whether this separation incorporates all the households of descent group members, some smaller cluster of households, or only the immediate family depends on where the decedent stands on a scale from 'important' (*beʔu baʔita*) to 'unimportant' (*beʔu sikaʔu*). So do the procedures and their articulation with other rites. In the case of an important decedent, the bereaved will constitute the entire descent group, and their affines, as ritual community; and they will be isolated from contact with outsiders by keeping taboos, as we will see. The *boni* sequence becomes incorporated within, and subordinate to, the sequence of desacralization rites. It is to these, in their full form following death of a priest, that I will now turn. These sequences represent the fullest elaboration of Kwaio ritual—and the most striking manifestation of a deep contradiction in Kwaio religious life, where the most sacred and otherworldly orientations and most worldly and material orientations are brought together.

10.3   Death of a Priest and the Quest for *Mamu*

The death of a descent group's priest, like crematory sacrifice, initiates a plunge into deep and dangerous sacredness in quest of powers for worldly success. This raises a theme in Kwaio culture that may seem fraught with contradiction. In their most sacred rites, in their communion with their ances-

---

2. Each ten day period includes "today," and hence is nine by our counting system.

tors, Kwaio seek, above all, earthly gain. Their most spiritual
and most materialistic moods and moments are juxtaposed,
even fused. This is nowhere more dramatic than in the quest
for *mamu* after death of a priest.

A Kwaio descent group, plunged into intense communion
with its ancestors by this opening of a door between living
and dead, must restore relations with the spirits, progressively
freeing themselves from dangerous sacredness and the social
isolation it imposes. But the death of a priest (or an important
senior leader, whose death will occasion a similar but less
drastic sequence of rites) culminates in a large mortuary feast.
And such feasts are important as major expressions of a descent group's prestige, the ascendancy or continued prominence of its entrepreneurial leader(s), and its political and
economic alliances and rivalries with other groups (Keesing
1978a). The group sponsoring the feast will go heavily into
debt accumulating the resources for the mortuary feast; acquiring large numbers of pigs and amounts of taro is a focus
of productive efforts of the descent group for many months
prior to the feast. Since attendance at, and contributions to,
the feast on the day it is finally staged can determine whether
the event yields a large profit or a crippling loss, it is no
wonder that Kwaio are concerned with attracting wealth to
the feast. It is this two-sidedness of concern—with spiritual
power and with worldly wealth—that characterizes the whole
ritual sequence.

The key concept here is *mamu*, the power to attract
wealth. Literally, *mamu* is the emanation of smell from bait
that attracts fish, or the scent of flowers that attracts insects—
in other words, the irresistible attracting power of which smell
is the perceptible medium. The whole sequence of mortuary
and desacralization rites seeks to elicit *mamu* from the ancestors: *mamu* to enable the living to produce taro, obtain fish,
and raise pigs so as to make the mortuary feast irresistibly
attractive to people far and near, and lure them and their
valuables. The objects manipulated in these rites include cordyline, coconuts, small entire taro plants, and other objects

commonly deployed in Kwaio ritual, but most centrally, the powerfully aromatic cultigen evodia (la?e), key symbol of attraction.

When the priest of a descent group dies, the body—unbound—must be taken up to the men's house, if death has not occurred there. The taboos that descend on the community begin the evening before burial. Louŋa describes the first stage in the long and complex ritual sequence.

> The son of the dead man goes into the men's house with sprigs of la?e [evodia]. He bespells the sprigs, then puts them into the nostrils and ears of the corpse [this is to kwasimaana, "decorate the face"]. He says . . . "Father, you've died and left me. I'm a man with no pigs or money, an unimportant man who can't accomplish anything. I kwasimaamu, 'decorate you', with this la?e, in order to attract fish and taro and pork for the feast for your death." . . . That's a very important, very abu thing.

The son then binds the arms and legs of the corpse. The next morning, he and the other buriers dig the grave and bury the body, which is wrapped in bark with its knees flexed. Louŋa continues, "When the corpse of his father is put into the hole, the son takes a single bead of shell and ties it, on a string of fiber, in the ear of the corpse." Then he and the other man or men who have buried the body come back to the men's house. The son, or some other man as his surrogate, will abuŋe?enia be?u, "taboo-ize the corpse," as suru?ai. This man, in Louŋa's account the decedent's son, "goes into his men's house by himself. He chews an areca [betel] nut, then breaks open a coconut. [He says], 'Father, I'm breaking open this coconut; I'm abu-izing you'. He will stay in the men's house by himself."

The next morning, he and the other maa?elaee, the buriers of the dead (lit., "section of the dead"), go to the shore taking shell valuables, to perform a rite called buule?ebe?u (lit., "standing on top of the corpse").

> They go down to the coast and meet a saltwater man they have arranged to meet there. . . . The suru?ai [taboo-keeper] takes the bag of valuables they have brought and hangs it up.

The bark-wrapped body of the old Gaʔenaafou priest is lowered into a grave dug in a shrine. Note the shaven head of the taboo-keeper (top).

"This is money for my *molaŋa* ['desacralization'], that is arranged for eight days from today [our seven]. People will come down for the fish in six days and will take the fish back up on the seventh day."

The saltwater man takes that bag of valuables—it may be two or three or even ten valuables. Then the taboo-keeper takes eight sprigs of evodia and eight sprigs of *alaala?ege* [a sweet-smelling flowering forest tree]. He twists and breaks these sprigs, and throws them into the sea. This is to *fa?amamua* [*mamu*-ize] the sea, to ensure that fish will come.

They come back. [The *suru?ai*] bites his areca nut.[3]

"Father, I have given money for your death, and come back. I gave so that fish would come back in return for the bag of valuables I have given."

The taboo-keeper, *suru?ai*, takes a cluster of ten coconuts; the other buriers (*maa?elaee*) each take a cluster of coconuts; and they put them into the sacred men's house where the taboo-keeper will be ritually isolated, out of sight of women. Louŋa's account continues:

From that time on, the *suru?ai* stays in the men's house. He has his own fire. His attendant feeds him, from that time on. No one can eat food cooked on his fire; no one else can sleep next to it. Firewood is brought and kept separately. The *suru?ai* eats taro harvested from two or three squares of the garden set aside for him. No one else, not even the *maa?elaee*, can eat from those plots.

On the day they are to go down for the fish, two days before the *molaŋa* [desacralization], *suru?ai* goes to the grave. He takes a coconut and husks it, then breaks it open.

"This is your coconut I'm burning for you, to make me *mola*" [he says]. He grates the coconut, then lights a torch and sets it on top of *?aifari* [the cradle of branches across the top of the grave]. He burns the coconut, the coconut of the dead [priest]. The *adalo* eats first.

The *suru?ai* goes back, and they [he and the buriers] go down to the coast. They get the fish [caught in effect on contract by the saltwater man] and come back. [*Suru?ai*] bites his areca nut. Then he pounds his *lakeno* [taro pudding], and the *maa?elaee* pound theirs separately. Then he comes outside the men's house [though still out of sight of women]. He reaches

3. Note how this serves, in ritual, to open a channel of communication to an *adalo*.

for the evodia for *ribaŋa*. He chews [the evodia] and counts
over each of the *maaʔelaee*.
"Two, four, five-six, seven-eight" [spitting the chewed
evodia on the chest of each]. He spits on his own shoulder.
Then he *riba* on the *lakeno* puddings and fish, counting and
spitting over them with the chewed *laʔe*. *Suruʔai* eats his first,
then the *maaʔelaee* eat theirs.

This rite of desacralization takes place the day before the
main *molaŋa*, which corresponds to the first wake of the normal mortuary sequence. What has been established through
the participation of one or more buriers from descent groups
other than the decedent's (groups with which the decedent
was linked by close kinship) is in fact a relationship in which
the descent groups square off vis-à-vis one another in mortuary exchanges (see Keesing 1978a). So each of the *maaʔelaee*
is backed by a cluster of kin and supporters, who in this and
later contexts bring food or other items as an assertion of their
prestige. In the *molaŋa*, each group brings taro puddings,
which are then exchanged with those brought by another
group.

When the *maaʔelaee* have arrived, and the puddings are
all set out, *suruʔai* comes outside. People see him for the first
time, including women. He [*suruʔai*] calls out who is to exchange puddings with whom:
"Your [puddings], so-and-so and so-and-so, you are to
face off and exchange them. And your puddings. . . ."
They divide them, and *suruʔai* goes back into the men's
house, staying unwashed and dishevelled. After that women
can't see him—that's the only time they see him. He is *abu*.
The next morning people go home.

This marks the end of the first ten-day period of the
hundred-day sequence of desacralization. The next crucial
ritual in the sequence takes place the day before the end of
the fourth ten-day period. At this stage the *maaʔelaee*, who
(with *suruʔai*) have been wearing garlands of cordyline leaves
(*laŋo*) around their necks, take them off; *suruʔai* keeps wearing his. Through this whole period, he has been in the men's
house, in his symbolic analogue of childbirth. On the morning

of the fortieth day, he and the *maa ʔelaee* go together to a taro garden that has been set aside for this purpose. Louŋa continues:

> They stand at the edge of the fence and look at the garden. They go inside to where they see the taro are mature. *Suru ʔai* reaches for a taro plant, tears the leaves, and says, "Father, I have come for the taro for the *lakenoniwane* [men's taro pudding] for your death. I'm tearing [the leaves of] the taro today. I am *olo*-ing [lit., "jumping"][4] with you. Tomorrow I will *ʔoto* ["jab" or "spear"] to you. I am marking off the taro for the men's *lakeno* for father's death."
>
> He tears the leaves, then marks off the section of taro [that will be harvested for the puddings]. They weed that section together, then they go back to the boundary fence [within the garden]. When they get to that boundary, the helpers [the *maa ʔelaee*] are *mola*.
>
> They [the *maa ʔelaee*] then go inside the dwelling house [for the first time since they become *abu*—they have been staying in their respective men's houses]. Then, the next morning, [*suru ʔai*] goes to that decedent [*be ʔu*—that is, to the grave]. He *ʔoto* there [by taking a pole he has cut and thumping it down on the ground at the grave].
>
> "*ʔOto* for the *be ʔu*, I [hereby] schedule the men's *lakeno* for your death, for a week from today. I *ʔoto* to you [father] for the men's *lakeno*. I will raise you [exhume your skull] for the women's desacralization [*maa ʔe ni geni*, lit., "women's section"]."
>
> He goes back. On the day before the one appointed they take the pigs to the shrine for sacrifice. Let's assume that the man who is to become priest for the shrine the decedent has left behind is not the one who is keeping the taboos for the dead.
>
> So the man who is to become priest goes to the shrine [to begin sacrificing for the first time to the powerful *adalo* of the descent group]. [The *suru ʔai*] stays in the men's house, and he kills a [small] pig there. Then he breaks open a coconut for his *lakeno*. First he husks the coconut, then he kills that pig [in the men's house, beside his bed]. He uses that pig he kills to talk to [*alasia*] the newly dead, to his father. He can't talk

---

4. The name for this ritual is a designation for which Louŋa and others could provide no explanation.

to the other *adalo*—no, only that one. After killing the pig and
making his *lakeno* pudding, he can't eat any of the pork.[5]
   Then they bring [a portion of] pork from the founding
shrine, the one [the priest] has left behind. They bring him a
piece of pork, and he [*suru?ai*] chews betel. He chews, then
chews evodia with it. Then he counts: "two, four, five-six,
seven-eight." He spits on [the piece of pork] and then eats the
piece of pork from the shrine. Then he is *mola* and he goes
to the *lakeno* pudding and the [meat of the] pig he has killed
in the men's house. He *riba* that too, then he eats it. It would
be improper for him [to partake of the *abu* food] without *riba*-
ing. *Riba*ŋa is for [making things] good, for straightening things
out.
   When the men come back from the shrine they make a
lakenoniwane [men's taro pudding]. It is cooked in a leaf oven
[most kinds of *lakeno* are not]. Then they take a section of
pudding as long as my arm, for the men's *riba*ŋa. In the morning, they take that *lakeno* and cut it up. The *suru?ai* comes out
of the men's house, bringing his bamboo of *lakeno*. There may
be ten, or twenty, men down there to undergo the *riba*ŋa. Each
one is counted over, then spat on, in *riba*ŋa; and each food
portion is *riba*-d, in order [these include pieces of pudding and
portions of the sacrificial pork].[6] *Suru?ai* eats first, then the
others. The man who *riba*-s them [the new priest] *riba*-s himself,
and eats last.

   This stage of the sequence of desacralization rites is also
called *molaŋaniwane*, 'men's desacralization', or *sifoŋaniwane*,
'men's coming down'. It is the second occasion on which
women of the group have seen the *suru?ai*. After this, he goes
back again into seclusion in the men's house, for another
forty days—making a total of ninety. In Louŋa's account, on
the eighty-fifth day the *suru?ai* exhumes his father's skull (this
is not a point in the sequence firmly fixed by all groups).
Louŋa continues:

   After eighty-five days, *suru?ai* goes to the grave and exhumes the skull. "I am raising you up, father. The time has
   come for me to *sifo* [lit., "descend"—that is, rejoin his com-

---

5. Although he cooks it at this stage, a process which—like the cooking of the
sacrificial pigs in the shrine, going on concurrently—takes several hours.
6. This is done by the new priest, who is not normally also the *suru?ai*.

The *lakenoniwane* for the death of Ga?enaafou priest Gooboo is carved.

Geleniu, as taboo-keeper, appears at *molaŋaniwane* for the death of his father Gooboo. His head had been shaved at the time of burial.

munity]. The women's *lakeno* will be done, and I'll go back down to the dwelling house."

He digs up the cranium and jaw, puts them in a cradle of split bamboo [beside the grave]. He schedules it [the next event]: "In five days I'll come back and wrap you up." On the fifth day [four by our counting] he comes back and wraps the skull and arranges the next step: "The [women's] *lakeno* for your death is in ten days."

He wraps the skull in a piece of bark and ties it with *lata* vine. There is an opening at each end of [the roll of] bark; each is bound shut with vine. Then he puts it in the cleft of a forked branch of *kwa ?u* or *?alabusi* tree [which he has cut, and implanted beside the grave].

A slight digression from Louŋa's account will be worthwhile at this stage. I was struck by seeing parallels between this Kwaio sequence of burial, exhumation, and the isolation of the bereaved community and the Borneo mortuary customs described by Hertz (1907) in a classic work in social anthropology. In the Borneo sequence there are, in effect, two funerals: one when the body is interred, after which the kin group becomes taboo and ritually isolated; and a second where, after the skull has been exhumed and purified, it is reinterred. At this point the spirit of the deceased is believed to go off to the afterlife, after remaining temporarily with the bereaved relatives, and the latter are freed from taboos. Hertz analyzed this sequence as a making of death into a rite of passage, with the liminality of the dead spirit and taboo kin group as a transitional stage of marginal isolation.

In 1969, in a betel-chewing break in a long discussion of Kwaio ritual, I explained to my mentors these Borneo customs. I pointed out that Kwaio exhumation of the skull was not at a point in the sequence fixed for all groups, and that the stashing of the skull did not necessarily correspond to the lifting of taboos from the community (although in Louŋa's version it does). The old priest Talauŋa?i then launched into an account of how his grandfather had told him that until the last two generations the exhumation was fixed (as in Louŋa's account) at a point that coincided with the lifting of taboos, and that the skull had been put in a limestone cave or fissure maintained by the priest for each kin group (a point supported by other evidence). He further volunteered the observation that although nowadays people did not know or care much about Anogwaʔu, the Land of the Dead, his grandfather had told him that it was after the skull had been interred that the shade of the dead went off to Anogwaʔu.

Let us go back now to the *suruʔai*, who returns from his father's grave to his men's house, bites an areca, and advises his father that the next stage in desacralization has been scheduled.

"This is your areca nut, father. I've scheduled the women's *lakeno* [*lakeno ni geni*] for ten days, so I'll be able to come down to the dwelling house."

Then the day before the women's *lakeno*, they take two pigs. One is a young women's-pig [*boo ni geni*], the other is an *abu* pig. They make a *taualea* [ritual pig-tethering shelter] and put fishtail palm leaves [*giʔa*] on it. They bring a cluster of areca nuts, and an immature coconut, and a branch of evodia [*laʔe*], with the fishtail palm leaves. The *suruʔai tania adalo* [lit., "takes the *adalo* in hand"].

"I *tania adalo* to *sifo* ["descend," i.e., become desacralized] with the *lakeno* pudding." He takes hold of the immature coconut, *siufa* [lit., "washing"—the liquid of the immature coconut]. He counts over the ten *siufa* [reciting a magical spell by naming ten items used in the rituals and feasting after a death]:

"*Siufa maamamu*, I *mamu* [magically attract] money, I *mamu* pigs, I *mamu alogalaua* [ritually baked taro corms], I *mamu ʔasauŋa* [packets of small fish, baked and used in *ribaŋa*] . . . ."

He counts over these and *ruufaʔi* [validates the spell by reciting the names of the ancestors]. Then the *suruʔai* and the priest hold the immature coconut and break it open. The *suruʔai* splashes the liquid over the [two tethered] pigs. He takes a young shoot of betel pepper, husks an immature areca nut, and squeezes the soft pulp in his palm, together with lime. Then he paints the *bou* [sacred post] of the lean-to, at its crotch, then paints his own chest and the priest's chest with the betel mixture, then paints the cheek of the sacred pig and then the women's pig.

We can pause to note that this phase of the ritual, a *fonulaanimae* or 'feast of the dead', is a condensed version of a segment for which a symbolic interpretation will be assayed in chapter 12. Louŋa's account continues:

> Then *suruʔai* goes into the men's house, bites his areca, talks with [*alasia*] his [dead] father, and pounds his taro pudding. This is the third pudding for finishing the sequence. The priest takes the *abu* pig and sacrifices it in the shrine to clear the way for the women's pig. Then he comes back and they make a *lakeno ni geni* ['women's pudding']. This isn't a rectangular pudding [as others are] but a round one[7]—one for the women, which will be baked.
>
> The next morning, *suruʔai* will 'descend' [*sifo*]. The day before, he finally took off the *laŋo* [cordyline garland]: everything was taken off the day before. The *suruʔai* goes down to where the women are gathered for *ribaŋa*—the oldest woman [called *ribaeteeta*, 'riba first', or *kwariʔulasi*, 'carve to open'] first, the others in birth order after her. They stand in a line.
>
> Then the 'women's priest' chews evodia, counts on each— "two, four, five-six, seven-eight"—and spits on the chest of each, going down the line. Then he goes back and *riba*-s each portion of taro pudding and [women's] pork. The women will eat their portions of pudding, but not the portions of pork. It is *abu* for them to eat the pork. That is for the *suruʔai* to "descend" with, to go down to the house, to become *mola*. The priest collects the pieces of pork that have been *riba*-d and burns them in the pig-tethering shelter. The body section of the pork is divided among the men and women and children from other groups, and they eat it. And then the *suruʔai* is *mola*.

This phase in the ritual sequence is also known as 'women's desacralization' (*molaŋanigeni*) or 'women's descending' (*sifoŋanigeni*), where "going down" symbolizes the transition from *abu*, in its sense of sacred isolation, to *mola*.

> The *suruʔai* goes back into the men's house and rolls up his bed, the piece of bark he has slept on. For a full hundred days he has been sleeping on it, he has been forbidden to roll it up. But now he rolls up the bark and his pandanus rain cape

---

7. Note the sexual symbolism here.

and puts them in the drying rack [above the fire]. The bamboo strip they have put across to block [symbolically] the section of the men's house he has been secluded in [which has its separate door behind, out of sight of women] is taken out by *suru?ai*, who takes it to their main ["founding"] shrine and throws it in there.

Then he is *mola*, and can go into the house. But he doesn't go straight into his own house. He must go to another person's house first, someone in a neighboring group. Then he comes back and goes into his own dwelling house. And he tells the women and children there:

"I've been *abu* but I've come into the house now. Now we have to stay and prepare for the mortuary feast for our dead. We have no pigs, no money, no taro; but our important decedent has left us. I've done all the *abu* things. Now we must prepare for the feast. And while we're preparing we must stay at our own places: we can't go to other people's mortuary feasts, can't eat pork, can't eat fish or coconuts with outsiders. You men can't eat coconuts or plantains, and can't go to any mortuary feasts. We're *abu*. . . ."

At this point the group begins to launch full-scale preparations for a mortuary feast that will be a major assertion of prestige. Although Louŋa's account continues, in comparable detail, we can summarize the subsequent ritual sequences.

The kin group still cannot go to other people's feasts until another desacralization feast, a kind of interim event before the main mortuary feast, called *fa?asafiŋa*, is held. We have already encountered this "recharging of ancestrally conferred power" in the sequence after crematory sacrifice. The *fa?asafiŋa*, like the 'men's desacralization' and 'women's desacralization,' may become a large-scale event entailing substantial quantities of food and elaborate reciprocal prestations (in the case of a large and wealthy group bent on public largesse to build up prestige), or may be a small event involving the local group and its members' immediate kin and allies. At this feast women of the group present small strings of shell valuables to the priest and taboo-keeper, to 'open' the way for the eventual mortuary feast. These become added to the bundle of sacred valuables that is brought out at various stages of the sequence as symbol of the group's earning powers.

The young Fanuabiri priest performs *ribaŋa* on *fousuu* pudding at *faʔasafiŋa* rite for death of his father.

By this time, the bereaved group has turned its productive energies to producing taro, raising pigs, and earning valuables. Not surprisingly they enlist ancestral support, using elaborate procedures. This collective effort brings together not only the resident members of the group, but the female members who have married out. These *ino rumaʔa* ('affine women'— that is, women domiciled with affines) and the husbands and children who work with them, play a central part.

One step along the way is *suufibooŋa*, 'pig bristle-plucking,' a rite in which pigs being raised for the feast are magically "treated" (with cordyline, coleus, and other vegetable agents) to make them grow well and quickly. The bristles plucked from the pigs are wrapped in special leaves. After fish have been procured from the coast, and edible insects gathered in the bush, a rite called "pig putting" (*arubooŋa*) is held. The men and women of the group who are raising pigs for the feast follow the priest and taboo-keeper to a special muddy place in the forest, each taking his or her packet of bristles and an insect; each one in turn buries the packet in the mud, telling the ancestors, "Here is your pig." Each one then takes the insect back and feeds it to his or her pig. Then the men eat fish and taro; the women eat insects.

Another complicated ritual sequence is carried out in planting sacred taro gardens for the mortuary feast. A special circle is marked out; the taro shoots planted inside are planted by the taboo-keeper, using a special sacred digging stick (sexual symbolism of the circle as female and the digging stick as phallus is transparent here). Subsequent gardening operations entail complex ritual procedures. Finally, when the taro is mature, a further rite is carried out for scheduling the feast. Here the *mamu* theme is so explicit it is worth quoting Louŋa's account:

> [The taboo-keeper] chews betel, then *tania mamu* ["holds mamu," as physically represented by aromatic evodia]. [He says], "I *tania mamu* for people to hear about our feast and be unable to resist coming—to make them break up their sacred valuables, if they haven't any other money; so that even someone with a bad infection will get better and will come, when they hear about our feast; so they'll break up their valuables to come, because they'll be attracted by the *mamu*."
>
> He chews the evodia, announces that "Our feast is ten days from today," and spits into the air: "Phhhh, phhhh, phhh, phhh." The feast is scheduled. The ancestors have taken that feast. The *adalo naa mamu* has taken the *mamu* he has spat up into the air, has taken it so that even a person who is having a hard time getting the money [that is the "price of admission"] will come, even if he has to break important valuables or make the shell beads himself.

At every stage along the way, taro and coconut puddings (of different varieties) have been made, blessed, and eaten. On this occasion the crusts of the baked taro are made into a pudding, a piece of which is ritually fed to each of the pigs to be killed for the feast.

In the final "countdown" to the mortuary feast, great attention is paid to purifying any hidden offenses that might

Arika explains to his ancestors that this offering of taro and coconuts is to ensure clear weather for his feast.

threaten ancestral support, and making magical presentations of taro plants and coconuts to the ancestors to prevent the calamity of heavy rain on the day of the feast (which can mean financial disaster).[8] The countdown intensifies on the second day before the feast, when a 'feast of the dead' (*fonulaanimae*) is conducted, on a more elaborate scale than the one prior to the 'women's desacralization'.

The 'feast of the dead' is ritually centered around a lean-to within which pigs to be killed by the feastgiving group are tethered—and within the lean-to, around a sacred "post of

8. Heavy rain is almost always attributed to someone's ancestor spoiling their mortuary feast (since a feast is held somewhere in the region at least once a week). An anecdote can illuminate the attitude of first generation Christians to their ancestors. I was talking to a Christian woman when thunder and black clouds showed heavy rain in the interior. "It's raining on Daŋeabeu's feast," I said (a feast being held the next day). "No," she said, "it's raining on Baʔefaka's" (to be held the day after that).

Sacred pigs are tethered in a *taualea*.

the dead." Ritual procedures, and particularly those relating to this post, vary considerably between descent groups. The full complex surrounding the *bou*, 'post' (or *bounimae*, 'post of the dead'), is practiced by descent groups for which Amadia is principal ancestor (figure 6.1) and, in somewhat different form, by descent groups for which ʔlgiʔigi is principal ancestor.

In this full form, the women's priest goes into the forest and cuts a length, some four to six feet, of cyathea palm (for Amadia) or *Alstonia scholaris* tree (for ʔlgiʔigi). The post is wrapped in sago fronds, then implanted on the upper slope of the settlement. Over it, a lean-to is constructed. The shelter is then covered with fishtail palm (*Caryota* sp.) leaves, "the thatching of the dead." Bundles of taro and clusters of areca nuts are put on the 'post of the dead'. The *foʔota* and purificatory pigs to be sacrificed, and the pigs of the 'affine women', are tethered inside, with the senior out-married woman of the group making the first speech of presentation. The pigs are tethered in prescribed order: first the *foʔota* to Amadia or ʔlgiʔigi, then a specially sacred women's pig, then pigs from the taboo-keeper and new priest, then the pig presented by the senior woman (*ribaeteeta*), then pigs presented by 'affine women', then those brought by men.

The women then retire to the dwelling houses; and a group of men and boys go off to the stream to wash. Having purified themselves and donned customary ornaments, they, led by the priest, go to a spot where they ritually rehearse together the magical spell for *mamu* they will recite. Then, each holding a bundle of cordyline leaves and a stick, they are led by the priest into the clearing (after first screaming to ensure no women have remained outside to see them) and up to the pig-tethering shelter. Crouching below the roof, they follow the priest around clockwise as he circles four times, stamping feet and counting out ("two," "four," "six," "eight") each time (see photograph). Then they crouch at the foot of the sacred post. The priest recites the magical spell, holding the immature coconut he has carried (which is re-

The men and boys of ʔAiʔeda circle inside the *taualea* in *beritauŋa*. Note fishtail palm on the right.

ferred to as *siufa*, from *siu*, 'wash'), while the others repeat after him:

Siufa maamamu, I *mamu*-ize the attracting of pigs;
Siufa maamamu, I *mamu*-ize the attracting of money;
Siufa maamamu, I *mamu*-ize the attracting of men;
Siufa maamamu, I *mamu*-ize the attracting of women; . . .

(the rest of the ten items being coconuts and ritually-used taro and fish). This whole procedure, referred to as "holding the ancestor," is followed by the validation of the spell, in which a line of ancestors is called out. Then the priest breaks open the coconut; the liquid is splashed on pigs, on the male participants, and on the sacred valuables hung on the post of the dead: this is *siufa*, 'washing'. The priest then husks an immature areca (betel) nut, crushes it with lime and evodia in his palm, and paints (*too*) the red mixture first on the cheeks of the pigs in prescribed order of sacredness, then on the 'post of the dead', and then on the chests of the participants. Then they go outside, undergo *ribaŋa* (chest-spitting) using bespelled evodia, then eat puddings that have been blessed in similar fashion. Only after this can the women come outside. This entire rite of circling the pig shelter, sprinkling, and painting with betel mix is called *beritauŋa* (lit., "secrecy of the men's house," but here referring to the *taualea*, the feasting shelter). The procedure is also referred to in terms of the circling of the *taualea* (to *garifela*, lit., "circle the ancestral skull repository") or in terms of the breaking open of the coconut (*ʔuiŋa* or *bakaŋa*, 'breaking open').

All these procedures other than the cutting of a 'post of the dead'—construction and thatching of *taualea*, tethering of pigs, circling of the *taualea*, "holding of the ancestor," "washing," painting of the betel mix, and *ribaŋa*—are performed by descent groups not propitiating Amadia or ʔIgiʔigi. The post, for those who use it, gives special powers of *mamu*; but the other procedures of the rite are efficacious enough.

The next morning, the pigs are killed—the *foʔota* and purificatory pigs by the priest, in the shrine; the women's pigs by the 'women's priest' at the margin of the clearing. The women of the group undergo *ribaŋa* (chest-spitting) before partaking of a first, sacred, women's pig; their portions of consecrated taro are collected again, and put at the base of the sacred post in the pig-shelter, "for the *adalo*." Then one of the group's sacred valuables is presented by the taboo-keeper to one of the buriers, who reciprocates with a valuable. Again aromatic evodia, symbol of *mamu*, is bespelled, and this time is spat in *ribaŋa* on the valuables, which are hung up on the pig shelter—opening the way for the secular transactions of the feast (which are described in Keesing 1978a).

I will use the symbolism of this *beritauŋa* rite to illustrate themes and meanings in Kwaio ritual, and some theoretical problems they raise; and so will shortly return to a closer look at painted pigs, sacred post, sprinkled coconut liquid—and open secrets. Before considering ritual meanings, we can return with new data and new insight to questions first posed in sections 6.1 and 6.3, about the way social relations of the living are defined with reference to the dead.

Chapter Eleven

The Sociology
of Kwaio Ritual

IN CHAPTER 6 I looked at ways in which relations of the living
to one another are structured in terms of their relations to
ancestors. I have touched on sociological implications of the
fo?ota system, and of commensality in sacrifice. Now, with a
more full ethnographic spectrum of Kwaio ritual spread out
before us, we can usefully return briefly to this theme.

11.1 Definition of the Ritual Community

We have encountered the sacrament of *ribaŋa* at several
points: where men *riba* prior to eating a sacrificial meal with
the ancestors, where men and women of a descent group *riba*
at the *fa?asafiŋa*, and now where men and women *riba* at
several stages in the rites of desacralization after an important
person dies. Particularly in these contexts where men and
women of a descent group line up in birth order to undergo
ribaŋa before partaking with the spirits of a sacred meal, this
ritual serves to demarcate and dramatize the membership of
a Kwaio descent group (Keesing 1971) clearly and unambig-
uously. Even the possibility of dual descent group membership can be dramatized in *ribaŋa*. I have recorded a rite where
ribaŋa was held twice, for men and women, by a group agnatically related to one territory but resident in, and strongly

attached to, an adjoining one where they are nonagnates. *Ribaŋa*, conducted separately for each territory and its ancestors, brought together different but partly overlapping rows of descendants.

There are few ritual contexts, and almost no secular contexts, where one cannot, sequentially or simultaneously, enact roles based on connection to two or more territories, their shrines, their ancestors, and the groups domiciled in them (Keesing 1968). An example will illustrate this.

> . . . An agnate in descent group A . . . is priest for the As though he has not lived with them since infancy. He grew up and has always lived with his mother's kin, from descent group B. In the course of a mortuary feast [he] was giving, a leader from group A approached from the left and presented him with a major valuable, which he accepted with his left hand. At the same moment, a man from B approached from the right and presented another valuable to him—which he accepted simultaneously with his right hand . . . acting at the same moment as both an A and a B. (Keesing 1968:83)

It is in the isolation of taboo, after *suuŋa* crematory sacrifice and following an important death, that an unambiguous commitment to territory and ancestors to which one has primary attachment must be made. One keeps, or does not keep, the taboos (although there are halfway degrees, for shorter periods, for husbands and children of out-married women). While one is keeping taboos, one is excluded not only from secular gatherings, but from the ritual observances of other groups.

For a priest, this can mean a separation from clients whose lives are in danger. Thus Kwaio avoid, if they can, a situation where the same person assumes two separate sets of priestly duties, for different congregations. An interesting case centered around Louŋa, the oldest son of an elderly priest. Louŋa's ritual expertise and high intelligence are reflected in these pages in his accounts of crematory sacrifice, mortuary taboos, and other matters. He was well versed in the knowledge needed to succeed his father as priest of Gaafolo. But a year before his father died, Louŋa's maternal uncle, the priest of Naalaʔe, died. There were no male agnates left at Naalaʔe, only a scattered array of cognatic kin. Louŋa was singled out in divination to assume the priesthood at Naalaʔe, and did so. When Louŋa's father Dikeafelo died, Louŋa was initially ruled out as his successor, on grounds that should one of the people related to Naalaʔe need to sacrifice an expiatory or fo ʔota pig while the Gaafolo people were keeping taboos, the Naalaʔe people would be without a religious officiant, and hence placed in jeopardy. So the oldest son of the brother of the dead priest Dikeafelo was chosen to assume the Gaafolo priesthood. But after the desacralization rites had been set in motion, difficulties in staging the rituals properly led the man chosen as priest to drop out, and Louŋa to step into the breach.

For the physically scattered, and conceptually overlapping, and fuzzily defined kin groups of the Kwaio mountains, these rituals provide a collective dramatization of who one is, with whom one stands, and where one's strongest interests and deepest ancestral attachments lie. A group that is normally dispersed comes together, physically and sociologically, as a religious congregation in contexts of close communion with the spirits, fraught with power and danger.

We have seen (in sections 6.3 and 9.2) how ritual relations between priests in sacrifice express relationships of common descent between the groups for which they act. Such linkages are enacted in crematory sacrifice as well. Thus one of the eight sons of the original Amadia (figure 6.1) is believed to be buried at Keto shrine. The priests of three descent groups, Naaŋari, Gaʔenaafou, and Funiʔalai, perform crematory sacrifices there. When any of these priests sacrifices, the other two priests go into liminal sacredness for ten days, because of their ritual bond. If the priest from Naaŋari performs a crematory sacrifice, the priests from Giruʔi, Dudu, and Namoriiridi will also be *abu* for ten days, because of their close ritual links.

If coparticipation in sacrifice is an expression of sociological and genealogical closeness, so the internal fission of a descent group is marked by separation of shrines and priest-hoods. When a quarrel divides two clusters of descent group members separated by some three to six generations from a common ancestor, a common response is for the segment which does not hold the priesthood to put forward their own priest, and sacrifice separately. A number of what now constitute separate but closely linked descent groups were bifurcated in this way, in the last two generations. One such rift appeared temporarily during my study when, because of a quarrel following the death of the octogenerian Ga?enaafou priest, the feastgiver ?Elota (Keesing 1978a) began to sacrifice separately to Amadia on behalf of his close kin. The rift was later smoothed over. A concomitant of this process is that what now is dramatized as ritual linkage between priests (as when the Kafusiisigi priest can share the head and sacred parts of pigs sacrificed by the priest of agnatically-linked Naala?e, which is the junior or derivative shrine) in fact resulted from a quarrel and consequent splitting of ritual communities, in a previous (in this case, grandparental) generation.

11.2 The Role of Women in Ritual

In section 8.4 the central part women play in childbirth, and the peripheral role men play, were outlined. I argued that these must be accorded full status as community rituals, not simply—as in much anthropological reportage—as "things women do." However, in ways glimpsed in the last three chapters, the participation of women in the community rituals primarily staged by men is both significant and vital to successful performance. The senior woman of the group, in particular, performs key acts: on behalf of her juniors, in *ribaŋa*, in presenting the first "opening" valuable in *fa?asafiŋa*, and in other contexts. The women of the group, including ones who have married out, *riba* together to free the group of taboos; they enact, with men, the pig bristle-plucking rite; and their presentation, as *ino ruma?a*, of pigs for the mortuary

The senior Gaʔenaafou woman undergoes *ribaŋa* at *fa ʔasafiŋa* rite after death of the priest Gooboo.

feast is symbolically as well as sociologically crucial in the whole proceedings. The man who *tania kwalo ni geni*, sacrifices women's pigs and *riba*-s women, represents a symbolic reinforcement of the critically important ritual roles of women, complementary to those of men.

It is as though, in all these acts and ways, what begin as male-focused procedures associated with ancestral power at the margins of the clearing are *brought back into* the clearing and the community through the ritual participation of women.[1] In this respect, as in the tenor of interpersonal relations between the sexes, the Kwaio system differs sharply from those reported for many societies in New Guinea and elsewhere in Melanesia where a similar symbolic polarization of the sexes prevails.

11.3 Ritual Expression of the Life Cycle

As we have seen, isolation in *abu* realms entails descent below the middle part of the clearing and ascent above it—both in periodic and cyclical temporary crossing from *mola* to *abu* (menstruation, sacrifice) and in sustained liminal isolation (childbirth, taboo-keeping after death of a priest or crematory sacrifice). The return transitions from *abu* to *mola*, by 'ascending' and 'descending', restore the marginalized to everyday life.

But if we consider the course of an individual's life, there is a more general trajectory through symbolically defined space. All infants are born below the margins of the clearing; all move upward to menstrual area, then to dwelling house. The life space of the very young child, boy or girl, is between dwelling house and menstrual hut. When a young boy is old enough, his life space moves upward, centered in dwelling house but extending to men's house and shrine. With adulthood and, particularly, old age the focus of life becomes the men's house, associated with ritual and war, the domains of death, and the ancestors. Finally, in death, mortal remains are

---

1. Shelley Schreiner, coparticipant in my 1974, 1977, and 1979 research, has pointed out that other rituals reincorporating marginalized members into the community also require participation of the opposite sex. In the case of childbirth isolation it is men who play this part.

The women of ʔAiʔeda in a rite to consecrate a new skull house. The senior woman holds *weewela*.

interred in the shrine, and it is into this upper realm of sacredness that an ancestor emerges.

In this life-trajectory, a women's path is more ambiguous. She begins below the clearing, like an infant boy; but through her childbearing years she cycles both to menstrual hut and childbirth isolation. When she reaches menopause, especially when she becomes *abu*, she moves upward in symbolic focus. But it is only in her ultimate death that she moves to the upper margin of the clearing.

Implicit in this symbolic trajectory,[2] I think, is a contrast between the *abu* realm of women and the *abu* realm of men and ancestors: the human beings women bring into the world are mortal, temporary creations; the ancestors men ritually bring into the world are immortal, unlimited by constraints

2. A point elaborated by McKinley (n.d.).

of time and space. Of course, it is the ancestors who bring death, and hence claim the living into their realm; but it is men who are entrusted by the spirits with the rites of transition through which mortal remains are returned to *wado*, the 'earth' of origins, and a new spirit emerges. Viewing life's trajectory and the transition from physical and mortal to metaphysical and immortal in this way can shed light on the symbolic mirror-imaging of skull and uterus, and on the meaning of exhumation.

The skull is an ideal symbolic vehicle for expressing the transition from the physical to the immaterial, from mortality to immortality, a process of death and rebirth. The skull physically survives for centuries, as a visible transformation of the known human individual. In size and shape, the skull lends itself to symbolically representing an infant; and exhumation itself becomes an analogue of birth—birth from the earth of symbolic origins to which mortal remains have been returned. In a cult principally practiced by the people of ʔAiʔeda,[3] an ancestral skull house is maintained and periodically rebuilt or renewed. In the attendant ritual, a woman of the group holds a sprouting, painted coconut kernel, called 'infant' (*weewela*), while the group's unmarried girls, clad in married women's pubic aprons, stand assisting her: the explicit symbolism is that the group is looking after its skulls as a mother looks after her infant.

We have moved toward the symbolic meanings of the acts and objects used in ritual. We need now to turn directly to questions of symbolic meaning.

---

3. This cult is supposed to have originated in Kwaraʔae, the neighboring language zone.

Chapter Twelve

Symbolism in Kwaio Ritual

WHAT DO THE objects and acts in Kwaio ritual symbolize? What are the covert symbolic meanings of cordyline and coconuts and evodia, of spitting and painting and planting and breaking and burning?

12.1 Iconic Symbols in Kwaio Ritual

We have encountered in Kwaio magic, and glimpsed in Kwaio ritual, a logic of analogy whereby objects and acts carry meanings because of some physical resemblance to the objects and acts they symbolically represent. Thus in childbirth, a slimy infusion is used to induce magically an easy passage through the birth canal; scrapings from the bark of a smooth, straight trunk of a tree are used in a poultice to induce a broken limb to mend straight and unblemished. And in ritual, an aromatic shrub represents the attraction of money, burning of a sacrificial morsel represents a transition from the physical world to the noumenal realm of the spirits. In such rites and magical procedures the symbol physically is modelled on its referent: that is, the symbolism is *iconic*. In language, symbolism is characteristically *noniconic*, in that words, as sounds, have an arbitrary relationship to their referents. (Some of the symbolism in ritual is noniconic and some of the symbolism in language is iconic; but as semiotic systems—systems of signs—ritual and language generally contrast in their preponderant use of iconic signs on the one hand and noniconic signs on the other.) A closer look at iconic symbolism in Kwaio ritual will be instructive. Given the Kwaio preoccupation with states (*ABU* and *MOLA*, HUMANS and ANCESTORS, PHE-NOMENAL and NOUMENAL), and transitions between states (purification, desacralization, sacrifice, etc.), it is not surprising to find iconic symbols of state transition. We have already encountered washing and head shaving (which is iconic in the covert symbolism in which head = genitals and shaving = castration) as dramatizations of purification and the reestablishment of sociality. Burning is an effective dramatization of the transition from phenomenal to noumenal realms. The spatial associations between UP and DOWN and *ABU* and *MOLA* make dramatizations of ascent appropriate symbolic expressions of sacralization or purification, and dramatizations of descent appropriate symbols of desacralization or isolation. When a kin group as ritual community is cut off from the outside world by sacredness when its priest dies or when the group undertakes crematory sacrifice, physical enactments of closing (e.g., setting up barriers) or opening serve to dramatize the social closure and progressive reopening of the ritual community.

Other pervasive iconic symbols express attraction (especially the attracting of valuables) or repulsion (the sending away of malevolent and destructive influences, particularly by planting or implanting barriers against invasion). Another theme is stability or permanence. Residential stability, in Kwaio society, is associated both with harmony with ancestors (since pollution or other serious disruptions of relations with ancestors frequently trigger a move) and harmony between the living (since quarrels may lead to dispersal of residential groups). The ritual quest for stable living is often dramatized by physical expressions of permanence: planting cordyline shrubs, or preserving the leaves; burying a coconut or piglet, or some physical representation of an offering (such as a stone). The latter illustrates again an important theme in Kwaio symbology that we have glimpsed at many points. The ances-

'Women's priest' Bono ritually washes the men who will undergo *ribaŋa* in desacralization after the death of Gooboo, the Gaʔenaafou priest. Washing here clearly symbolizes desacralization.

tors, in the noumenal realm, are on a separate plane of existence from the physical objects—pigs, shell valuables, coconuts, areca nuts—they crave. To represent transition of a sacrificial pig from phenomenal to noumenal realm, a hair or piece of flesh can be burned; and to represent the presentation to the ancestors of a major shell valuable, a short string of beads thrown into the shrine as a token will suffice. A stone is characteristically used to represent a coconut; sometimes it can represent a piglet. A Kwaio man on his way to a feast puts a sprig of fern in his hair, saying over the sprig, "Here is an areca nut for you, ancestor X: Protect me."

Living in a lush and diverse sea of vegetation, with an array of ancient cultigens and wild plants which are associated with the sacred throughout a vast belt across south and southeast Asia and into the Pacific (e.g., cordyline, ginger, evodia, coleus), the Kwaio understandably depend heavily on the plant world to provide vehicles for symbolism. Trees that ooze red, bloodlike sap or white, milklike sap provide symbols of bodily substances, in medicinal magic and ritual procedures. Flowers and aromatic shrubs provide symbols of attraction, beauty, desire. Ginger is associated with heat—hence it is used in curing, used to symbolize malevolent and uncontrolled forces or, in other contexts, the heat of anger. *Cordyline fruticosa* serves (as throughout Melanesia) as a vehicle both for color symbolism (growing as it does in many varieties of red and green) and as a symbol of continuity and permanence (since the leaves, kept dry, are rot resistant and last for many years; and the plant takes root easily and lives for many decades, marking old sacred places and settlement sites). Areca nuts also can be preserved, kept dry, for decades, and serve as physical symbols of ancestral presence and powers. Nuts that sprout when mature (particularly coconuts) serve to symbolize regeneration.

This raises questions of sexual symbolism. In all symbolic systems, it seems, a logic of iconic symbolism is used to carry covert sexual meanings. Kwaio magic and ritual are by no means dominated by sexual symbolism, but the presence of sexual themes is unmistakable. For Kwaio, as for other peoples, the head is a symbolic focus of sexuality; and that gets tangled up with ideas of sacredness. Thus the heads of ritually senior men (and their knees and teeth, which in Kwaio carry latent sacred—sexual—meanings as well) are a focus of their sacredness. As in other parts of the world (Leach 1958), hair serves as vehicle for sexual symbolism. In mourning dishevelment, Kwaio are temporarily expressing withdrawal from sociality (and sexuality); by shaving the head, a Kwaio mother is removing the pollution of childbirth (and being reborn herself); and the 'taboo keeper', her mirror image, is desacralizing himself and being reborn in a *mola* state. The equation head = genitals is expressed in the custom whereby a boy has a small tuft left on his head if it is shaved.[1] The equation tuft = penis is made more transparent in the marking of men's water bamboos: a triangular projection, cut on the rim of the top internode, is called by the same term as the head tuft. Transparently sexual meanings underlie some of the ancestral rules and categories. Thus, for instance, females are prohibited from eating bananas (whose phallic shape is unmistakable) except during part of their menstrual periods.

Most of the sexual symbolism in Kwaio ritual is "unconscious" in the sense that native actors can proffer no explicit account of the sexual referents. This then raises several questions. Some are methodological. How do we know if our interpretation is "right" if these meanings are unconscious? Do all participants in ritual unconsciously perceive the same meanings, whether sexual or not? Some of these questions have to do with the nature of ritual symbolism. If an act or object symbolizes phallus or copulation, can it symbolize something else as well? In Hindu symbology, representations of genitals or copulation are used to symbolize the creative forces in the universe; could this be true in tribal religions such as that of the Kwaio? And where rituals are performed

---

1. Kwaio do not share the notion, reported for Small Malaita (Ivens 1927) and San Cristobal (Fox 1924), that the fontanelle is the aperture through which shade comes and goes.

to achieve practical goals—to desacralize, to enlist ancestral support, to induce ancestral forgiveness—what is the relationship between the explicit goals of ritual and covert symbolism? We need theoretical clarification before looking more closely at symbolism in Kwaio ritual.

12.2   How Symbols "Mean"

In a series of papers, Victor Turner (1967, 1968, 1978) has argued that ritual symbols are characteristically *multivocal*: that is, an object or act used in ritual has not one referent, but a range of them. Such a spectrum of meanings, Turner suggests, includes physical referents related to primary experience (sex, maternal nurturance, etc.) and more abstract referents having to do with society and the moral order (the solidarity of the lineage, collective responsibility, etc.). Thus the *mudyi* tree, canonical "milk tree" in the symbolism of the Ndembu of Zambia, exuding a milky sap, "stands for" a range of referents: "breasts, breast milk, the mother-child relationship, the novice's [lineage], matriliny, womanhood in general, married womanhood, childbearing, and even Ndembuhood" (Turner 1978:577). Turner suggests that rituals "work" partly in connecting these abstract social and moral ideas to the primary, hence emotional, experience of individuals. That the head of a Kwaio priest symbolizes both genital sexuality and the sacredness of the ancestors may be fundamentally important, not incidental.

  Understanding of this kind of multivocality has been carried further by Gregory Bateson. In a brilliant paper on art, Bateson (1972) suggests that iconic symbolism is not only different in kind from the noniconic symbolism of language, in the way it conveys meanings, but that it depends on different faculties of mind. Bateson suggests that art—and, I would add, ritual and metaphor—depends on an integrative/aesthetic capacity to perceive *patterns* and *relationships*. These relationships are *by their nature* inexpressible in language, except by indirection.[2] In his analysis of a Balinese painting, Bateson views it not as "about" death or sex, but "about" a relational pattern manifest in both death and sex—of which death, sex, and other relationships in human experience are expressions. When we say, as interpreters, that the painting is about death, or sex, or both, we are moving, as it were, out of the dimension in which iconic relationships are expressed, and into a different dimension, where "things" exist and can be described in words.

If this is generally true of the iconic symbolism of ritual (and I think it is) then the process of "translation" in analyzing meanings is not only formidable; it inevitably distorts as well. Moreover, the ability of native actors to explain what symbols "mean"—to give an *exegesis*—involves a similar distortion. Whether some, all, or no members of the society explain to one another or an anthropologist what the ritual "means" may be incidental to native actors' unconscious comprehension of the relational patterns dramatized in ritual; yet these deep meanings, relational and abstract, may not be expressible in words or representative of "things" at all.

The problem of covert meanings has concerned many recent analysts of symbolism, notably Sperber (1974) and most recently, Gilbert Lewis.[3] Lewis' careful interpretations of ritual among the Gnau of Sepik New Guinea pose the issues squarely. Lewis notes at the outset that specified *procedures*— what he calls "the ruling"—are what is distinctive about ritual, rather than shared understanding of symbolic meanings:

> . . . People know clearly how to perform their rituals, assert that they know right from wrong performance, yet they do not necessarily provide an explanation in words of what they express, what they communicate or what they symbolise by their

2. As Isadora Duncan is supposed to have said, "If I could tell you what it meant, there would be no point in dancing it."
3. The original version of *Kwaio Religion*, written under contract to Mayfield Press, was completed prior to publication of Lewis' (1980) book and Brunton's (1980) comparative analysis of Melanesian religion. I regard as significant this independent confluence of ideas on Melanesian religion.

rituals. The ruling is explicit but its meaning may be implicit; may be esoteric, or established for all to know, or forgotten and unknown; tolerant of interpretation on many levels and by many individuals, or intolerant of any but the single "true" meaning established by tradition within that culture. The ruling is public, clear and social; its meaning may be so, or it may be indeterminate, private, various and individual. (Lewis 1980:19)

How, then, are we to proceed in a quest for covert meanings, and with what cautions? Lewis is unwilling to limit himself to Nadel's dictum (1953:108) that meanings that are "uncomprehended"—in the sense that native actors cannot explain them—are private and nonsocial, hence irrelevant. He points, as Bateson does, to the qualitative difference between what is expressed in acts and through objects, in a logic of iconicity, and what can be conveyed in words:

> . . . We cannot put a perfume into words. . . . It may not be possible to translate some expression adequately into another medium, or into words. We must expect our informants to be at times inarticulate or silent about part of what the ritual means to them, or does to them, or makes them feel. But we can get closer to it by careful study and analysis, just as we could convey something about . . . a perfume if we paid close attention to it and had skill with words. (Lewis 1980:24)

If we are prepared to go beyond what our informants can tell us about the meanings of the often elaborate pageantry of their rites—and we seemingly must—how are we to assess our interpretations, and what constraints should bind us? When we find a people such as the Umeda (Gell 1975) who stage elaborate rites yet have no exegetic traditions, we must go beyond overt acts and objects to seek covert meanings. But the anthropologist who would see in ritual a languagelike code of meanings may construct a spurious order, a theology that distorts social realities. Symbolist anthropology can become a kind of "cultural cryptography." There are several sides to this danger.

First of all, the anthropologist seeking covert meanings begins with theoretical assumptions—derived from structuralist, psychoanalytic or other traditions—that predispose him or her to find some particular sort of structures of meaning, whether of dyadic oppositions, triads, or covert sexual reference. A people's rites, like their myths, can become a pattern of ink blots in which the analyst sees what he or she is looking for. The symbolist anthropologist, by training and inclination, has a virtuosity in interpreting covert symbolism, and an access to the whole Western tradition of symbolic decipherment and literary and art criticism, which individuals in a tribal society do not. The rare tribal philosopher may share the anthropologist's gifts and commitments; and symbolic anthropology becomes a collaboration between a Melanesian Muchona[4] and ethnographer. The ethnographer, professionally rewarded for cleverness in decipherment, is motivated to seek meanings in ways native participants are not.

Moreover, as Brunton (1980) has argued, Melanesian religions differ widely in the extent to which they embody a global, theological order and systematization. A "cultural theology" can too easily—by filling in missing pieces, imputing meanings to symbols, piecing together partial accounts, and attributing the insights of the odd tribal philosopher to "the culture"—create what Brunton calls "misconstrued order." A quest to find order and coherence, in an anthropological tradition of "cultural theology," may not only lead to spurious overinterpretation, but may in the process obscure significant variations in the degree to which different peoples order their universe. I have suggested that the Kwaio, living pragmatically with their ancestors, unconcerned with ultimate explanation and origins, yet enacting complex rituals, represent an important variant on the theme of order and disorder in Melanesian religions.

There are deep problems in imputing meanings to "the culture," when, as Lewis suggests, understandings may be differentially distributed within a population. One of the most

---

4. The reference is to Victor Turner's Ndembu informant, Muchona the Hornet, whose virtuosity in exegesis provided Turner with crucial evidence.

serious problems of a conceptualization of culture as public and social, unless it is counterbalanced by a "distributive" conceptualization as well (see Keesing 1981: ch. 4; and Schwartz 1978), is that it leads us to impute meanings to "the culture." We might better say that ritual symbols, like other cultural symbols, *evoke* meanings, which may depend on who individuals are, what they have experienced, and what they know. As Lewis puts it, "We may say that a people perceive a meaning or intend one, but not that things apart from people have meanings . . . independently of someone's understanding them. . . . Meaning is present not in things but in people's minds" (1980:221–22). And thus the distribution of knowledge on the basis of which meanings are evoked in the minds of participants becomes a crucial question, both within a society and in comparing the ritual traditions of different peoples. Lewis continues to say that societies "differ in the ways they teach, diffuse or control the interpretation of their rites and symbols as something to be clearly established, or left open and unexplained, or made mysterious, or kept secret" (1980:222).

The Bimin-Kuskusmin of New Guinea, who have an extensively developed exegetic tradition, liken symbolic meanings to a nut which is layered like an onion (Poole 1982). Women and uninitiated boys have access to the outermost layer; and the layers of hidden meaning are progressively stripped away in the revelations of male initiation. Similarly, among the nearby Baktaman (Barth 1975), an initiate is provided at each stage of the cult hierarchy with symbolic "keys" that unlock new and previously hidden meanings. If we commit ourselves to a position that it is in the nature of the human mind to decipher covert symbols, and that these meanings are public and cultural even though no one can tell us about them, we become unable to conceptualize effectively the social control of information on which understandings of covert meanings depend—a matter central in the politics of societies such as Bimin-Kuskusmin and Baktaman (see Keesing 1982).

Finally, the very assumption that ritual is a system of *com-*

munication predisposes us to seek meanings, where native participants are primarily engaged with ritual as a mode of *action*, a form of collective work for social ends. Kwaio crematory sacrifice is performed to induce the *adalo* to *nanama* the living; a *sifoŋanigeni* desacralizes the women of the bereaved group, a spitting of evodia in the air attracts guests to the feast. Not only do rituals "work" in the eyes of the participants, they bring humans and real (though invisible) and awesomely powerful beings into intimate contact, sharing food and carrying on conversations. These rites evoke emotions of awe, concern, communion, and fear, not necessarily because the participants understand meanings, but because they have placed their lives desperately at risk to achieve good living and prosperity. In our concern with uncovering covert meanings, we can easily distort these compelling subjective realities, can over-intellectualize what is probably—for most people most of the time—a primarily emotional experience, and a collective enterprise, not an intellectual communion of shared meanings. Kwaio ritual is crucial, dangerous, collective work. Here Barth's observations about the Baktaman of Papua New Guinea provide an apt warning:

> . . . rites . . . *do* something as well as *say* something. . . . An analysis [of] . . . ritual events *merely* as communicative events constructs spurious problems and invites the use of inappropriate concepts. . . .
> . . . To have persons—such as novices and women—participate . . . in a (mystical) productive enterprise which they do not understand is rather different from merely speaking to them in a secret language which they cannot interpret. It is the *concerns* of Baktaman ritual—taro, growth, pigs—that integrate even the most passive and excluded categories . . . into the cult and make of the whole population one unified congregation with a common purpose. . . . (1975:209–10)

Lewis expresses a similar concern with the paradigm of ritual-as-communication: "To limit ritual to its communicative aspect would exclude and falsify its significance to those who perform it. Ritual is not done solely to be interpreted: it is . . . done . . . to resolve, alter, or demonstrate a situation"

(1980:35). He notes, in symbolist anthropology, "a desire to find an intellectual or cognitive component in everything people do at the expense or neglect of the emotional, expressive, and functional components" (1980:222).

We need to look very closely at what Kwaio can tell an ethnographer, and what they do tell one another, about what they are doing in ritual, why they are doing it, and what it means.

12.3   Meanings and Exegesis in Kwaio Ritual

Kwaio occupy a middle position on a Melanesian continuum, in terms of the degree to which they can explicate ritual meanings. Like the Gnau, Kwaio can—at least by indirection—provide interpretations for some ritual acts and objects and not for others. These mainly have to do with the *goals* of ritual acts as they are enacted using objects. Kwaio adults know (and teach their children) that the reason they undergo *ribaŋa* is to make them and the food *mola*, before they partake, with the spirits, of a sacred meal. Similarly, all or most Kwaio adults know that the goal of the *beritauŋa* rite in which coconut liquid is sprinkled on pigs, sacred valuables, and the male participants, is to achieve *mamu*, the attraction of wealth by drawing guests to the feast to be held two days later. Kwaio similarly know that the ritual planting of cordyline and other sacred plants at the margins of the clearing is to *oria*, 'send away', malevolent influences; and that rocks, spoken of as coconuts, are "planted" behind the men's house of a new settlement as offerings to the ancestors that will ensure stable living and the permanence of the settlement.

As I have demonstrated, many of the objects and acts in Kwaio ritual have to do with effecting changes between states (*ABU → MOLA*), with preventing undesired invasions by dangerous outside forces, with transferring material objects into the NOUMENAL realm, or with opening a "channel" between PHENOMENAL world of humans and NOUMENAL world of

the spirits. Underlying such ritual operations are some pervasive assumptions, ones that only the few most gifted and
reflective Kwaio philosophers (chapter 13) could make partly
explicit, that burning or burying transfers material objects to
the NOUMENAL realm; that washing removes invisible danger
or sacredness as well as physical dirt; that breath and spittle
are special agents for communication with ancestors and the
infusion of ancestrally conferred power; and that breaking
open an areca nut and chewing betel opens a channel of
communication with the spirits.[5]

The rituals we have glimpsed obviously draw on and express the cosmological schemes sketched in section 5.1. Thus
desacralization entails descending, purification entails ascending, and the seclusion of the taboo-keeper is an inversion
of the seclusion of mother in childbirth. The extent to which
Kwaio adults perceive this symbolic scheme as a kind of global
system—and hence perceive details of ritual procedure as
expressions of this scheme, or as systematically interrelated—
apparently varies considerably, a problem to which we will
shortly return.

Some of the objects used in ritual carry meanings which
are made quite explicit in the accompanying procedures and
verbal commentaries. Perhaps the clearest example is evodia.
It would be hard for a Kwaio participant in ritual not to perceive the symbolic expression of attraction-through-scent—
of *la?e* as magical "bait" to draw people and their money. But
the use of *la?e* in *ribaŋa*, where the plant is chewed and spat
on participants in a sacred meal (and on the food to be shared
with the ancestors) is less transparent. The *la?e* in effect makes
the ancestors safe to eat with, but how and why is nowhere
made explicit. Those Kwaio who have unconsciously formu-

---

5. A person's 'breath' (*maŋona*) is viewed as a kind of life force, but also as vehicle
for the power of (ancestrally transmitted) words, and spittle is a kind of agent of this
power. The association of betel chewing with the ancestors almost certainly reflects
its dissociative effects: when you are "high" you have a communion with the sacred,
an association given greater importance by people, such as the Yanomamö, who have
powerful hallucinogens.

lated a "theory" of this, if there are any (no informants have produced an explicit interpretation), may well have reached quite divergent interpretations.

Another commonly used object or substance, as we have seen, is *Cordyline fruticosa*. This cultigen is an ancient and sacred plant used very widely throughout the Asian–Pacific zone as a symbol of stability and permanence and (through its green and red varieties) a vehicle for color symbolism. Cordyline is used pervasively in Kwaio ritual—planted in the shrine after crematory sacrifice, carried in *beritauŋa*, used for divination, and employed in scores of other ways (red cordyline in vengeance magic, bundles of ancient dried cordyline leaves to invoke the spirits after giving first fruits of yams, planted around graves, planted around settlements to ensure permanence and to ward off malevolent powers, etc.). Most adult Kwaio probably have some unconscious or semiconscious sense not only of the sacredness of cordyline but of its "rootedness" in the past (hence its expression of permanence and continuity).

A similar perception of meaning (in this unconscious or unverbalizable Batesonian sense) probably is derived from the physical acts of breaking open and implanting in the ground in Kwaio ritual. Over and over again, the coconuts or areca nuts to be shared with the ancestors are opened not in a perfunctory way, but in a prescribed way (hitting the coconut with a sharp stone, biting the areca husk off) that is attributed special significance. As representations of opening—removing taboos, opening transactions or events, opening channels to the spirits—such physical acts express important nonverbal ideas about states and transitions. The reverse process of closing is physically represented by acts of blocking off (as when, after crematory sacrifice, the path leading to the shrine is blocked by felling branches and saplings across it). In a social world where settlements are moved every few years, and group solidarity is vulnerable to quarrels, acts of burying, implanting in the ground, or planting, express stability and continuity with the past. Although Kwaio have no explicit folk

Offering of immature coconut and areca cluster hung in a *taualea*.

theory that acts and objects "stand for" such themes of opening, closing, or stability, they are seemingly attuned to such
iconic, analogic symbolism by their experience of magic,
where the procedure is so often modeled analogically on the
desired effect.

But if some symbolism is at least partly transparent to
Kwaio participants, some of the acts and objects deployed in
the rites seem not to be. Why are fishtail palm leaves put on
the pig shelter in *beritauŋa*? There are no obvious clues, no
transparent meanings, no explanations proffered by experts.
The pith of *giʔa*, the fishtail palm, like cyathea tree fern pith
and sago pith, is used as pig fodder. Are we to interpret the
fronds on the *taualea* as symbols of women's nurturant role
in raising pigs to the ancestors? The heart of the palm is used
for making bows, and *giʔa* is sometimes used as a generic
term for men's weapons. Is the symbolism about death and
war, not nurturance? The rare Kwaio philosopher tells us that
giʔa is "the thatching of the ancestors." Can we—should we—
guess at deeper covert meanings?

The same problem arises with regard to the more global
meanings of ritual sequences. How far should we be prepared
to go beyond the explicit goals of rituals—the removal of *abu-
ness*, the solicitation of *nanama*-ization, the inducing of (supernaturally aided) growth of pigs—to find meanings Kwaio
do not? And how confidently? In commenting on the original
version of this manuscript, Robert McKinley speculated that
the *arubooŋa*, "pig-putting," rite is a "mock sacrifice" which

> ends with men eating taro and fish while women eat taro and
> insects. In other words this mock sacrifice adumbrates the
> resolution of the entire mortuary sequence, namely, that men
> will be able to resume secular exchange only after the blessings
> of the ancestors have reached all the way to the women of the
> descent group. The association of the men with a product
> acquired through trade (the fish) and the women with a food
> just fed to the ancestors (insects) shows that the final release
> of the bereaved group depends on a successful accommoda-
> tion between ancestral power and women. Holding the mock
> sacrifice in the forest allows this touchy accommodation to
> begin to take effect on neutral ground. (McKinley n.d.)

He may be right. But if decipherment of covert symbolism is to be solidly grounded in ethnographic realities, what are we to take as evidence, and with what confidence in the meanings we see and native actors do not? Are such meanings "part of the culture"? Such questions can be posed in a more focused way if we look in greater detail at a single ritual sequence.

12.4   The Symbolism of *Beritauŋa*

The *beritauŋa* rite is worth looking at more closely to illuminate these questions. At one level, the meanings of *beritauŋa* are clear enough. The rite takes place a week or so after the bespelled evodia has been spat into the air to induce the *adalo* to "take" the *mamu* and exert powers of magical attraction. *Beritauŋa* further develops the *mamu* theme, once more enlisting ancestral powers to attract guests and their money.

But in *beritauŋa*, the *mamu* theme is given a different turn. This rite is the initial phase in the 'feast of the dead' where the ancestors will eat sacrificial pigs before the feast of the living commences. The rite points in two directions: to the ancestors, to whom offerings are being made; and to the guests who, with ancestral aid, will be attracted to the feast. The dual orientation is physically represented by the pigs tethered in the shelter where *beritauŋa* takes place. These are the pigs that will attract guests to the feast, and they are also the pigs to be sacrificed to the spirits to enlist their support. The taro plants and immature coconuts and areca clusters tied to the 'post of the dead' and/or to the rafters of the pig shelter are at once offerings to the spirits and symbols of the food and conviviality that will attract guests from far and near.

The *mamu* theme, explicit in the magic spell recited in *beritauŋa*, could hardly be missed. But at another extreme, as we noted, the fishtail palm fronds that are the prescribed "thatching of the ancestors" convey no obvious meanings. What about the 'post of the dead' bespelled and ritually implanted in the pig shelter? What about the breaking open of the coconut and the sprinkling of liquid on pigs, valuables, and participants? What about the painting of betel mix on the snouts of pigs and the chests of participants? What constructions might Kwaio (male participants and spectators, and the excluded women, many of whom know these procedures which they cannot see) place on *beritauŋa*?

The term *beritauŋa* (lit., "secrecy—or stealing—of the men's house") points to the secrecy of the circling, sprinkling, and painting in the *taualea* from women: the root of the verb *beria*, 'steal', implies something done in secrecy. *Garifela*, "circle the ancestral skull repository," the alternative term for this rite of circling, splashing, and painting, points to the ancestral locus in the *taualea*; but any further meanings are shrouded in the semantic history of the language.[6] The other terms for segments of the rite—"taking hold of the ancestor(s)," "breaking"—offer no clues to a covert global symbolism. What, then, of the objects and acts in *beritauŋa*? And what more global themes, beyond the explicit ones, can we uncover?

The 'post of the dead', as we have seen, is highly sacred to descent groups tracing close relationships to Amadia and ʔIgiʔigi. It is used in a more perfunctory and partial manner by other groups. It is not, in either case, either physically prepossessing (usually being a four-foot length of tree fern) or visibly phallic (wrapped as it usually is in sago fronds or forest leaves). It is salient to Kwaio participants, at a surface symbolic level, as the locus of ancestral presence. The post "is" Amadia, and other ancestors. More abstractly, the post would seem to symbolize continuity with the ancestors, a kind of physical representation of the line connecting the founding ancestors, through the intervening priests, to the living. (The priest, having led the participants in reciting the spell for *mamu*, has validated the magic by naming this line of ances-

6. E.g., *fela* apparently is cognate with the north Malaita *fera/fela* meaning 'village' or 'island', and Bogotu *vera*, meaning 'plaza'.

tors, from most ancient to more recent, standing beside the 'post of the dead'.) Perhaps the 'post of the dead' *is* phallic (though there is no compelling evidence for this); but if so, the phallus would seem itself to symbolize the descent through males that connects ancestors to the living, and the generative powers of nature (hence the green?) rather than human sexuality per se. But there seems to be a female theme in the symbolism, as well, associated with sago, the tree fern or "milk tree" as symbol of nurturance, and the green on which the red of blood, war, and death is painted.

The sprinkling of coconut liquid is, in Kwaio view, an expression of the *mamu* theme. The sprinkling as "washing" is explicit in the term *siufa*. But even at this surface level, Kwaio interpretations are inconsistent. One Kwaio explanation is that "washing" the pigs makes them desirable to the potential guests; but why, then, splash the liquid onto the participants as well? Another Kwaio interpretation is that the coconut liquid "washes the minds" of potential guests, making them want to come to the feast. Yet another Kwaio interpretation is that the coconut is offered for the ancestors' pudding, with the liquid representing the making of the pudding. At a more covert level, the coconut liquid could symbolize semen . . . or breast milk?

The painting of the betel mix, in which a sprig of evodia is substituted for the usual betel pepper, also is given varying interpretations. Most obviously, it is betel chewed by and with the ancestors, to enlist their powers of attracting guests and money. Or does it represent the attractions of the feast itself, where guests will be drawn by the conviviality which betel chewing expresses? Is the red paint on pigs and participants blood as well as betel? To the extent Kwaio place such constructions on the events and objects in ritual—in addition to having diffuse senses of pattern buried deep below consciousness—the constructions of individuals are often divergent, often idiosyncratic. There seems to be no reason to expect that all the details of Kwaio rites would be laden with meaning for most participants. With their pragmatic orientation to acting in the world, not explaining it, there is no impetus for Kwaio participants to seek (consciously or unconsciously) a host of covert, hidden meanings. The objects and acts used in dealing with the ancestors were originated by the ancestors in ancient times and have been required by them ever since. To seek to explain them, to seek human reason in ancestral rules, would seem unnecessary, even presumptuous, to most Kwaio most of the time.

Are there wider covert themes in *belitauŋa*? The 'feast of the dead' of which *belitauŋa* is a key sacramental segment is, as Kwaio participants and the women sequestered in dwelling houses are well aware, a time when the powerful ancestors are *with* the living in the settlement: with them in a more direct, awesome, and dangerous sense than in their everyday roles of watching, protecting, and punishing. In this sequence leading to the final mortuary feast after death of a priest, the feast of the dead brings a group's ancestors into communion with them at a time of heightened activity and excitement. The mortuary feast itself is a critical assertion of a descent group's wordly power and prestige, and the culmination of many months of heightened productive effort. The ancestors that join the living were themselves the priests, leaders, and feastgivers of the group, and powerful feastgivers of olden times. The quest for *mamu* is in this case an incorporation of these ancestors into the group's enterprise. Blessed with this support, the efforts of the group will be rewarded with a profusion of valuables and pigs, with good weather, with an absence of fighting, theft, or malevolent magic. And after the feast, when members of the group have ended their mourning dishevelment and isolation and reentered the networks of feasting exchange and politics, the support of the ancestors ensured by the sacrifice of *foʔota* pigs will bring worldly success. This large-scale sacrifice of *foʔota* pigs in the feast of the dead also brings the full installation of the new priest in place of the one who has joined the ancestors; the religious congregation centered around the group's shrine is, through this final rite in the desacralization, reconstituted.

In this vein, McKinley (n.d.) sees the symbolic joining of ancestral power and women's power in the 'post of the dead' as occurring

> at a time which calls for a total synthesis and renewal of rela-
> tions between human and ancestral members of the descent
> group. . . . Some meaningful synthesis is required [for] the bes-
> towal of the sacred and eternalized powers of the ancestors
> back upon the living, whose temporal existence is epitomized
> in the reproductive powers of women, could never be com-
> plete. It would remain locked away in skulls and shrines.

McKinley sees *beritauŋa* as a crucial moment of ritual transition after which the pigs that go to their death serve to link
the living to their ancestors. In *beritauŋa* "the brief union of
the three, pigs, men, and ancestors, methodically shifts to
become a separation, marked in red against green, between
mortality and the timeless grip of ancestral presence" (Mc-
Kinley n.d.). McKinley's interpretation generally accords with
my own. But it is possible to distort Kwaio realities by imagining *beritauŋa* in its fullest and most dramatic form. A 'feast
of the dead' with much less ritual drama is held on other
occasions prior to the sacrifice of 'women's pigs', often on a
very reduced scale with only a small local group taking part
and only two or three pigs. A *taualea* is built for any mortuary
feast, and for descent groups related to Amadia it will include
a 'post of the dead' when any important man or woman—not
necessarily the priest—has died.

    The *mamu* theme is enacted for any mortuary feast, even
though it may be a very secular occasion—and indeed, need
not follow a death at all.[7] Thus while *beritauŋa* in its full enactment is a time of heightened sacredness, the elements of
which it is composed—*taualea* thatched with *giʔa*, tethered
pigs, invocations of *mamu*, areca nuts and taro for the ancestors, *ribaŋa* over people and puddings—are familiar from ritual episodes of lesser drama and danger, where the ancestral

---

7. If a group's resources have built up and no appropriate death has occurred, a
mortuary feast may be given to honor the long-dead member of another group, the
father or other kinsman of a rival to whom prestations are made (see Keesing 1978a).

presence is less immediate and compelling. Such understandings as these acts and objects evoke among participants and onlookers must come from this full range of contexts, more and less sacred, more and less dramatic, more and less crucial to life and prosperity.

They must depend as well on the knowledge individual participants bring to these rituals; and they depend on the different vantage points of male and female, young and old, priest or peripheral participant. We need now to look more closely at who knows what, in Kwaio society. And we need to ask who preserves, creates, and modifies the symbolic structures we have examined.

Chapter Thirteen

Structures, Meanings, and the Sociology of Knowledge

AT SEVERAL POINTS in the preceding chapters I have suggested that there is considerable variation in the way individual Kwaio interpret the nature of ancestors and their involvement in everyday life. I have also shown ways that men and women, young and old, have different perspectives on social life; and noted how individuals vary in their degree of sacredness and ritual seniority and in the roles they play toward the ancestors. Here I will look more closely at the sociology of knowledge in Kwaio society: at who knows what, and how that knowledge is used and controlled. In the process, I will examine the possibility that different individuals participate in different ways and degrees in preserving, transmitting, and changing the religious practices and symbolic structures of the community.

13.1 Access to Knowledge

Recall that magic is distinguished from other kinds of knowledge about the sacred because it constitutes *property*. Magical spells, procedures, and validations can be bought and sold, and are supposed to achieve their ends even if the person performing the magic is not related to the ancestor from whom the powers have been transmitted. Other kinds of knowledge about ancestors, about the past, and about ancestral rules and ritual procedures can usefully be lumped together as sacred lore, or simply lore. Bear in mind that this is not a single Kwaio category, but a composite of separate categories: 'genealogies', 'taboos', 'stories', 'epic chants', and so on.

Access to magic and access to lore are, by their nature, different. Epic chants are publicly performed; genealogies are always accessible from those senior members of the group who are responsible for seeing that knowledge of them is preserved. These and other forms of lore are valuable, in some cases vital, resources of the group. Seniors are concerned that juniors will let this knowledge lapse, and are happy to find willing hands into which it can be safely passed. This is true not only of the senior generation of one's *own* group, but that of one's mother's group, one's father's mother's group, one's mother's mother's group (especially if any of these are dwindling in number and seen as vulnerable). One has particularly direct access to the lore of one's mother's descent group, as well as one's father's.

A man is more likely to acquire lore than a woman, an oldest sibling more likely to acquire it than a younger, the child of a specially knowledgeable person more likely than others. Partly these patterns reflect responsibility for preserving knowledge: an oldest brother acts as a sort of custodian on behalf of his siblings; a potential priest is assigned a heavy weight of responsibility to learn ritual procedures, taboos, and ancestral stories.

But learning large amounts of lore requires both special talents and special dedication. Imagine both the task of rote memorization and the *organization* of memory needed simply to acquire what for Kwaio is a reasonable middle level of genealogical knowledge, and be able to reproduce it. Many families include six, eight, even ten or more children. Imagine knowing all the family members of your father's five siblings, knowing all the children of your paternal grandfather's three or eight siblings, and knowing all *their* children. Add all the spouses, and then go through the whole procedure again for your mother and her siblings. Many Kwaio, in addition, can go back six or seven (or in the case of a priest, fifteen or twenty) generations in a single line, and know the genealogies of their father's mother's siblings and their descendants, their mother's mother's siblings and their descendants, and more. . . . To be really unusual in genealogical knowledge, like the feastgiver ?Elota (Keesing 1978a), one would know in detail the genealogies of half a dozen groups, would know much of the information about a dozen more, and would know the marriages (some five or ten generations ago) that link them together. These feats of memory are rendered more difficult by the naming system, whereby a single individual may have as many as three names, and where the same name may be passed down across several successive generations. In addition to powers of rote memory, sheer analytical intelligence enables a person to see connections between elements of lore or symbolism that would otherwise be hidden, to see global patterns where others see parts.

In addition to unusual talent, learning lore requires dedication. ?Elota's autobiographical account is instructive here:

> When [Fuita] used to recite genealogies the others all got bored and went away. . . . I was the only one of us young people who stayed and listened to him. He told stories about the old days, and I would stay and listen. . . . He used to ask us all, "When I recite these genealogies and stories to you all, why do you just run away? . . . Even if it sounds worthless to you now, some day you'll search to find out." (Keesing 1978a:119)

The period of irresponsible youth lasts, at least for young men, well into the twenties—the time when, if ever, broad foundations of sacred knowledge must be laid. For young men, learning lore competes directly with hunting birds, stealing pigs, flirting with girls, gambling, going to plantations, and sleeping in the men's house (all likely to be preferred to hard mental exercise with old men).

Women can acquire a high degree of expertise about taboos, about ancestors, and about ritual procedures—including those they can never see performed. Sometimes this reflects a woman's stepping, in effect, into a structural position a man would normally occupy. Thus Fenaaori, daughter of an important warrior-priest, has stepped as far as a woman can into her father's shoes—as ritual expert, custodian of magic, and even as feastgiver. Others, such as ?Eteŋa, may be both successors to normally "male" expertise and to a heritage of women's power and magic. Yet others may carry a heavy burden as the last agnates of descent groups, who feel responsible for preserving the genealogical and ritual procedures and passing them safely to their sons. (One such woman went so far as to stand at the edge of the shrine and prompt her son, who was assuming the priesthood as a teenager, in sacrificial magic and genealogies.) Other women, forceful, ambitious,curious, and intellectually gifted, may simply have sought out lore and mastered it. Thus Fa?afataa, a brilliantly able woman in her forties, commands tremendous amounts of lore, much of it from her warrior grandfather and his contemporaries; most of her male kin know much less than she about the ancestors, their rules, and their deeds in olden times.

Young men who do not begin in a structural position where such knowledge is thrust upon them, or even extended to them, may still seek it out. Maenaa?adi is a young man in his mid-twenties, the youngest of nine children of a relatively knowledgeable priest, now about seventy, who is the only surviving male agnate of his descent group and generation. The two oldest sons are in their late forties, and have been instructed for years in the knowledge needed to succeed their father as priest; but neither is particularly bright or energetic. Maenaa?adi, in contrast, is already an incredible repository of knowledge, gleaned not only from his father but from the priests and experts of surrounding descent groups. His command of genealogies is staggering, he has distinguished himself as a singer of epic chants, and his knowledge of stories of ancestors and old feuds is encyclopedic. He is also keenly analytic. Maenaaʔadi has achieved this formidable expertise through a rare confluence of talent, inclination, and commitment.[1] In talking about such expertise, Louŋa of Kwaŋafi—himself very knowledgeable, and a person of rare gifts—commented that "in every group there is only one person who really knows about sacred things, about ancient times, about the genealogies and the ancestors." There might, in some groups, be two or three; but often there is none.

The openness of Kwaio lore can be contrasted to the closure and secrecy of sacred knowledge in many societies. In many tribal societies, religious knowledge is controlled by men's cults, often through initiatory hierarchies (here such Amazonian peoples as the Mundurucu and Mehinacu, such Papua New Guineans as Baktaman and Iatmul, and many Aboriginal Australian groups come to mind). In such societies, entry into closed cults entails the revelation of secrets.

While access to lore is relatively open, magic—as *property*—is less freely available. But in practice, a person such as Maenaaʔadi (or his female equivalent) is likely to be taught magic by relatives, even distant ones (and in some cases nonrelatives as well) who perceive in energy and cultural commitment the manifestations of ancestral power and the promise of future success. To understand the process of reinforcement or positive feedback where ability is construed as ancestrally conferred, and success breeds success, we need to look at personal relations with ancestors.

13.2   Dream, Possession, and Personal Relations with Ancestors

We saw in section 2.1 that a child has close personal bonds, formed in life and reinforced through dream experience, with attachment figures (parents, parents' siblings, grandparents).

---

1. In 1977 Maenaaʔadi accompanied me on a three-day trip into a remote area where he had distant relatives. Wherever we paused he probed our hosts for details of ancient happenings and remote genealogical skeins that connected to his.

Fuamae, an old priest, goes into a dissociated state during sacrifice. His psychological instability was regarded as a manifestation of ancestral power: he was virtually a shaman in a society that does not institutionalize the role.

These then may serve as intermediaries in seeking powers from more distant ancestors.

One of the processes whereby a person, male or female, comes to be attributed special ancestral powers (and to believe he or she possesses them) is the development of a personal bond with a distant ancestor (La?aka, Kwateta . . .). Partly this is a matter of life experience. A girl or woman who falls into coma, then returns to consciousness, will be deemed to have been saved by the ancestor to whom prayer has been made. This will be taken as a sign that she is to become 'sacred' (section 6.6), and that she has a special and personal bond with the ancestor that returned her to life. A man may have similar experiences, perhaps ones where prayers have been answered in some dramatic way, or where a compelling encounter in dream or experience of possession has been taken as a sign of a special bond.

A person may have predispositions to experience dissociative states, or other unusual psychological states. But how these are interpreted by the community—as signs of special ancestral bonds and powers, or as illness—depends not only on the symptoms (and culturally conventional interpretations of them) but also on the personal qualities of the individual involved. An incompetent or insignificant person experiencing severe psychological or neural disturbances (such as an epileptic fit or a psychotic episode) would be viewed as ill. A knowledgeable and able person in the same condition will be viewed as specially chosen by the ancestors as a vehicle (although the ancestors may use such a person for destructive and antisocial or positive social ends). Here, two quotations from the autobiographical account by the feastgiver ʔElota are revealing.

> At a mortuary feast ʔAlaʔota was . . . chanting. While he was singing . . . ancestors Firilae and Akalo possessed him. He used their real names. . . . [We said] "He's . . . out of his mind and saying whatever comes into his head." He sang and sang, while we all went to sleep. In the night he got up and left, taking his knife. . . . And in the morning he went into the men's house and killed Faʔalalai. . . .

> We were all afraid: we thought a fight was close at hand. It was ancestor Kwateta that was making us afraid. I went outside. Ancestor Kwateta took possession of my body, rose up in me, spoke through my voice. "You, Riufaa, have forsaken me [speaking of a man who had almost been killed]. I Kwateta, am afflicting you: I exposed you to death today. But if you consecrate a pig to me, even if a fight starts and is as wide as the sky, as big as the ocean, it will all pass away." The ancestor spoke through my voice. (Keesing 1978a:150, 153)

Whether a person experiencing dissociation, or what we would call a private world of fantasy, is deemed *kakaru*, in a state of ancestrally altered consciousness, or simply *kaku*, 'crazy', depends on who the person is, and what she or he knows, as well as on the behavior the person displays.

Although the shades of all people (and indeed of pigs and dogs) wander in dream, only those Kwaio who have close, special bonds with powerful ancestors are thought to be given important information in dream encounters. Such a person will encounter his or her ancestral ally in the guise of, say, a friend or neighbor; and will receive information—an impending death, a hidden pollution violation (which if not expiated will bring misfortune), the success or failure of a planned venture. Such messages are given in the form of signs, partly conventional, partly requiring insightful interpretation. A person who regards him or herself as having such a special bond, hence as dreaming "true" dreams—and is so regarded by other members of the community—will communicate these messages upon awakening. Most people view their dreams as "just rubbish," filled with spurious or doubtful messages. If they communicated them, others would respond with doubt or derision. We are dealing, then, with a situation where close bonds with ancestors, command of lore, control of magic, form a self-reinforcing complex.

Different individuals may reflect both different degrees of expertise or power and very different styles for expressing it. There was a vast gulf between the old wizard Fuamae of Tofu (see photograph, p. 203) a shaman in a society that accords shamans no conventional role, a man on the borderline of psychosis whose command of magical powers was regarded as awesome and dangerous—and the great feastgiver and savant ?Elota (Keesing 1978a), whose vast knowledge was deployed in strategic investments, whose ancestral powers were manifest in worldly pursuits, and who was ultimately skeptical about theological matters.[2] This connection between sacred knowledge and secular power calls for closer examination.

13.3   Sacred Powers, Secular Powers

As ?Elota's case suggests, those who succeed in growing taro, raising pigs, and giving feasts, are deemed to have special

2. If we view the Kwaio social system as reproducing itself, we could envision a Fuamae and an ?Elota as eventually becoming powerful *adalo* to whom very different powers are attributed. To these two we might add a Basiana or a Tagailamo (Keesing and Corris 1980), each a great warrior in life, and each destined to be *adalonimae*, 'war spirit', had pacification not intervened.

magical powers and special ancestral support. The concept of *nanama* provides an explanation not of how the universe works, but of why some people succeed and others fail. Ancestral support is both in the eye of the beholder and in the eye of the able and ambitious leader who lives with risk and employs bold stratagems.

The same was true of warriors in the previous generation. Only imbued with confidence in his ancestral powers to kill in combat, to ward off blows or bullets, and to avoid vengeance would a man plunge boldly into confrontations. And here too success bred success, since a feared warrior would force many issues by sheer intimidation (Keesing 1978a; Keesing and Corris 1980).

In these realms, then, the connection between a command of magic and lore, a presumed special and close relationship with an ancestor (who conveys powers of prosperity or destruction), and worldly power and success is very close. One might want to say that the sacred, ancestral powers are a mystification of real, physical ones; but in a world where ancestors are everyday participants in and controlling forces of life, this conveys political insights only at a great cost to subjective realities. It is a step we will want to take—but not yet. For the moment, we need to see how a young man such as Maenaaʔadi—in learning genealogies and ancestral lore, and acquiring magical powers—is acquiring not only an intellectual command of his culture, but powerful instruments for pursuing secular ambitions as feastgiver and leader as well. It is no surprise that Maenaaʔadi has begun to be a formidable political presence in his neighborhood cluster of descent groups, both in traditional pursuits and contemporary manifestations of Maasina Rule neotraditionalism (Keesing 1978b).

Some men are oriented primarily toward the sacred, as custodians of ritual knowledge and intermediaries between their group and the spirits. Such priests are not necessarily attributed power in secular pursuits, and have no substantial political role in secular life except as channels through whom the ancestors communicate. Thus mild ꞌAiniuo of ꞌAiꞌeda or Talauŋaꞌi of Fouꞌalabusi used sacred knowledge primarily to sacred ends. But in a number of other cases, a man who in his seventies or eighties was a revered and sacred priest had decades earlier been a feared warrior or renowned feastgiver: Iꞌelamoof Ɖudu and Siꞌowane of ꞌAiꞌeda (Keesing and Corris 1980; Keesing 1978a) are striking examples. Secular power deemed to be ancestrally conferred is, as it were, sacralized by age in the life cycle, as a strong man approaches ancestorhood.

13.4 Expertise and Powers of Understanding

I have suggested that Kwaio vary in their understanding of symbolic structures and ritual procedures. The constructions individuals place on the rules and arrangements of everyday life and transactions with the spirits depend, it would seem, on what they know. There is considerable evidence that men and women who command extensive knowledge of lore and magic are able—both because of their expertise and their intellectual gifts—to perceive a grammar of symbolism of which most Kwaio see only segments and elements. This is manifest in the ability of at least some ritual experts, men and women, to give metatheoretic interpretations of cosmology and ancestral rules.

Fenaaori, the elderly woman who acquired the expertise and magic of her warrior-priest father, has given a number of global metatheoretic interpretations that will serve to illustrate. In discussing with men a series of taboos applying to menstruating women, that prohibit their chewing betel, breaking open a coconut, or making a taro and coconut pudding, Fenaaori viewed them as the inverse of the ritual acts following high sacrifice or death of a priest: to perform these acts in the menstrual area "on top of" the acts performed in ritual would by implication defile the latter. She was similarly strikingly incisive in viewing childbirth and the seclusion of the taboo-keeper, and the attendant taboos and rites of purification/desacralization, as mirror images.[3]

A concern with global interpretation, with intellectual coherence, may lead such gifted and committed individuals to perceive overall cultural patterns that remain partly hidden to most people. But it may also lead Kwaio "philosophers" to ask questions that are not, as it were, culturally standard (or even culturally relevant); and they may be led, as a result, to reach different conclusions. This would seem to be the case wth ideas of souls and the Land of the Dead. Only Kwaio "philosophers," it would seem, have reflected on the apparent contradiction between the shades in the Land of the Dead and the shades that afflict; and they have resolved it in varying ways that we can only uncomfortably call "cultural."

The keys to understanding ritual symbolism may—despite the relative openness of Kwaio knowledge—lie not in the "public domain," but in magic. Thus the dark purple leaves of coleus are used in a number of ritual procedures. But there is no apparent key to the symbolism unless one has access to magic in which coleus is used as an iconic symbol of the darkness of night; hence a means whereby the living can hide from ancestors, or where a kin group against whom vengeance is sought can be made to disappear from people's consciousness. Coleus, then, symbolizes *invisibility*; but the symbolism would be clear, I think, only to one who knows the magical uses of coleus and the verbal formulae employed.

It is worth distinguishing between two levels of sacred knowledge: what we can call an *operational* level, and an *interpretive* level. It is possible for a ritual officiant to have detailed step-by-step knowledge of how to conduct a rite without a coherent understanding of the symbolic grammar of which it is an expression. One can know a catalogue of

---

3. A similar incisiveness underlay the turn of phrase I recorded in which Faʔafataa portrayed death as the inverse of childbirth: "When a person is struck down by an ancestor," she said, *"beʔu ka futa"*—a dead person is born.

ancestral rules without having the kind of insight Fenaaori displayed about the logic the rules express. Kwaio themselves make similar distinctions, especially in contexts where procedures are to be modified.

We can illustrate by returning to the procedures after death of a priest, or crematory sacrifice. Because keeping the full array of taboos for the full period is both burdensome and dangerous, there is a recurrent temptation to shorten the period or modify the taboos or the procedures of desacralization. Such departures from normal ritual procedure often evoke criticism from outsiders. Sometimes these criticisms reflect niggling and rigid traditionalism. But more interestingly, they sometimes reflect a deeper metatheoretic understanding on the part of the critic, and an inappropriate permutation of procedure. I overheard my ritual mentor Louŋa discussing with another expert the modified form of burial ritual a descent group used after death of their priest:

> They didn't know what they were doing. Step one when you bury a priest is [such and such]. Step two is [——]. Step three is [——]. Step four is [——]. Step five is [——]. They decided to leave out three and four and to do five. But you know as well as I do that it doesn't make any sense to do five unless you did three and four.

Such "ungrammatical" changes of procedure probably can become more widely adopted, and in the long run may contribute to permanent changes in normal procedures. But in these and other contexts, failure to understand the meaning of ritual is commonly attributed by experts to the nonexperts who often must stage ritual performances. A Kwaio officiant need not understand the deep symbolic structure and meaning of a rite to stage it properly; but to create appropriate permutations of standard procedures requires a deeper understanding.

This, then, leads us squarely into a question first raised in the early chapters: how, and by whom, structures of symbolic meaning are preserved, transmitted, modified, and created.

13.5 The Preservation, Modification, and Creation of Symbolic Structures

There are two related contradictions we must examine in considering the processes of change in ritual and cosmology. The first is that by Kwaio dogma the system does not change: it 'originated from the ancestors' and it is the duty of humans to follow ancient rules, not modify them. The second is that by Kwaio dogma the rules are imposed by ancestors, not created by humans. This means that to understand how symbolic structures are continually modified, and by whom, we must step outside these Kwaio dogmas to analyze the realities they disguise; and must examine how Kwaio resolve the contradictions between dogmas of ancient permanence and ancestral will and the realities of human intervention.

The latter question will provide an opening wedge. In Kwaio theory, the ancestors—though they lived long ago— are ever-present participants in contemporary social life. Their rules and wishes, though ancient and timeless, are continuously *applied to* the changing and varied circumstances of everyday human life by the ancestors themselves, who communicate their wishes through divination, dream, or possession, through human intermediaries.

Comparative evidence of language, prehistory, and anthropologically recorded customs in Melanesia, and Malaita in particular, indicates that the basic ideas and ancestral rules expressed in Kwaio religion are indeed ancient. Yet in countless and potentially cumulative ways, new taboos and modifications of ritual forms are going on in local kin groups. I have written about one such mode of innovation, the tabooing of words associated with ancestors' names (Keesing and Fifi?i 1969). Descendants of a particular ancestor are also subject to special restrictions on eating particular varieties of fish, taro, and insects. Such local variations, subject to progressive augmentation and modification (based on divination, restrictions imposed by a curer, etc.), extend into the way a rite (such as *faʔasafiŋa* or *beritauŋa*) is performed, what special taboos apply, and how they are lifted. Ancient cultural *forms* are permuted and expressed in locally distinctive ways.

This raised several questions. What human "intermediaries" introduce changes into the local community? What constraints limit changes if they are to be accepted by the group as ancestral will? By what mechanisms do local innovations spread? What factors promote or inhibit the acceptability of locally introduced innovations within a wider region? How are symbolic structures preserved in this process?

I have sketched the outline of a systematic cosmological scheme (chapter 5); and I have suggested that those individuals who by talent, inclination, and opportunity have acquired an extensive command of lore are likely to have a global perception and deep understanding of these symbolic structures. It is men such as Fuamae, Louŋa, Talauŋaʔi, and ʔAlabai, women such as Fenaaori and ʔEteŋa, who have the greatest understanding of cosmological structures and ritual meanings, the most effective command of the symbolic grammar. And it is precisely such individuals who are likely to be viewed, and to view themselves, as intermediaries through whom ancestral wishes about rules and rites are communicated. We can guess (though we cannot know) that the individual or individuals who introduced into the community the rules prohibiting menstruating women from chewing betel, opening coconuts, or making puddings perceived, because of their command of the symbolic grammar, what Fenaaori perceived (section 13.4): that these can be construed as polluting because of the mirror-image relationship between menstrual isolation and men's rites of desacralization.

Other members of local kin groups may understand the symbolic grammar less globally and systematically, but they will certainly perceive the appropriateness of some modifications and the inappropriateness—ungrammaticalness, we might say—of others. We have noted that eight is a ritually salient number; eight acts or objects (or four, counted by twos) appear over and over again. But some rites, for some groups, and some magical spells, use ten, not eight; or, more rarely, twelve or twenty. Multiples of ten are also a standard pattern, as in reckoning periods of desacralization. A modification of procedure which entailed the use of eight, or ten, objects or acts fits into this pattern. But one entailing an odd number, say nine or thirteen, would be ungrammatical. Thus the plausibility and acceptability of an ancestral message, conveyed through an intermediary, will depend both on the plausibility of the human intermediary and the grammaticalness of the message.

The two, of course, are likely to work together. The mind of a Talauŋaʔi or Fenaaori will be a creative source of culturally coherent ideas and interpretations and a filter straining out the inappropriate. Here we need to look more closely at both the psychology and the micropolitics of this intermediation with the ancestors. Dream, as fantasy process, draws creatively on the unconscious mind. But placing *constructions on* the experiences of dream is very much a matter of conscious interpreting and editing, in which analytical powers and cultural knowledge (and, of course, repression) are brought into play. Conveying the meaning of dreams to one's group, as ancestral messages, entails the translation of private experience into the realm of cultural symbols. It also depends on powers of persuasion and plausibility. Converting private experience to public policy is inevitably a political process. Both dream and possession are substantial sources or channels for the introduction of new ideas and procedures into the group. The possibility is always open that a leader could invent spurious messages from ancestors for his own purposes (Keesing 1978b). (Kwaio would be more likely to suspect that a *buru*, or malevolent alien spirit, may be impersonating the would-be leader's ancestor and misleading him with false prophecies or promises; see Keesing 1980a).

Most often, my data suggest, new rules and procedures are conveyed to the group through divination. This is likely to be a more public and open procedure, and one where the outcome depends heavily on chance. What is most important, for our purposes, is how—in the case of some situation where members of the local kin group consider themselves to be in dire danger—the group's assembled resources of sacred expertise are focused on the problem. The senior or most knowledgeable men and women of the group will discuss the possible sources of anger, or the wishes, of the ancestors. The possibilities put to the test of divination may represent mainly the imagination and cultural knowledge of the group's most qualified expert or respected leader; or may represent the collective creation, through dialogue, of an array of possibilities. The final outcome of divination may, in different circumstances, reflect random chance, some conscious or unconscious structuring of possibilities, or the imagination and perception of the diviner (who may "see" an answer rather than testing a series of proffered questions). But whatever the process in a particular case, the answer will never be one the living are unprepared to accept (since only acceptable possibilities are explored) or unable to imagine; and it will never be unconstrained by such expert knowledge of ritual and symbolism as the local group can marshall.

Such processes probably were at work when the old rule that prohibited a man whose mother was still alive from becoming priest was changed (apparently before the turn of the century). No one has clear information about just how and when this occurred (some speculate that it was a result of dwindling population, but it seems to antedate sharp decrease in bush populations). Since ancestors are supposed to designate successors to priestly duties, through divination, one can imagine a scenario where this change in the rules could have occurred. The oldest son of a priest, his logical successor and the person who has acquired greatest command of the group's lore and magic, is unable to succeed to the priesthood because his mother is still alive. In seeking confirmation of a successor, the concerned elders put successfully to the test of divination the query of whether the rule about a living mother could be waived. If the group then prospers, and no dire consequences are seen, other groups faced with choosing replacements put the same query, and (perhaps less than by chance) get the same answer. The ancestors clearly have, in concert, decided to change the rule. If, as some claim, the original rule prohibited men with living mothers from eating *fo?ota* pigs, senior men would have had an added incentive to follow new procedures once someone had put a foot in the door. Sometimes magic is "discovered" that permits a procedural change, which eventually can lead to a change in the rule for many or most people. Thus one ancestor is supposed to have discovered, by accidentally eating his sister-in-law's child's placenta, a magical protection against some kinds of pollution. For groups related to that ancestor, the rules against post-childbirth isolation have been made less stringent. A similar process apparently accounts for the virtual disappearance of a custom whereby a woman spent the night after the first day after her menstrual period in a special halfway hut (*rigi*). For all women but a few related to one of several "traditionalist" ancestors, the rule has been changed to allow her to enter the dwelling house in the evening, having spent the day outside. The general rule that a man who eats *fo?ota* pigs cannot partake of a portion of food a woman has eaten is waived in the case of women's pigs at a mortuary feast. A man who is ritually mature but who does not partake of *fo?ota* pork at this particular feast can eat a share of women's pigs. But he cannot do so if he is related to one of several ancestors from the ?Are?are border zone. Perhaps this is a case where an original rule (like that of the *rigi*) was waived for all but a few; perhaps it is a case where a rule that has been dropped, or never applied, in Kwaio has been (re)introduced through a neighboring language group.

I noted earlier (section 13.4) the temptations for kin groups to try to simplify and reduce periods of sacredness and the taboos and ritual sequences they entail. In these and other ways, and simply by error and failure in the transmission of lore and variations in personal style and knowledge, small changes are being introduced into local groups. Individuals— all individuals—are in small ways changing and contributing to "the system." But this process of corner-cutting, error, convenience, and style would seem to erode structures as well as preserve them. We can think of a kind of informational or behavioral entropy at work in the way individuals apply and modify the cumulated ways of the group. How, then, are order and coherence maintained? Where do new forms that *conform to* existing structures, even render them more elegant, come from? For the Kwaio, my data strongly suggest that despite continual small and local shifts in procedure, structural coherence and the overall order of the symbolic grammar are maintained across generations largely because of the impress of expertise, construed as ancestral will.

We need finally to return to the politics of innovation. Once a new rule or procedure has been adopted by a local group, what determines whether it will spread and become general, or will remain localized? We have already seen some hints in speculating about the change in rules of eligibility to become a priest. If an innovation created (i.e., legitimized) by one ancestor or set of ancestors would provide an advantageous solution for others—such as a way out of overly restrictive taboos—then the chances that other ancestors will adopt it are enhanced by the processes of earthly politics. In time, a local pattern may spread because the group in which it was adopted proliferates, and visibly prospers. Women of the group, marrying out, bring with them rules and taboos that apply to their children. In this process, the grammaticalness and plausibility of the innovation, the spiritual and visible advantages it confers on those who practice it, and the political power and sacredness of the human medium through whom the message was introduced, and his successors, all play a part.

The symbolic neatness and appropriateness of a new rule—one that fits into or fills out an existing framework—may be important. Presumably such processes have been at work in producing, neatening, and maintaining the kinds of symmetrical symbolic schemes discussed in chapter 5. The rule forbidding menstruating women from eating special puddings and related foods seems to be a case in point. But note that there is another side—a side to which I will now turn. If men are politically dominant in a society such as Kwaio, if they are the primary custodians of sacred knowledge and sacred responsibilities, then the possibilities are open for the "ancestors" to impose rules that further subordinate or restrict women, that give men privileged access to desired resources, or that give women more work, and men more leisure.

Chapter Fourteen

Ancestors, Celestialization, and Earthly Politics

14.1 Celestializations and Realities: The Politics of the Sacred

EVERY SOCIETY DRAPES itself in veils of illusion. To depict the veils as "cultural symbols," and leave it at that, is to take the illusions as reality. We must lift them and probe beneath.

In tribal societies, a characteristic veil presents the past as a charter for the present: a people's way of life is portrayed as eternal enactment of ancient customs, expression of cosmic truths. The illusions have been partly unveiled by functionalist and symbolist analyses that show how the cosmic is a mirror of the social, and how cultural symbols reinforce the integration of the social order and hence perpetuate it. But illusions remain. An anthropological preoccupation with how society and cultural systems are integrated, how elements reinforce one another, has disguised the fact that tribal societies *have histories* (though histories we seldom can learn about directly). Our theories have led us to pay more attention to the ways societies perpetuate themselves than to how they change.

Yet we know that they do change. The religious system broadly common to the northern Malaita peoples is indeed ancient: at least a thousand years old, perhaps two thousand. Many elements—the propitiation of ancestral shades by sacrifice of pigs, magic using cordyline and ginger and coleus, the quest for *mana*-ization—are much older, apparently going back at least four thousand years. But substantial changes have taken place across this time span, both in religion and social structure. Change is constantly occurring, in the local modification of rules and procedures. We need ways to understand the processes of change—processes that are disguised by a people's dogmas about themselves and their world.

And we need ways to conceptualize how "the system" perpetuates "itself" that do not trap us in functionalist circularities. We cannot assume without critical analysis that "a culture" such as that of the Kwaio constitutes a single unitary system to which all members of the society are committed in equal degree, to which all have access in equal degree, in which all have an equal stake.

An emerging anthropology inspired by Marxist social theory presents the change and the self-perpetuation of social systems as two sides of the same problem. That is, the progressive transformation of societies can be understood only in terms of the processes of their self-perpetuation; and their self-perpetuation can be understood only in terms of potential forces of change. I will draw on Marxist perspectives to seek to probe further beneath the illusions with which Kwaio religion and society are veiled. We begin with the assumption that even in a classless society such as Kwaio—where there are no rulers or ruled, no owners, landlords, serfs, or proletarians—different categories of people may have divergent or conflicting interests. The simplest division of labor, between men and women, young and old, places these segments of society in potential opposition.

Pervasively, in Melanesia, men control intergroup politics and prestige economies based on feasting, exchange, and bridewealth; and women, excluded from or subordinate in these realms, nonetheless do the bulk of work of feeding pigs and producing horticultural surpluses. Senior men use the structures of kinship not only to control female labor power (of wives, sisters, daughters, daughters-in-law) but to control young men. Control over the prestige economy enables senior men to keep young men obligated and economically dependent. In marrying and becoming adult, men become enmeshed in obligation to their seniors.

Senior men, in Melanesia as elsewhere in the tribal world, have depended heavily on control of *sacred knowledge* to maintain their control of earthly politics. By keeping in their hands relations with ancestors and other spirits, by commanding magical knowledge, senior men could maintain a control mediated by the supernatural. Such religious ideologies served too, by defining rules in terms of ancient spirits and by defining the nature of men and women in supernatural terms, to reinforce and maintain the roles of the sexes—and again, to hide their nature. This is not to say that we can understand such symbolic systems by viewing them cynically as deliberate, conscious, creations of a Melanesian version of a "ruling class." Symbolic systems have an intellectual logic of their own, and a force of their own, as the Kwaio material amply illustrates. We need to work toward a theory that takes into account the way cosmological schemes operate to infuse human life with meaning, and preserve a logical structure, but that at the same time shows how these schemes are anchored in political and economic realities and serve ideological ends.

Kwaio ancestors do not simply represent a supernatural reflection of the authority of senior men (cf. Fortes 1960); they at once reinforce that power and disguise its nature and sources. Marx described this function of disguising and reinforcing, as well as reflecting, as "celestialization." Writing of the "misty creations of religion," he saw the analytical task as "to develop from the actual relations of life the corresponding celestialized forms of those relations" (Marx 1938: 1:367).[1]

---

1. Feuerbach had argued that religions represent illusions in which supernatural orders are posited that correspond to earthly ones. Marx sought to go beyond this in constructing an economically grounded theory that renders systematic the nature of this "celestialization" under different modes of production.

Marxist perspectives lead us to expect that, both to understand how a Melanesian society changes and how it perpetuates "itself," we must look at the divergent and potentially conflicting interests of men and women, young and old.[2] We need to look particularly closely at the battle lines of sexual politics and their celestialized expression. In a Melanesian society, we are likely to find men and women having contrasting and ultimately conflicting perspectives on the social order. At stake are symbolic issues, such as dogmas of descent (C. N. Modjeska has suggested that it is revealing to think of patriliny as "men's project" and matriliny as "women's project"), and sociological and economic issues (such as rules of postmarital residence, property rights and, most important, who does what work and who has control over what is produced). The contradiction men face is that their quests for prestige and instruments of power depend on extracting the labor of women for male ends. They can do so by control of marriage as a mode of political alliance through which they bring women from outside groups; by systems that define women's roles in terms of the production of children, sustenance, and surplus; and by systems of polygynous marriage, which set women into competition as cowives or as wives of competing men. And they can do so by actual or threatened violence.

But men conduct their campaigns—whether consciously or not—on the symbolic level as well. One of the recurrent focal points in the unfolding of sexual politics in small-scale societies is the nature of women's power to bear and suckle children (which men must contend with not only in relationship to their own power, but because in bearing children women are the producers of labor power, as well as being workers themselves). Symbolically, men can create cosmological schemes that define men's powers in begetting children as active, and women's as passive. They can create re-

2. In a particular system, there may be other more specific strainlines (e.g., between group members and dangerous affines; between initiands and initiates; between cowives, etc.).

ligious ideologies that, by portraying women's nature as polluting and inimical to social order, exclude them from public politics and ritual. And ideologies can serve to define male and female nature as radically contrasting, and define the essential fulfillment of women's nature as childbearing, domestic labor, pig-raising, and garden work.

Rules imputed to ancestors, ideologies about male and female nature, do not spring forth full blown—either as rationalizations of what people are doing anyway or as magical solutions to ecological problems (see Keesing 1981: ch. 9). Humans invent them, assert them, accept, or reject them. We need to ask *who* invents them, and what political ends are served by asserting them. We need to ask about the contradictions that give rise to such assertions, and about the cleavages—between men and women, young and old, commoners and chiefs, etc.—that are widened or narrowed by them. We need to ask about the real-world consequences, and economic and political roots, of conceptions of the supernatural and rules attributed to the spirits. Where we know no history, we approach these questions most effectively by looking at how a symbolic complex such as the ideology of women's polluting powers is used and lived in: how it is perceived by men and women, how it is expressed in the politics of everyday life.

14.2   Ancestors and Sexual Politics

The Malaita system, separating women's realm from male and ancestral realm, appears to subordinate women and define their essential nature as dangerous to social life. But in addition to giving women dangerous weapons, it establishes a separate spatial base for women's power. Women in the menstrual hut or clustered in support of a mother in childbirth isolation have a solidarity in their *abu*-ness which they do not have in everyday domestic life. In their liminality they are free both from male domination and from the heavy work burdens of everyday life. In some ways reproductive power, mystified as dangerous and potentially antisocial, represents women's victory, not women's subjugation. In their menstrual isolation, women have a world of their own: a world where they work only for themselves, a world where they have a social life of their own independent of (and sometimes counter to) that of men. Girls and young women in a neighborhood visit one another in their menstrual huts, work with one another in menstrual gardens for their own subsistence. Even mortuary feasts include a kind of secondary gathering of menstruating women. If childbirth is the inversion of extreme sacredness, it too is ritualized, and it entails a celebration of women's powers as well as a quarantining of dangerous emanations.

By mystifying women's reproductive powers in the ideology of pollution, Malaita men have exposed themselves to danger. They have placed their lives at risk. Men worry that their wives and sisters and daughters, and in-marrying affines, may pollute them—by accident, by carelessness, by irresponsibility or malice in not reporting a violation or, worst of all, by deliberately poisoning their husbands with feces or menstrual blood. Men have placed dangerous powers in the hands of women; and their concerns and energies are continually diverted to trying as best they can to police the way women use these powers.

Women, in turn, are able to use an ideology which they cannot challenge to build a counterinterpretation of the scheme of things, in which they are pillars of moral responsibility. They may portray themselves as responsible, through their careful following of taboos and their careful teaching of their daughters, for the well-being and the lives of men and children. Such a depiction of women as the moral keystones of the community does not challenge the ideology of pollution: it stands it on its head. The women's depiction is if anything more apt, in terms of where responsibility lies, than the men's.

By celestializing political powers and rules, men have in one sense reinforced "the system" in rendering it beyond challenge. But if men maintain primary political and ritual control, dominate the prestige economy, and exploit women's labor fairly effectively, the outcome in everyday social relations is far from one-sided. The religious ideology certainly has not demeaned women's self-image. There is some evidence that, rather than seeing their bodies as polluted and dangerous, women see them as pure and sacred, and use the rigid rules enjoining chastity (which the men see as controlling women's sexuality and reproductive powers) to sustain this counterinterpretation.

It is worth pausing briefly to note a theoretical implication of the way women may place different constructions on ideologies of pollution and chastity than men do. The pollution system, the rigid sexual code, constitute—in the terms of symbolist anthropology—a *cultural system* of symbols and meanings. I have suggested at several points in the preceding pages that individuals may have widely variant knowledge of, and place divergent constructions on, rituals and cosmological schemes. The contrasting perspectives of Kwaio men and women show how a shared "cultural system" may be open to differing, even conflicting, constructions. The same "cultural symbols" may have different "meanings," not only for individuals, but for categories of people with structurally opposed perspectives and interests.

Among the mountain peoples of northern and central Malaita for whom we have data, symbolic systems that would seem to polarize the sexes sharply and place them in structural conflict are, in daily interpersonal relationships, expressed and lived in without discernible strain and hostility. Before the Pax Britannica, when the threat of death for pollution violations and other breaches of virtue hung over women (at least among the Kwaio), stress must have been greater than it is today. But we would badly misrepresent the Kwaio system if we extrapolated from the symbolic forms to assume interpersonal conflict between the sexes. Relations between brothers and sisters, husbands and wives, are usually close and mutually supportive, substantially free of the strain reported for many New Guinea societies. If conflict between the sexes in terms of economic, political, and religious roles and symbolic forms has been an important formative process, it has been a subtle dialectical process rather than an overt "battle of the sexes." (It is instructive that of the Malaita peoples for whom we have solid data, it is the Lau peoples of the northeastern lagoons who use the ideology of pollution most directly as an instrument of the exclusion, subordination, and denigration of women [Maranda 1976]. On densely populated islets and coral platforms the northern Malaita pattern of social organization has become more strictly patrilineal, hierarchical, and male dominated. Women, outsiders by virtue of exogamy, are "alien spirits.") The characteristically free and easy interpersonal relations between the sexes in Kwaio society can usefully serve to remind us that assessing the "status of women" or relations between the sexes is exceedingly complex, and can never be based directly on symbolic systems or institutional forms. We must seek understanding in the texture of actual social relations, in the way real humans live their lives.

A religious ideology, while disguising the nature of political and economic realities, is closely geared to them. And the realities of Kwaio society are that the ascendancy of men is far from complete, in almost every realm of life. In the kinship system, ties through women may be as important as ties through men (Keesing 1970). Economically, women may control many of the fruits of their labor: a woman herself can earn valuables from selling pigs or craft items. She can assert herself in the prestige economy, by making major contributions to mortuary feasts or even sponsoring one herself. We have seen (chapter 13) how a strong and able woman like Fenaaori or ?Eteŋa can acquire sacred knowledge and magic and become a power in the ritual and political life of the community. I have heard Fenaaori on center stage at a mortuary feast giving an eloquent speech, in complete control in what is supposed to be a male domain. ?Eteŋa speaks with pride of her ancestresses who, when their male kin were unable to secure revenge, themselves entered the enemy camp and killed its male defenders. Several years ago, when she tethered a pig as a contribution to a feast, a man who had been demanding compensation from her in litigation seized the pig. Tiny ʔEteŋa went after him with a machete, and he fled in terror.

Kwaio women are, then, not radically subjugated, drastically demeaned, or consigned to exploitative labor without recognition or reward. But they are locked into a system that defines their reproductive powers and bodily functions as dangerous to the community, that separates them from control over the group's relations with the ancestors (although their periodic ritual participation is required), that places jural control over their sexuality in the hands of men, and that diverts much of their labor power to serve male ends in the prestige economy. A woman's duties as provider anchor her into domestic production, where male labor, and time, can be deployed in the quest for prestige. Women have to work for, and in many contexts subordinate themselves to, men—fathers, brothers, fathers-in-law, husbands. The constraints that in precontact times bound Kwaio men and women, young and old, into this system fell into two broad classes. One was physical force or the threat of physical force; the other was the rules of the ancestors.

The threat of execution kept young men, and girls and women, within strict bounds of conduct. A young man who put his group in jeopardy of ancestors or other groups by cursing, for example, a young woman who stole, a seducer, a girl who was propositioned—any of them might be summarily killed by their own kin or given up to another group to be killed. A girl or woman who violated pollution taboos, however inadvertently, could be killed for purification. Such weeding out of undesirables was most likely to occur when blood feuding had put a group in jeopardy and/or when a tempting bounty of blood money had been put up as reward. The men of a group could then save their own skins, or collect a lucrative reward, by killing a member of their own group or giving her or him up to be killed. The threat of sudden death made sexual adventuring tremendously dangerous, adultery almost suicidal; made obedience to one's seniors, and avoidance of verbal defiance and confrontation, matters of mortal concern. If you challenged the strong, you had to be prepared to risk immediate death.

There was no escape from this system. There was certainly no way in which women, without weapons, could challenge the men who had them, on their own grounds. Fei?a, who grew up in the latter days of blood feuding and watched her own innocent mother shot down by strongmen,[3] recalls how women were "locked in" by the system:

> Women were often killed for things men did. The men would accuse a woman of stealing taro or greens, or urinating in the house and not reporting it. And so they'd kill her. Or a man would proposition a girl, and the men would say "Let's kill her." . . . The men . . . would lie about a woman. They'd find some excuse to kill her; but what they were really after was the blood bounty—the money and the pigs. "That woman had an affair with a relative." "That woman urinated in the house." "Let's kill her for purification."
>
> I saw that when I was young. . . . The women talked about that. They said to the men: "You have to accept compensation for that sexual offense, not kill her."
>
> "No, we have to kill her."
>
> So they'd kill her and then put up a blood bounty to avenge her death. . . . The women mourned the death of their sister, or their daughter, or their mother. They cried, saying "They've killed our sister." Then they'd say, "I'm putting up my pig for the bounty to get revenge for her. . . . I'll put it up for the death of the man who caused the death of my sister." Another woman might get killed then. That's the way killings went on and on.

3. Fei?a's mother's only "wrongdoing" was that her husband (Fei?a's father) had violated the most drastic secular rules of Kwaio society by seducing his sister-in-law (the real younger sister of Fei?a's mother), and then running away with her. Kwaio strongmen tried unsuccessfully to kill Fei?a's father and the woman he had run off with, but they were too strongly protected. So the aggrieved and deserted wife was both symbolically sullied by this act and was a visible reminder of the inability of feared bounty-hunting strongmen to secure justice and claim the reward. So they decided to kill Fei?a's mother, then claim that honor had been done.

Old Aiʔarifu who, fifty-two years earlier, had cut down a policeman in the 1927 massacre, recalled without visible emotion how his Gounaakafu people had made a practice of killing a girl or woman who had violated a pollution taboo, however unintentionally:

> Our grandfather's sister had urinated in the house. My grandfather Basiberi had said, "Let's give a pig in purification for her—she's an old woman. You can't kill her." Basiberi went out to hunt, with Fanuaeʔafu. Fanuaeʔafu said "Let's go and kill her now." She was down at the stream washing, and they went down and killed her there. That was our way. If a woman urinated in the house, or was propositioned, they'd kill her, for their purification. They refused to give pigs for purification. Only killing was good enough for our ancestors.

A young man could break clear of the constraints of his elders only by proving himself as fearless warrior: only by joining the system, not by challenging it.

The physical strength of mature adulthood sustained the power of adult men, whose control of weapons and command over younger followers in their debt placed them beyond challenge by women or young men. But so, too, did the power of *adalo*. Physical intimidation by strong men entering middle age was backed by the powers of magic they were believed to command, and by the support of powerful war spirits.[4] This control of ancestral knowledge and power gave seniors a political power in the community far beyond their sheer physical strength.

In a more direct sense, the ancestors and their rules constitute a second set of sanctions. Even paternal authority over children is sustained by the ancestors: a father or ritually senior man can prohibit some act by swearing on his head, or his tooth, or his knee. To violate the injunction is to invade the father's sacredness, and it calls for purification as well as compensation. But it is the dominance of men over women that

---

4. Old men, as repositories of sacred lore and magical powers and as intermediaries to the spirits (close themselves to death and ancestorhood), also played an important part in the ventures of the group in fights and feuds.

is most directly sustained by the ideology of pollution, and the myriad rules that bind women's lives—rules invented by humans but rendered cosmic and impervious to challenge. Kwaio had evolved a self-perpetuating, self-reinforcing, self-justifying system. Real-world social relationships were cast as ancient truths of the cosmos, laws laid down and enforced by the ancestors.

We have seen that Kwaio religious practices were changing continuously, in small, potentially cumulative ways. Yet the fundamental premises and cosmological structures of the northern Malaita pattern of religion and social organization had apparently existed for many centuries—probably at least ten, perhaps twenty.

Yet it seems likely that in an ancient past dimly remembered through the mists of oral tradition, this Malaita pattern emerged from a quite different one. There must have been generations in which the fundamental rules about sacredness and its converse, the potentially polluting power of women, were created by human rulemakers, and where distinctive Malaita variations on more ancient themes of *mana* and magic and sacrifice were codified. Are Kwaio elders celebrating in their epic chants and in invocation and sacrifice the powers of the *ta?a ba?ita*, 'the people of olden times' (lit., "big people"), hearkening back to a formative period of the Malaita cultural pattern and its distinctive Kwaio variant?

Does this Malaita pattern represent any substantial modification of still older ones? The evidence is meager and indirect, but it seems likely that it does. The closest linguistic relatives of Malaita peoples on San Cristobal, Gela, Guadalcanal, and southeastern Santa Ysabel, all have matrilineal descent systems; and none, apparently, had similar ideologies about isolating the dangers of menstruation and childbirth.[5]

---

5. In some places a woman in childbirth was briefly isolated because of her heightened sacredness and dangerousness (Bogesi 1948); speakers of Kaoka, Guadalcanal (a language of the Cristobal-Malaita subgroup) have a more developed ideology of the dangers of childbirth (Hogbin 1964:84). But all of these peoples treat menstrual blood as innocuous.

I have speculated, in a long, unpublished paper (Keesing n.d.) written in 1976 about the processes through which a system of matrilineal descent might have changed into the Malaita pattern where agnatic/cognatic principles are complementary, and male and female are sharply polarized cosmologically. We have no need here to go out onto this thin ice of speculation. But it is worth reflecting that the Malaita pattern, while very old, probably did emerge out of a quite different one; and that changes in descent system from matri- to patri- and the emergence of dogmas of the polluting powers of women were probably closely connected.

For our purposes, it is more important, in understanding the hidden dynamics of the Kwaio social system and the place of religion in it, to examine what happened when the sailing ships appeared on the horizon, when steel tools and firearms and alien ideas began to transform the economy, and eventually when colonial power brought an end to the threat of execution in the name of purification and vengeance.

14.3 Transformations in the Colonial Period: The Power of Weapons, the Power of Ancestors

In the early decades of the labor trade (1870–1910), firearms transformed blood feuding; but if anything, they increased the power and wealth of the bounty-hunting warriors and their control over women and young men (Keesing 1978a; Keesing and Corris 1980). The development of an internal plantation system after 1910 began to erode this control, making young men more independent of their elders, at a time when the ancient rifles, half a century old, were disintegrating and ammunition was running out. When the Kwaio strongmen assassinated Bell in 1927, it was the last blow of an old order whose foundations were threatened from within, as from without.

Both colonial power and Christian presence on the coast

had, by 1928, taken firm hold. After the 1927 massacre and the bloody punitive expedition, the surviving Kwaio strongmen were forced into retirement; those who killed faced death or life in prison. The disarming of men lifted a pall of fear from women, from the young, and from the weak and marginal. While sporadic killings have taken place in the decades since, they no longer constitute socially sanctioned responses to sexual offenses, curses, pollution, or other violations or provocations. Those who commit mortal offenses cannot be killed; those who kill cannot be targets of blood vengeance.

Boori?au, an elderly and respected woman, reflected on the contrasts in temperament between men and women, as culturally construed, and the changes brought about by pacification:

> Women's minds are different from men's. A man goes on the rampage and kills a man or steals a pig or seduces a girl. A woman thinks only about getting married, and about work. Men are different . . . they are given to troublemaking; they kill, they steal, they seduce. They aren't placid. . . . We have two different temperaments, not just one. Even a man who is good-natured and fun-loving will turn around and kill his sister or his wife over some trouble. At least, that's the way it was in the old days.
>
> Now things are better. Now, if something happens with a man's wife [i.e., adultery] they straighten it out with money and she is left alive. If a girl gets pregnant, they pay compensation and then she has the child and they raise it. Nobody is angry in the long run. In the old days, anger rose over these things. Men turned around and killed their wives or sisters or daughters if some trouble happened. We Kwaio did not know how to be placid and peaceful, in the olden days.

But the effects of the disarming of Kwaio strongmen and the government-imposed peace have filtered only slowly through the structures of Kwaio society, gradually changing them. In the first decade after pacification, there were a few sexual affairs between close kin that could not be punished, a few disapproved marriages between relatives. By the fourth decade after pacification, more than half of the marriages were disapproved; and in the fifth decade the figure had risen to about nine out of ten. Among today's young people a sexual revolution is a fait accompli. The elders, trying to impose the old rules about purity, compensation, and marriage payments, are left to manage as best they can: by being outraged by what has been going on under their noses, pressing angry demands, paying compensation, and eventually negotiating a marriage; by trying to get a girl married to a reasonable young man (even a close relative) after her second or third affair, to get a young man who has been costing a lot of valuables through his sexual adventuring settled down. Morals, the moralists say, are in disarray.

But the ancestors' rules remain. The *adalo* may be weakened by Christian incursions and defilement, but they still hold powers of life and death. The complex interconnections between physical force and religious ideology as buttresses of the traditional social order have come progressively into view as the pressures of physical threat have been pulled away under colonial rule. The power of weapons as direct instruments of male ascendancy and the subordination of women and children has disappeared. But the mystified form of (male) political power, the life-threatening and *nanama*-ing power of *adalo*, remains inviolate. As long as contemporary Kwaio remain in their mountain communities, they must follow the ancestral rules as articulated by their seniors and adumbrated in precept and religious practice. The women whose accounts of their lives and of women's taboos and virtues have been recorded[6] have at no point challenged the legitimacy and binding force of these ancestral rules; they portray female virtues and appropriate paths and styles of life in terms of them.

Many Kwaio have, over the last fifty years, opted to break clear of the ancestral rules and punishments: but never by challenging them, only by seeking sanctuary from them, by moving down to the coastal villages where ancestral power is neutralized, where pollution rules are suspended, where the white people's God holds sway.

6. Extensive autobiographical and cultural accounts by sixteen Kwaio women, collected by Shelley Schreiner and myself, will be analyzed in a forthcoming monograph.

Chapter Fifteen

The Struggle for Autonomy

WE NEED NOW to place the Kwaio traditionalists, still living in a world of *adalo*, sacrifice, and magic, in the wider world of Christians, copra, cash, capitalism, colonialism, and now Commonwealth.

Why have so many of the Kwaio maintained their commitment to old ways? In neighboring Kwara?ae, Christianity has taken hold in almost every community; by World War II, there were few traditionalists left. In many parts of Melanesia, conversion to Christianity came swiftly (although often superficially). Why, and how, have so many Kwaio resisted? We need first to look at the Christianity that has been their alternative.

15.1 The Kwaio Encounter with Christianity

The main Christian impact on the east coast of Kwaio country has been by two varieties of fundamentalism: the nondenominational South Sea Evangelical Mission (SSEM, now SSEC as an indigenous church), and the Seventh Day Adventists. The SSEM established Christian villages at Uru, Sinalagu, and ?Oloburi prior to 1910.[1] The SDA mission established a base

---

1. Roman Catholics (Marist) established a strong base in west Kwaio in 1913, but did not operate in east Kwaio until 1958 (Laracy 1976). Their influence there has been mainly confined to the Uru area. The Melanesian Mission (Anglican) tried only fleetingly and unsuccessfully to establish a foothold at Sinalagu.

at Uru, with resident white missionaries, in the early 1920s; it was later abandoned. In the mid-1960s, they returned to establish a large hospital complex in Uru Harbor. The two missions have had rather different strategies. The SDAs had their center in the western Solomons. Their strategy has been to work through white missionaries and black teachers and pastors from the western Solomons in the villages, using pidgin as a medium. The SSEM has had a few European missionaries at key posts on Malaita. But their main strategy since Queensland days has been to train local Christians as Bible teachers and have them provide Christian teaching and leadership in their home communities.

In some important respects, both fundamentalist missions have taken similar stances toward Kwaio culture. Both characterize the cosmos in terms of a struggle between forces of good and evil, the latter personified in Satan. Both take for granted that Kwaio ancestral spirits are real and exert an influence in daily life: but they are manifestations of the devil (in Solomons pidgin, ancestors are "devil-devils"), whose evil powers are fought by God and angels, as Judgment Day nears. Only by praying for God's intervention can people be free from the devil's powers. Elements of traditional culture associated with the "devil-devils"—mortuary feasting and associated customs such as pan-pipe music and chanting, as well as religious rites—have been prohibited. Rules associated with the *adalo*, notably pollution taboos, have been systematically transgressed, and new sets of Christian taboos (about swearing and stealing, and in the case of SDAs, Old Testament food taboos, and rules about the sabbath) have been substituted.

The Roman Catholic Mission (Marist) has long been strong on the west Kwaio coast, but since stationing a priest in Uru Harbor in the 1950s has achieved only limited success, mainly around Uru and up the Kwaibaʔita River valley. The Catholics, with priests who learn the local languages, seek to create a synthesis of old and new rather than insisting on a clean break with old ways. Some Kwaio have seen in this the best of both worlds—access to schooling while still going to mortuary feasts. But more, on the conservative east coast, have feared to leave themselves under the power of both ancestors and Christian God.

Before, during, and since the 1927 invasion and desecration of the Sinalagu heartland, the primary motive leading Kwaio to move to the coast and become Christian has been the desire to escape from ancestral wrath. In the face of sickness and death, families have fled to Christian villages for sanctuary. In prayer in their churches, Christian communities have challenged the power of the particular *adalo* deemed to be causing the illness, with the saving power of Jesus. Since the 1920s, all non-Christians have been aware of the essential elements of Christian theology. And they have been aware that the rules of the ancestors have been "successfully" flouted in the Christian villages: women menstruate in their houses, and men share food with them; childbirth is at most fleetingly isolated. (Christians—at least until the SDA hospital provided sophisticated medical care—died at least as often as non-Christians, particularly along a swampy and malarial coast, with concentrated villages and inadequate latrines and water supplies. But a people prepared to see *adalo* as giving and taking life are prepared to believe in Jesus saving it, if the occasional seriously ill patient recovers.)

This has an interesting implication for the dynamics of Christian–non-Christian relations. The non-Christians have to "believe in" the power of the Christian God—within the Christian villages—to explain how people violate the most important ancestral rules, and live. And the Christians have to "believe in" the power of the ancestors—characterized as "devils"—in order to justify having become Christian, and in order to sustain the solidarity of the community in resistance against the powers of evil.

The Christians, prior to 1927, had been at the mercy of the lions of the interior. With the punitive expedition, the power swung toward the government and the missions. Prior to World War II, Christians were aligned against *ta?a i ?itini,* 'heathen people' (or *wikiti*, 'wicked', a term also used by the non-Christians to characterize themselves). The Christians had every hope that they would soon gain control of the bush areas (as they had in Kwaraʔae). The SSEM white leadership sensed the impending Christian triumph:

> In Koio [Kwaio] two new places in the mountains behind Sinorango [Sinalagu] are making a vigorous beginning for the Gospel . . . PRAISE GOD! There is a healthy stirring among the Koio heathen. I have just heard that they have asked for another Christian centre among them.

. . .

> A great door is opened in Koio. . . . Three new places are starting in the bush behind Sinorango; one is about two and a half hours' walk inland! (Keesing 1967:88)

With the experience of World War II, many volunteers in the Labor Corps perceived that the power of the whites was not inseparably linked to Christianity, as they had been led to believe (many Americans were as irreverent about theology as they were about colonialism). Some of the Malaita Christians perceived that in giving them Bible teaching without education, the SSEM had withheld the keys to real power. Finally, in the emergent doctrine of Maasina Rule, "kastomu" (custom) became a symbol of anticolonial struggle, and the unity of Christians and "heathen" against colonial oppression became a central theme (Keesing 1978b).

To the surprise of their European missionary "masters," Malaita Bible teachers took the lead in Maasina Rule in many areas. White missionaries were physically ejected from their churches. Although the split has been healed over on the surface, and a new generation of well-educated young leaders (including the first Solomon Islands Prime Minister, Peter Kenilorea) has emerged, the SSEC has been a genuinely indigenous church since World War II. (The SDA continues to rely on massive investment by the Church in medical and educational work, and an infrastructure operated by Europeans and western Solomon Islanders.)

So the Kwaio are beleaguered on two fronts. At home, Christians increasingly press to use their ancestral lands in the interior. Christians represent the bush people in the Provincial Assembly and the national Parliament. Christian lawmakers impose taxes that exceed mean annual income in bush areas, pass bylaws that forbid keeping pigs in settlements or houses, and pronounce platitudes about "a Christian country." The SDA hospital offers the sick miraculous means to life,[2] but— for men, at least—only by deserting their ancestors and exposing themselves to massive pollution.[3]

The temptations to life are strong. So are the temptations of education: government primary schools (taught, of course, by Christians) have been established on the coast at Uru and Sinalagu. Why, then, do the non-Christians maintain their stubborn commitment to ancestors and their ways? There are no easy answers. Defiance to the new ways, commitment to the old, remains strong. Thus, in 1977, traditional priests from ?Ere?ere along the Kwaio-Kwara?ae border were seeking to use the pollution rules to end the SDA flights to and from the mission hospital. Through the Christian scribes on whom they rely when writing needs to be done, they wrote:

> Dear Director of S.D.A. and the pilot of S. Steck [Piper Aztec] Plain.
>
> I just want to let you know that I don't want want your plain to fly over my village including Ere ere area from now on. I stop in for the following reasonable reasons:
> 1. The plain carry women with bloody babies.
> 2. He always fly over our most Holy Alters where we burnt offering to our devil.
> 3. It always cause death to our people because the devil get angry and kill people.

2. Especially since penicillin dramatically and almost instantly cured the symptoms of yaws, a crippling and disfiguring disease, Kwaio have attributed to Western medicine great powers in treating the symptoms of disease (though not the ancestral causes).

3. The childbirth ward of the hospital is physically attached to the men's ward. Kwaio non-Christians firmly believe that the afterbirth and bloody materials are burned by the hospital (although hospital policy is supposed to prohibit this).

4. Many pigs are kill to mean the plains fly over our devil
   . . .
   On behave of majority of headen [heathen] people who
are living here if you are Christians please don't set your
flyth over our area for it cause us death.
Thank you,
Yours sincerely Ere ere Devil Priests
1. Timikooliu
2. Maerora
3. Maealea

Explanations of continuing conservatism cannot be found
solely in negative factors—the absence of coastal land, the
lack of development and education. They must, I think, be
found in large measure in the traditional system itself. There
are deep satisfactions in being able to produce with one's
own hands, through work in family groups, virtually everything one needs to live. There are enormous satisfactions in
living in a physical landscape filled with ancient landmarks,
surrounded by history: gardening, living, worshipping in the
settings where one's parents, one's grandparents, and one's
great-grandparents spent their lives, and being bound to them
by direct social bonds.

15.2   The Economics and Politics
of Kwaio Conservatism

Europeans committed to law and order, Christianity, or development have been prone to see the Kwaio and ?Are?are
as more nasty, intractable, innately conservative, or unrea-
sonably hostile than other Malaita peoples (a stereotype reinforced, for the Kwaio, by the 1927 attack on Bell and his party,
and the 1965 assassination of a white missionary). But a close
reading of the historical evidence suggests that in Kwara?ae,
To?abaita, and other areas where Christianity and development have been particularly successful, initial hostility to
Western influence was equally strong.

A look at the geography of Malaita quickly reveals some partial bases for Kwaio conservatism. If we look at only two variables—the availability of coastal land suitable for development, and the proximity to the early European centers (the administrative headquarters at Auki and its satellites, Malu?u and Su?u)—we see that the southern half of the east coast was maximally disadvantaged. The government has spent very little money on this stretch of coast, and virtually none in the mountains. Movement to the coast has been, all along, a precondition for westernization; and where the coastal shelf is narrow or nonexistent, the inducement to abandon traditional lands is reduced. Because of land scarcity on this southern east coast, moving to the coast has meant a reduced standard of subsistence in many areas, scarcely compensated for by availability of fish and coconuts, and has precluded the prosperity achieved in other areas from production of copra or other cash crops. The lack of economic development of this "forgotten coast" may have a more insidious side, in terms of government policy. A senior British administrator in the Solomons, whose experience on Malaita dates back to 1947, has observed to me that it was unwritten government policy throughout the colonial period to leave the mountainous south-central zone of Kwaio and ?Are?are undeveloped so that it would be a reservoir of unskilled, cheap labor.

If this has been the policy, it has been successful. As noted in chapter 1, it is mainly the peoples of culturally conservative bush Malaita who continue to do unskilled physical labor on plantations and in town. Meanwhile, the peoples of the Kwaio and ?Are?are coastal villages have begun to enjoy visible economic rewards from education, and the Christianity that has provided, until recently, the only means to it. Plantations, as worlds in miniature where workers created their own social order, have largely given way to urban centers where power and wealth reside in the people with cars and trucks and motorcycles, in people—black and white—who work in offices and live in elegant houses. The pleasures of town, of drink and gambling and movies, depend on access to money, and Kwaio laborers have too little of it to enjoy the bright lights, except vicariously. There are satisfactions in following ancient ways and rules, in living the life of one's forebears. The means to prestige and prosperity—raising pigs, growing big gardens, earning or fabricating shell valuables—lie in people's own hands. If we can measure a standard of living in cultural and human terms, the traditional way is highly satisfying (see Keesing 1980c, 1980d).

But what about the pollution taboos? Would women not go to the Christian villages to escape burdens of menstrual isolation and restrictive rules, to avoid bringing death or illness on their familes, and the burden of guilt? Many have done so: mothers taking their children to sanctuary, widows taking children to a new life. But my data would suggest that of those who have done so, more than half have returned to traditional life in the mountains: to their ancestors, sustaining as well as punitive, to a life where ancestral rules provide structure and a sense of virtue and moral responsibility. Kwaio religion may in some objective and historical sense be a means of reinforcing male domination. But it provides deep satisfactions; it gives everyday life—the experiences of dream, of sickness and health, prosperity and paucity—a meaning and structure, a value beyond immediate pragmatic and worldly concern, for which an alien religion centered around a white God, a white Jesus, and a white people's heaven provides, for many Kwaio, no adequate replacement.

To appreciate the values and sustaining strengths and rewards of traditional life requires a large measure of wisdom and a perspective that would be difficult to maintain in a coastal village where trucks and ships and shiny radios were a reminder of European wealth and a source of material temptation. In areas where the material rewards of a commitment to Western ways, and Western-style education, are visible on all sides, some adults may choose to follow old ways (as in the Lau Lagoon); but even those who do are likely to send their children to school, so that the passing of the traditional religion becomes inevitable. The richness and value Kwaio non-Christians perceive in traditional life remain in view because, in their mountain settlements, the new temptations are partly hidden. As long as the Kwaio traditionalists remain in the mountains, on their ancestral lands—and the narrow coastal margins are already overcrowded and under ecological pressure from overcultivation—they are likely to continue to value old ways: at least until the outside world, through roads and development, becomes more accessible and more economically advantageous.

Finally, there is a crucial symbolic element in Kwaio resistance to Christianity. In the course of anticolonial struggle, "kastomu" and commitment to ancestral ways have become symbols of identity and autonomy (Keesing 1980c, 1980d). Kwaio see that all over the Solomons peoples have lost their cultures and, in losing them, their ties to the land and to the past. Alienated from their customs, alienated from their ancestors, they have become like the white colonists, have become outsiders in their own homeland. Kwaio traditionalists see their culture not simply as their grandparents did—as *the* way of life. They see it from the outside, as it were; "kastomu" has become a symbol of personal and group identity. Resistance to Christianity and westernization is perpetuated, and articulated, through this ideology: following the rules of the ancestors is a mode of political struggle, as well as a way of life.

Conclusion

IF ANTHROPOLOGISTS ARE to deepen our understanding of humankind, of human natures socially and culturally expressed, it must be by illuminating the general through the particular. What can the Kwaio, bespelling evodia, sacrificing pigs, following rules about fires and food, tell us about humanity, and about ourselves?

The Kwaio, like the Yanomamö or the Balinese or the Tikopia or the Trobrianders, add, in their singularity, to our understanding of cultural diversity and human possibility. The Tylorean constructions Kwaio place on dreams, shadows, and reflections, the logic of magic, the conception of *nanama*, the symbolic inversion of ancestral power and women's power, death and childbirth, express in cultural form modes of thought and interpretation that illuminate the human mind and the life experiences of a universe they share with us. Their singularity can cast light on our own.

Each new accretion to our understanding of cultural possibility may be valuable in its own right. But anthropology, whether we characterize it primarily as a science or an interpretive quest (Geertz 1973), must seek more powerful theoretical understandings and interpretive modes as well as documenting particulars. Kwaio religion can perhaps contribute more to our ways of *thinking about* cultural traditions than to our catalogue of diverse patterns of life and thought.

Kwaio religion as a system of meanings uses the surface evidence of nonphysical states—the experiences of dream,

coma, and memory, the physical signs of shadow and reflection, the transmutations of smoke and steam, the processes
of birth and death—to create the implicit terms and categories
of a metaphysic and an eschatology. Positing a noumenal
world controlled by the spirits behind the visible one they so
imperfectly control, Kwaio acquire explanation for failure and
success, life and death. They can treat death as a converse of
birth, a rite of passage; and they can attribute meaning, a
measure of controlability, to what would otherwise be meaningless ending, whether by sudden death or wasting illness.
As Leach puts it,

The concept of the Other World is generated by direct inversion of
the characteristics of ordinary experience. This World is inhabited
by mortal, impotent men, who live out their lives in normal time in
which events happen in sequence, one after another. In this world
we get older and older . . . and in the end we die. The Other World
is inhabited by immortal, omnipotent [beings] who exist perpetually
in abnormal time in which past, present and future all coexist. . . .
"Power," conceived as the source of health, life, fertility, political
influence, wealth . . . is located in the Other World and the purpose
of religious performance is to provide a bridge, or channel of communication, through which the power of the [ancestors] may be
made available to otherwise impotent men. (Leach 1976:81–82)

The ancestors, who can surround the living with a mantle
of protection or withdraw it, who can convey powers or visit
punishment, are part of the social system. One cannot reason
with, solicit benefits from, or appease, abstract random forces
in the universe. By rendering these forces at once human and
superhuman, the living gain a control—albeit imagined—over
events; and they acquire access to a magical technology that
joins them, through lines of ancestors, to an ancient past
when great deeds were possible.

Kwaio religion makes awesomely powerful ancient spirits
both personal and accessible, in portraying the shades of dead
parents as confidants and intermediaries, and in portraying
familiar humans encountered in dream as the shades of these
ancient ancestors. This association between an individual's
attachment figures and the ancient ancestors controlling life

and death provides a kind of cognitive linkage between the *adalo* and the primary experience of infancy, in which mother, father, and parent-surrogates were givers of nurturance and gratification, sources of frustration and punishment. This linkage may well be a central source of the emotional power of Kwaio religion.[1]

Kwaio religion shows vividly how cosmological schemes—the oppositions of male and female, the living and the dead, *abu* and *mola*, nature and culture, childbirth and sacrifice—can be expressed in everyday life and ritual action even where they are not developed into an explicit metaphysic or explained in myth. These polarities implicitly structure the spaces in which one moves, the places one sits, the water one drinks, where and what one eats. Religious meanings can be given abstract expression by the analyst: but it is a religion of the concrete and immediate, a way of living and acting, not of explaining.

We need to move above this plane of subjective realities to see a patterning more global and coherent than the individual's view. But we do so with risk. Too easily we piece together from our own inferences, and bits and pieces from the rare folk philosopher, a coherent theology that is too far removed from the lives and thought of individuals to illuminate them. If we elevate this theology, artifact of analysis, into a system of "cultural symbols," we not only run a danger of creating what Brunton (1980) calls "misconstrued order." We may in the process lose the power to understand how religious ideas express and disguise political and economic interests, and to understand how these ideas are perpetuated and progressively modified.

The distribution of knowledge in Kwaio communities, the

1. Such interpretations would require for substantiation much more evidence than I have on infancy and on dream experience and other fantasy. Such hypotheses draw on psychoanalytic theory, but they do not require a reductionism where cultural patterns are explained as psychological projections. Primary experiences do not *produce* systems of cultural symbols, but they may infuse them with emotional meanings and hence contribute to their perpetuation and their salience.

varying constructions individuals appear to place on ritual and cosmology, and the lack of systematic theology and concern with ultimate explanation can serve to warn us of the dangers in creating a composite, coherent, and intellectually tidy scheme of symbols and meanings and calling it a "cultural system." Men and women may follow the same schemes of rules and categories, but they characteristically place different constructions on them. Ritual symbols do not "have meanings": they evoke interpretations and understandings that depend on the perspective and knowledge of individual actors (see Lewis 1980).

I have suggested that the creation, preservation, and progressive transformation of Kwaio cosmological structures depend on the distribution of knowledge: on access to and command of sacred lore and magic, on intellectual capacities and personal commitments to understanding, and on the processes of local politics. That individuals contribute differentially to the cultural heritage of their community is not a radically new insight. The phenomenon, and the theoretical problems it poses, were glimpsed in the realm of Melanesian religion almost half a century ago by Gregory Bateson. Characteristically well ahead of his time, he had written in 1935 of the role of experts in defining and modifying the rich and intellectually elaborated cultural tradition of the Iatmul of New Guinea. He was struck by "how the stimulation of a small number of specialists can react on the culture as a whole." Bateson noted that:

these specialists constantly set themselves up as unofficial masters of ceremonies, criticising and instructing the men who are carrying out the intricacies of the culture. . . . Thus the culture is to a great extent in the custody of men trained in erudition and dialectic and is continually set forth by them for the instruction of the majority. . . . We may be fairly certain that [these] individuals . . . contribute very much more than their fellows to the elaboration and maintenance of the culture. (1958:22)

In contrasting male and female ethos in Iatmul society, Bateson further anticipated some of the insights of the modern anthropology of women: the experts who most centrally contributed to the definition and modification of Iatmul culture were senior men, whose control over knowledge gave them political control over women and young men (see also Tuzin 1980).

Religious systems like that of the Kwaio do not simply infuse human life with meaning. Like other ideological systems they serve political ends as well: maintaining relations of dominance and submission, power and privilege. Ideologies of women's pollution and men's control of sacred knowledge may serve, as in many New Guinea societies, to sustain male subordination and exploitation of women. Ideologies in New Guinea that semen is necessary for growth sustain male homosexual cults in which seniors dominate, brutalize, and sexually exploit juniors (see Herdt 1980, 1982; Keesing 1982). Trobriand commoners had to crawl prostrate in the presence of a high-ranking "chief." Sexual dominance and prostration before chiefs, like pollution, are certainly meaning-laden; but the view from the bottom and the view from the top are very different. A symbolist anthropology is necessary; but we cannot let it blind us to earthly political and economic relationships by a wave of the analytical wand, telling ourselves that meanings are shared. Cultures are not simply accretions of countless generations of human thoughts, like polyps on a coral reef.

An anthropology of tribal religions requires a delicate balance between two perspectives, either of which by itself is seriously inadequate. On the one side we need to view religions as shared orientations to the cosmos, collective symbolic constructions that give order and meaning to the lives of mortal humans. And on the other side we need to see how religions, as ideologies, celestialize earthly realities, disguising their nature and ensuring their perpetuation.

If we concentrate on religions as collective symbol systems we are prone to give them a spurious coherence, and to analyze them on an ethereal plane floating above and beyond the diverse subjective experiences of individuals and the political interests of groups and classes. We become the theologians of worlds where, as for the Kwaio, theology may have no salient place. If we go too far in the opposite direction, we can fall into either of two equally dangerous traps. By concentrating on the fragmentary beliefs and diverse subjective orientations of individuals, we can become trapped in an empiricist flotsam of analytical debris, unable to see coherent symbolic structures. If instead we take a kind of vulgar Marxist perspective on religions as mystifying ideologies, we become blind to both their symbolic coherence and their subjective meanings; from this trap we can see only false consciousness and political conspiracy in people's deepest and most compelling experiences and emotions (Asad 1979).

I have tried, in describing Kwaio religion, to situate symbolic systems both in individual experience and in the political life of communities, without obscuring their coherent and elegant, though largely implicit, structure. It is a difficult anthropological balancing act, and many will feel I have leaned too far to one side or another. I hope at least that in depicting Kwaio magic and sacrifice, sacredness and pollution, the ancestors and the living, I have illuminated both sides and conveyed some sense of what it is to live in such a world.

Kwaio Glossary

ʔ: Is treated as last letter in alphabet.

abu: forbidden; sacred (Eastern Oceanic *tapu*).

adalo: shades of the dead; ancestral ghosts who observe and take part in Kwaio life.

alasia: pray to (*kwaialasi* is the intransitive form).

ariŋa: divination, using knotted cordyline leaves.

aruʔia: to bespell.

bata: valuables made from strung beads fabricated from cone shells.

baʔe: shrine.

beritauŋa: a ritual sequence in *fonulaanimae* in which the pigs are blessed to attract wealth to the feast.

bisi: a menstrual hut.

boni: A wake, held every ten days after a death, at which relatives of the decedent gather and spend the night with the bereaved family.

bounimae: the "post of the dead" used in *beritauŋa*.

fanua: a territory comprised of land tracts clustered around a focal shrine.

foʔota: "offerings"—pigs consecrated to ancestors, and named with the ancestors' pseudonyms.

kaakaba: women's area, including menstrual area and latrine (also used, =*bisi*, for menstrual hut).

kaloŋa: bush, forest (the realm of nature).

kwaialasi: pray.

lafiŋa: childbirth (nominalized form of *lafi*, 'give birth').

lakeno: a taro dough and coconut cream pudding, usually eaten ritually.

lamo: warrior, bounty-hunter (north Malaita *ramo*).

laʔe: an aromatic shrub (*Evodia* spp.) used in attraction magic and *ribaŋa*.

Maasina Rule: the rule of brotherhood, a post-World War II anticolonial movement centered on Malaita.

mamu: magical attraction; a complex of magic for attracting wealth.

mana: Eastern Oceanic term (Kwaio *nanama*) for ancestrally-conferred powers or state of sacredness or efficacy.

mola: secular, ordinary, permitted, mundane (contrasts with *abu*).

nanama: sacralized or rendered effective by ancestral power; of ancestor, render human effort *nanama*.

naruŋa: washing, purification; sacrifice in expiation (=*siuŋa*).

nunuiʔola: shade of a dead person.

nununa: shadow, "shade," of a living or dead person.

omea: mortuary feast.

ribaŋa: a rite, using bespelled and chewed *laʔe*, spat on the chest or on food, for desacralization before a meal or communion with spirits.

siuŋa: A washing, purification; sacrifice in expiation (=*naruŋa*).

sua: polluted, defiled (=*kwaʔa*).

suruʔai: the "taboo-keeper" who goes into liminal isolation after death of a priest or crematory sacrifice.

suuŋa: crematory sacrifice, burning a piglet for an ancient ancestor (the high act of sacrifice).

tele: pray.

umu: sacred ovenstones used in sacrifice.

wado: ground, land, earth.

walafu-: relative four or more generations removed from ego; used as a kin term and in referring to ancestors.

ʔokoeʔenia: attend to the physical needs of a woman in childbirth seclusion, or *suruʔai* in sacred seclusion.

References

Asad, T. 1979. "Anthropology and the Analysis of Ideology." *Man* (n.s.) 14:607–27.

Barrau, J. 1965. "L'Humide et le Sec: An Essay on Ethnobiological Adaptation to Contrasted Environments in the Indo-Pacific Area." *Journal of the Polynesian Society* 74:329–46.

Barth, F. 1975. *Ritual and Knowledge Among the Baktaman of New Guinea.* New Haven: Yale University Press.

Bateson, G. 1958. *Naven.* Stanford, Calif.: Stanford University Press. (First published 1936; Cambridge: Cambridge University Press.)

———— 1972. "Style, Grace and Information in Primitive Art." In G. Bateson, *Steps to an Ecology of Mind.* Philadelphia: Intext.

Bell, D. 1980a. "Daughters of the Dreaming." Ph.D. dissertation, Australian National University, Canberra.

———— 1980b. "Central Australian Aboriginal Women's Love Rituals." Paper read at Wenner-Gren Symposium on the Sexual Division of Labor, Burg Wartenstein, Austria.

Bogesi, G. 1948. "Santa Isabel, Solomon Islands." *Oceania* 18:208–32; 327–57.

Brunton, R. 1980. "Misconstrued Order in Melanesian Religion." *Man* (n.s.) 15(1):112–28.

Codrington, R. 1891. *The Melanesians: Studies in Their Anthropology and Folk-lore.* Oxford: Oxford University Press, Clarendon Press.

Cooper, M. 1971. "Economic Context of Shell Money Production on Malaita." *Oceania* 41(4):266–76.

———— 1972. "Langalanga Religion." *Oceania* 43:113–22.

Coppet, D. de and H. Zemp. 1978. *ʔAréʔaré: Un peuple Mélanesién et sa musique.* Paris: Seuil.

Corris, P. 1973. *Passage, Port and Plantation.* Melbourne: University of Melbourne Press.

Douglas, M. 1966. *Purity and Danger.* London and Baltimore: Penguin Books.

———— 1970. *Natural Symbols: Explorations in Cosmology.* London: Cresset.

Durkheim, E. 1912. *Les formes élémentaires de la vie religieuse: le système totemique en Australie.* Paris: Presses Universitaires.

Evans-Pritchard, E. E. 1956. *Nuer Religion.* Oxford: Oxford University Press, Clarendon Press.

Firth, R. 1963. "Offering and Sacrifice: Problems of Organisation." *Journal of the Royal Anthropological Institute* 93:12–24.

Fortes, M. 1960. "Ancestor Worship in Africa." In M. Fortes and G. Dieterlen, eds., *African Systems of Thought.* London: Oxford University Press.

Fox, C. E. 1924. *Threshold of the Pacific.* London: Routledge.

Geertz, C. 1973. *The Interpretation of Culture.* New York: Basic Books.

Gell, A. 1975. *Metamorphosis of the Cassowaries: Umeda Society, Language and Ritual.* London School of Economics Monographs on Social Anthropology, 51. London: Athlone Press.

Goodenough, W. H. 1957. "Cultural Anthropology and Linguistics." In P. Garvin, ed., *Report of the Seventh Annual Round Table Meeting on Linguistics and Language Study.* Monograph Series on Language and Linguistics, vol. 9. Washington, D.C.: Georgetown University.

———— 1961. "Comment on Cultural Evolution." *Daedalus* 90:521–28.

Herdt, G. H. 1980. *Guardians of the Flutes.* New York: McGraw-Hill.

Herdt, G. H., ed. 1982. *Rituals of Manhood: Male Initiation in Papua New Guinea.* Berkeley and Los Angeles: University of California Press.

Hertz, R. 1907. "Contribution à une étude sur la représentation de la mort." *l'Année Sociologique* 10:48–137. (Translated in R. Needham, ed. 1960. *Death and the Right Hand.* New York: The Free Press.)

Hogbin, H. I. 1936. "Mana." *Oceania* 6:241–74.

———— 1939. *Experiments in Civilization.* London: Routledge.

———— 1964. *A Guadalcanal Society: the Kaoka Speakers.* New York: Holt, Rinehart and Winston.

———— 1970. *The Island of Menstruating Men: Religion in Wogeo, New Guinea.* Scranton, Pa.: Chandler.

Hogbin, H. I. and C. Wedgwood. 1953. "Local Grouping in Melanesia." *Oceania* 23:241–76; 24:58–76.

Howells, W. 1973. *The Pacific Islanders.* Wellington, N.Z.: A. H. and A. W. Reed.

Hubert, H. and M. Mauss. 1897–98. "Essai sur la nature et la fonction du sacrifice." *l'Année Sociologique* 2:29–138.

Ivens, W. G. 1927. *Melanesians of the Southeast Solomon Islands.* London: Kegan Paul, Trench and Trubner.

———— 1930. *Island Builders of the Pacific.* London: Seeley Service.

Keesing, R. M. 1965. *Kwaio Marriage and Society.* Ph.D. dissertation, Department of Social Relations, Harvard University.

———— 1967. "Christians and Pagans in Kwaio, Malaita." *Journal of the Polynesian Society* 76:82–100.

———— 1968. "Chiefs in a Chiefless Society: The Ideology of Modern Kwaio Politics." *Oceania* 38:276–80.

———— 1970. "Shrines, Ancestors and Cognatic Descent: The Kwaio and Tallensi." *American Anthropologist* 72:755–75.

———— 1971. "Descent, Residence and Cultural Codes." In L. Hiatt and C. Jayawardena, eds., *Anthropology in Oceania.* Sydney: Angus and Robertson.

———— 1972. "Simple Models of Complexity: The Lure of Kinship." In P. Reining, ed., *Kinship Studies in the Morgan Centennial Year.* Washington, D.C.: Anthropological Society of Washington.

———— 1976. *Cultural Anthropology: A Contemporary Perspective.* New York: Holt, Rinehart and Winston.

———— 1978a. *?Elota's Story: The Life and Times of a Solomon Islands Big Man.* St. Lucia: University of Queensland Press.

———— 1978b. "Politico-Religious Movements and Anticolonialism on Malaita: Maasina Rule in Historical Perspective." *Oceania* 48:241–61; 49:46–73.

———— 1978c. "The Kwaio of Malaita: Old Values and New Discontents." In E. K, Fisk, ed., *The Adaptation of Traditional Agriculture.* Canberra: Development Studies Centre, Australian National University.

———— 1979a. "Linguistic Knowledge and Cultural Knowledge: Some Doubts and Speculations." *American Anthropologist* 81:14–36.

———— 1979b. "Cultural Symbols and the Political Economy of Knowledge: Some Problems in Analyzing Kwaio Religion." Paper read at Stanford University, April.

———— 1980a. "Antecedents of Maasina Rule: Some Further Notes." *Journal of Pacific History* 13(2):1–6.

———— 1980b. "The Uses of Kinship: Kwaio, Solomon Islands." In S. Beckerman and L. S. Cordell, eds., *The Versatility of Kinship.* New York: Academic Press.

———— 1980c. "*Kastomu* and Anticolonialism on Malaita: 'Culture' as Political Symbol." Paper presented to the Annual Meeting of the Australian Anthropological Society, Brisbane, August.

———— 1980d. "Traditionalist Enclaves in Melanesia." Paper presented to the annual school seminar, Research School of Pacific Studies, Australian National University, October. In H. Nelson, ed., forthcoming. *Melanesia: Beyond Diversity.* Canberra: Research School of Pacific Studies, Australian National University.

———— 1980e. "Rethinking *Mana*: The Kwaio Evidence." Paper read at the annual meeting of the Kroeber Anthropological Society, Berkeley, California, May 1979; and presented in extensively revised form at the Department of Anthropology, University of Sydney, Australia, February 1980.

—— 1981. *Cultural Anthropology: A Contemporary Perspective*. 2d ed. New York: Holt, Rinehart and Winston.

—— 1982. Introduction to G. H. Herdt, ed., *Rituals of Manhood: Male Initiation in Papua New Guinea*. Berkeley and Los Angeles: University of California Press.

—— n.d. "Kwaio Pollution and the Politics of Ideology." Unpublished ms.

Keesing, R. M. and P. Corris. 1980. *Lightning Meets the West Wind: the Malaita Massacre*. Melbourne: Oxford University Press.

Keesing, R. M. and J. Fifiʔi. 1969. "Kwaio Word Tabooing in its Cultural Context." *Journal of the Polynesian Society* 78:154–77.

Laracy, H. 1976. *Marists and Melanesians*. Canberra: Australian National University Press.

Leach, E. R. 1958. "Magical Hair." *Journal of the Royal Anthropological Institute* 88:147–64.

—— 1976. *Culture and Communication: The Logic by which Symbols are Connected*. Cambridge: Cambridge University Press.

Lewis, G. 1980. *Day of Shining Red: An Essay on Understanding Ritual*. Cambridge: Cambridge University Press.

Lindenbaum, S. 1972. "Sorcerers, Ghosts and Polluting Women: An Analysis of Religious Belief and Population Control." *Ethnology* 11:241–53.

McKinley, R. n.d. "Commentary on Keesing's *Kwaio Religion: The Living and the Dead in a Solomon Island Society*." Unpublished ms., 46pp.

Maranda, E. 1976. "Woman is an Alien Spirit." In C. Matthiesson, ed., *Many Sisters: Women in Cross-Cultural Perspective*. New York: Free Press.

Maranda, E. and P. Maranda. 1970. "Le crâne et l'utérus: deux theorèmes Nords-Malaitans." In J. Pouillon and P. Maranda, eds., *Echanges et Communications*. The Hague: Mouton.

Marx, K. 1938. *Capital*. 2 vols. London: Allen and Unwin.

Meigs, A. 1978. "A Papuan Perspective on Pollution." *Man* 13:304–18.

Nadel, S. F. 1953. *The Foundations of Social Anthropology*. London: Cohen and West.

Needham, R. 1977. "Skulls and Causality." *Man* (n.s.) 11:71–88.

Poole, F. J. P. 1982. "The Ritual Forging of Identity: Aspects of Person and Self in Bimin-Kuskusmin Male Initiation." In G. H. Herdt, ed., *Rites of Manhood: Male Initiation in Papua New Guinea*. Berkeley and Los Angeles: University of California Press.

Rappaport, R. 1967. "Ritual Regulation of Environmental Regulations Among a New Guinea People." *Ethnology* 6:17–30.

Ross, H. M. 1973. *Baegu: Social and Ecological Organization in Malaita, Solomon Islands*. Urbana: University of Illinois Press.

Salmond, A. 1978. "Te Ao Tawhito: A Semantic Approach to the Traditional Maori Cosmos." *Journal of the Polynesian Society* 87:5–28.

Saunders, K. 1975. "The Black Scourge: Racial Responses Towards Melanesians in Colonial Queensland." In R. Evans, K. Saunders, and K. Cronin, eds., *Exclusion, Exploitation, and Extermination: Race Relations in Colonial Queensland.* Sydney: Angus and Robertson.

Schneider, D. M. 1968. *American Kinship: A Cultural Account.* Englewood Cliffs, N.J.: Prentice-Hall.

——— 1976. "Notes Toward a Theory of Culture." In K. H. Basso and H. Selby, eds., *Meaning in Anthropology.* Albuquerque: University of New Mexico Press.

Schwartz, T. 1963. "Systems of Areal Integration: Some Considerations Based on the Admiralty Islands of Northern Melanesia." *Anthropological Forum* 1:56–97.

——— 1978. "Where is the Culture? Personality as the Distributive Locus of Culture." In G. D. Spindler, ed., *The Making of Psychological Anthropology.* Berkeley and Los Angeles: University of California Press.

Smith, W. R. 1889. *Lectures on the Religion of the Semites.* New York: Appleton.

Specht, J. and J. P. White. 1978. *Trade and Exchange in Oceania and Australia.* Sydney: University of Sydney Press (*Mankind*, vol. 11).

Sperber, D. 1974. *Rethinking Symbolism.* Cambridge: Cambridge University Press.

Turner, V. 1967. *The Forest of Symbols: Studies in Ndembu Ritual.* Ithaca, N.Y.: Cornell University Press.

——— 1968. *The Drums of Affliction: A Study of Religious Processes Among the Ndembu of Zambia.* Oxford: Oxford University Press, Clarendon Press.

——— 1978. "Encounter with Freud: The Making of a Comparative Symbologist." In G. D. Spindler, ed., *The Making of Psychological Anthropology.* Berkeley: University of California Press.

Tuzin, D. 1980. *The Voice of the Tambaran: Truth and Illusion in Ilahita Arapesh Religion.* Berkeley: University of California Press.

Tylor, E. B. 1871. *Primitive Culture.* London: Murray.

Index

NOTE: Glottal stops have been ignored in alphabetization.